An
AUTOBIOGRAPHY

An AUTOBIOGRAPHY

"Cast your bread upon the waters, for you will find it after many days."

[Ecclesiastes 11:1]

JACK P. LEWIS

Published by Gospel Advocate Co.
1006 Elm Hill Pike, Nashville, TN 37210
www.gospeladvocate.com

ISBN 10: 0-89225-598-6
ISBN 13: 978-0-89225-598-6

Back cover photo by Cindy Putnam McMillion

DEDICATION

To my sons, John and Jerry

Table of Contents

Foreword

I am very pleased that Dr. Lewis has chosen to publish these reminiscences of his journey. I have heard some of these stories through the years from him and his brother Clyde. On those occasions, I always wanted to hear more.

Dr. Lewis gives a detailed picture of a small Texas town during the Depression and the lives of its inhabitants. More specifically, he relates the inspiring story of a devout Texas farm family and the hard work and frugality it took to make it through this era of U.S. history; they not only persevered, but all five of the children were able to get a college education. His entertaining stories about his five seasons (1938-1941 and 1944) of selling Bibles during his college days illustrate the work ethic acquired on a farm in the Depression – a work ethic he has maintained throughout his life.

At its commencement each year, the Harding School of Theology presents the Jack P. Lewis Ministry of Study award to one of its graduates. Dr. Lewis's story of his years at Abilene Christian, Harvard University and Hebrew Union College reveals why this award is appropriately named. His anecdotes from the mid-1940s Harvard years about its leading theological scholars, the rigorous course work, and theories and perspectives that challenged his conservative background in the Church of Christ are enlightening. His story of earning two doctorates will inspire anyone who thinks he knows all he needs to know after four years of college or even after one Ph.D. Of course, this was all done in an era when there was little appreciation for the need for theological education within the Churches of Christ. The chronicle of his first trip to the Holy Land in the early 60s reveals the effort he was willing to take to see as much as he could that related to the biblical story so he could not only understand the text better but also make it come alive for his students.

Dr. Lewis also tells of the founding, growth and significance of the Harding School of Theology (formerly the Harding Graduate School of Religion). He has been a part of the Harding community since the beginning of the graduate program in 1954 and relates stories about its early years that few have heard.

Over the last year or so, I have heard Dr. Lewis's presentation on his 80 years of ministry at least three times. Each time I have been inspired and challenged. It's a story of a scholar who never lost his commitment to the church or his desire to tell the Gospel story to others. It's a story of someone who always tried to do what was right and was willing to do whatever necessary, no matter how menial or demanding, to bring someone to Christ. Some of his actions may have seemed insignificant at the time, but as he says in the last line of the book, "A Christian life is composed of the insignificant things one does as opportunity comes." I think you will enjoy reading about these "insignificant" events in the life of a scholar and servant who continues to practice the ministry of study and share its fruits in his teaching and lecturing, even at the age of 93.

Don L. Meredith, Librarian
Harding School of Theology
July 24, 2012

Preface

Joshua Loth Liebman (1907-1948) described life as being like a day in the park: some days are short, and some days are long. This book is the story of my day in the park.

I am reminded of what a debt I owe: to my father and mother who were generous, sacrificial people; to the Midlothian church for letting me practice on them; to those who made possible the fellowships which I enjoyed; to the teachers who shared their time so generously; to the students who were so tolerant and taught me so much; to the members of the Church of Christ at White Station, who have made me an elder and have allowed me to continue teaching in the auditorium Bible class on Sunday mornings; to the University for the intellectual stimulus of preparing and teaching; to those who have graciously invited me to speak; to the audiences that came to hear. I am a product of sacrificial people who went before; others have labored, and I have entered into their labors.

As is true of several of my recent books, I am indebted to my niece Mrs. Jean Saunders for computerizing and editing these reminiscences, saving them from molding forgotten in the file.

These chapters were written at different times over the past several years. They are a record of my journey and not of personal details.

Memories of Midlothian were recalled when I was asked to speak at the celebration of the congregation's 90th year. My studies at Hebrew Union College were recorded when I was invited to speak at a graduation ceremony. Many opportunities to speak in chapel at the Harding Graduate School and for numerous occasions at the White Station congregation have given rise to a collection of more life stories.

It makes an old man's heart glad to be given the opportunity to reminisce. One has to be amazed at how far back into childhood one's memories go. The years have not quieted the dreams or dampened the tingle of the spine. I cannot say with certainty that this is exactly how it happened. I can only say that this is how I remember it.

Jack P. Lewis
July 3, 2012

Chapter 1

NO SMALL GIFT

Both my paternal and maternal grandfathers had passed on long before I came into the world. My knowledge of them is quite scant, gained only from stories I heard repeated. William Donnel Lewis worked as timekeeper in a coal mine in Sequatchie Valley, Tenn., before migrating to Grapevine, Texas. My father told of memories of awaking as a small child with the wagon backed up to the door for moving and of his bed being all that remained unloaded. Eventually, the Lewis family moved to Midlothian, Texas, and had a farm about two miles to the southeast of town.

Another of the stories was of Grandfather's cleaning out the well when he was barely able to climb back to the surface, an experience to which he attributed the breakdown of his health. Upon doctor's advice, he tried a visit to West Texas to recover from tuberculosis but returned in worse condition, hardly able to speak. On one occasion, I heard of relatives named Lewis, but we never really had contact with any of Grandfather's people and knew nothing of them. My Uncle Don claimed that four brothers had come from Wales.

Amanda Jane Hackworth had been a teacher prior to her marriage to W.D. Lewis. She was a Hard Shell Baptist and he a Methodist. To them were born seven children: Fred, Walter, Pearl, Amber, Jasper, Don and Robert. The children all followed their father into the Methodist church. Life was a struggle, and the children worked in the fields, not getting to start school in the fall of the year until after the crops were gathered. There were stories of walking two miles to town to spend five cents received for Christmas for licorice candy.

We never saw much of Grandmother Lewis's family. They were back in Tennessee; but on occasions, her brother Bob would come for a visit. He was a Hard Shell Baptist preacher. On another occasion, a car full of her people, including Bob, came, and it led to a picnic in our pasture of the entire Lewis clan – all that were in the area.

Though my father, Pearl, had one year in Southwestern at Georgetown, Texas, the demise of his father brought him home to work on the farm, and he never returned to college; he dreamed of it until his dying day. He never intended to be a farmer, but circumstances drove him that way. He did a turn at being a rural mail carrier, but that came to an end in some dispute among the carriers over whether to motorize the horse-drawn routes. I sensed that had he found another option, mail carrying would have been his preference over farming. That preference may have led my brother Roy into a career with the post office.

My grandmother lived on her farm until the end of her life in her 90th year. First, she was with her unmarried children. Jasper married late, and for a time he and his wife lived with her. Then her brother Joe and his wife, Mattie, came for a time in the depths of the Depression. Amber and her family lived with her for a while; and finally, Don and his family moved in and cared for her to the end. In this way, the family farm passed to Don and his descendants.

Going to Grandmother's house was a great treat during my childhood. Rural electricity had not yet come, so there were kerosene lamps to learn of when visits were made after dark. My father visited her frequently, and that was only after the day's work was over. But every Sunday afternoon brought a visit to Grandmother of all her children and grandchildren that were in the area.

Christmas was also a family gathering time. Names were drawn and presents exchanged between the adults, and children were given a quarter each by Grandmother, which was no small gift to the recipient in Depression days and no small gift for a widow in pre-Social Security days. But more joyous was the abundant Christmas dinner with their share brought by each family in the group. The Depression years and the increase in the size of the clan brought an end to the exchange of gifts.

The one missing person was her son Robert (Bob). Prior to my memory, he had moved to California. At every visit to Grandmother, the question was asked her by a son or daughter, "What have you heard from Bob?" On rare occasions, he visited home, and that was the highlight of the year to the whole clan to be anticipated long in advance. Once, he drove through in a Packard Straight 8, and that was some car to all of us who knew Fords best. Finally, Bob married and brought his bride, Louise, with him. She worked in the registrar's office of the university at Berkeley. I never knew what sort of work Bob did; but I do know that at a late period, he had to do with real estate. I last saw him when I was in college. He unexpectedly stopped by Abilene on one of his trips, and I had lunch with him. He and his wife had no children, but they volunteered graciously to finance my sister's staying in the dormitory for the remainder of her school years. Bob died early of a heart attack, and it was a sad blow to all of the family.

H.T. Holland, my maternal grandfather, reputedly came by wagon train from Illinois to settle in Pleasant Valley, about five miles north of Midlothian. After a period of farming, he and his family moved into Midlothian, and he was in the hardware business. The Hollands acquired a house, located on the peak of Sharkey Hill at the west end of Midlothian, which had an excellent view over the valley to the west. The pasture of the place was the city's slope for sledding when snow fell, though that did not happen every winter. The railroad from Dallas to Cleburne crossed that from Fort Worth to Ennis at Midlothian. The town had been named by a Scotsman working on the railroad who came from the Lothian district of Scotland.

There had been a congregation meeting in the school house in Pleasant Valley; but my grandfather gave the lot in Midlothian on which the church building was built, and mother was present on its opening day in 1903. He included the clause in the deed that should an instrument of music ever be used in the building, the property would revert to his heirs. That later created some problems when the congregation wanted to borrow money with the land as security. However, eventually, when the congregation needed more room and a new building, the lot became the site for the preacher's home, which it still is today.

My grandfather was known as a man of his word. When an angry man called him a liar, without any retaliation, my grandfather said to bystanders, "He called me a liar!"

My grandfather's family included Jim, Walter, Claudia, Anna and Gillie plus Annie Hardesty and Roland Hartin, whom they reared. Gillie died in childhood, but her picture drawn by Claudia graced the wall and was later in my mother's room in our home until her death. She had stories of Gillie.

The Holland family scattered. Jim and Walter married sisters and went to Lubbock, Texas. One of my memories of pre-school days is of a train trip to Lubbock with Mother and Aunt Claudia to bring their mother home from her visit there. Walter had three children, but Jim had a very large family. However, it was only Colene of them that I ever knew. She taught school in Texas and occasionally visited us. She ultimately married and had a large family. Walter later moved to Harlingen, and Jim and his family went to Eugene, Ore. We knew little of them except from letters. They did come to their mother's funeral. And Aunt Betty came to her sister Berta's funeral, during which time Walter's family was staying briefly at our house. While I was away in Harvard, Jim surprised my mother with a visit. They had not seen each other for 25 years. Later, my brother LeMoine took mother and Aunt Claudia in their late years to Oregon for a brief visit.

Aunt Claudia had married J.S. Dunn and lived in Oak Cliff in Dallas. I was told that my mother suffered a nervous collapse following my birth and that I was cared for by Aunt Claudia for a period of undetermined length. Dunn was a capable preacher; but in my early years, he died of pneumonia, leaving three children. Aunt Claudia's income came from dress making. It was a delight to visit her. She learned that children liked spaghetti; so when we visited, as we always did when we went to Dallas, we could count on spaghetti for lunch. It was always a drop-in affair. My parents did not use the telephone to inform her that we were coming. They patronized a doctor in Dallas called Dr. Davis. He was adept at administering sugar pills. The patient got pills on which Dr. Davis had poured some liquid, and the other children in the party got sugar pills. Whether his treatments did any good or not, I will never know. We all survived.

In my earliest memories, the Emory Holland family (cousins) was living with my grandmother in her house. They had experienced a tragedy in which their house had burned and one child was lost. The Hollands had three surviving children of comparable ages to those of my parents, and that made a visit to Grandmother's a special pleasure. We visited regularly. Grandmother had a gentle horse named Old Bell, and my first horse rides were on her. Her back seemed to me as a small child to be the widest thing one could be expected to put legs on each side of.

When I was about five, it was decided that Grandmother could no longer live alone, and so she was moved in to live with us. But on a windy March day, she fell in the yard. She lived on until Christmas morning. For my mother, Christmas was always a sad occasion.

My mother, Anna Elizabeth Holland, was adept in piano, which she had studied in Dallas at Saint Mary's. Lessons involved a roundtrip train ride from Midlothian. She did not finish high school but did spend a year at Gunter Bible School.

The Farm in Midlothian

I have no memory of stories of how my father and mother first met. They studied the Bible together attempting to reconcile their differences. He wrestled with the fact that often at the mourner's bench in the Methodist church, he could not receive salvation. He asked preachers questions, not always receiving satisfactory answers. It was finally in conversations with Horace W. Busby that he was satisfied what his duty was and was baptized. Despite many discussions in which each tried to convince the other, his mother remained a Baptist throughout her life, and all of his brothers and his sister remained Methodists.

In anticipation of their marriage conducted by Busby, my mother and father built a small bungalow on the southwest corner of the block north of Kimbell Park, a house that still stands. But with the mail-carrying job ending, farming was inviting. They purchased a farm of about 120 acres from Clayborn Rutledge located on the east side of Midlothian, part of it within city limits. The house was an impressive white house with white posts holding up its upstairs and downstairs porches on the front. The lane, bordered by hackberry trees, led squarely into the front door but at the last moment veered around to the south. Both the north and south sides of the house had large porches. The high ceilings, when the doors and windows were open on both the north and south, made for a cooling breeze even in the hot season. Midlothian could go to 110 degrees in the summer. No effort was ever made to heat all the house in the winter. The kitchen and one bedroom about did it. At first, the heat was from burning coal in the fireplace; but reasonably early, natural gas came to Midlothian, and my folks paid the price to have the house piped and the gas brought down the lane. The railroad ran along most of the northeast side of the farm, and train watching was always exciting. This section of the single track had a siding where trains passed each other; but it also made our house, though a quarter- to a half-mile away, convenient for hobos who needed a handout.

Unlike many farm families, we had electricity as far back as I can remember. That was one of the advantages of living at the edge of town before rural electrification became a reality. The outhouse was a regular part of life both in town and on the farm in those days. We never had a water heater until I sold books in Dallas prior to my going to Harvard. I gave my parents a water heater, and they at that time put in an indoor toilet. During my high school years, the town had put in a sewer system. The line ran along the west side of our farm, and the digging of the tunnel provided much rock to be disposed of. My father acquired a sufficient supply to rock our drive the entire length of the lane; and for the first time, we could get out even when it rained. The city did not have rocked streets until during the Depression when the WPA made them possible. Asphalted streets came only after the war.

The farm had a garage painted red, but most distinctive was a silo. I remember it being filled only once; but it did distinguish this farm from others nearby. The source of water was a long way off; but there was a windmill with pipes to the barn for water for the cattle, and there was a cistern in the yard. Lowering butter and other perishables into the cistern could serve for preserving them. Ice could be had from the iceman who came around once or twice a week. But we also went to the ice house and brought home our own ice in a 100-pound block.

My father could put such a block into the ice box. The visit to the ice house was a delight for one could pick up the "snow" from the ice saws and eat it.

Quite early, it was possible to get water in the house from the city with the pipe coming down the lane. Like many farms in central Texas at that time, the farm had its "Negro House" 100-200 yards away from the main house. It was a one-room affair. I have a memory of going there as a small child with my Aunt Amber, who was living with us, to see a new baby; but most of the time, the building was unoccupied. It became used for storing seed, and then sheds were put about it for farm machinery and for sheep.

My father was quite resourceful as a farmer about repairing and operating his farm equipment in a pre-mechanized period. Fixing the windmill and its pump offered him no problem. The planters, the binders and the plows he could manage unless welding was needed. Then he could turn to the local blacksmiths, of which the town had two. Motors seemed beyond him, and so cars had to be taken to mechanics. John Milton, another farmer and jackleg mechanic, was depended on for motor repair.

Slaughtering pigs and calves for food was within my father's skills. He and my mother were adept at curing meat and at canning vegetables. He was interested in progressive farming. His was one of the early farms in the area to have terraces built to control erosion. He and his brother Don bought a cross-plow which was supposed to eliminate labor in chopping cotton. However, the irregular stand of cotton made the plow somewhat impractical. He went to two-row equipment as early as it was available. His farm power was mules until sometime around World War II when he got a tractor. My younger brothers joked about his saying "Whoa" to the tractor.

The location of his farm near town made it the learning field for all the town kids who thought they wanted to earn money by chopping, hoeing or picking cotton. Putting up with all of them took unlimited patience. He could figure hours and wages in his head in a period when calculators were undreamed of. The Depression years made ends hard to meet. The bank would loan money only with security, so the mules without which the land could not be plowed were put up for security for winter and summer loans until crops were gathered. Work clothes were patched and repatched. One dress suit did him across the time I can remember.

He understood that diversified farming was the only hope for the family farm. Although cotton was the basic crop of Ellis County at the time, he also had corn, wheat, oats and barley. He had cattle and sheep. He had a pecan grove. There were chickens and turkeys; however, the turkeys often found the railroad their place, and the loss was staggering. These various activities kept work going the year around but also brought in a bit of money at different seasons. There was an orchard for fruit (peaches and plums); but when the trees died out, we lost ground in trying to replace them.

We did not have grapes in our immediate area; but some 10 miles away, mustang grapes grew in sandy soil. With our clan, it was a yearly outing to go to the Mansfield area to pick mustang grapes. The grapes were crushed, the juice strained and placed in bottles which were sealed with corks and paraffin. The juice remained fresh for drinking through the year. Money was in short supply, but the larder was kept well stocked.

My father's basic philosophy is to me best expressed in his remark on a rainy day: "It is too wet to work today, so we will fix the fence." Or there was that time when he thought money could be made by feeding out cattle. The calves were bought, reared on pasture, and then put into the feed lot. When market time came, the expenditure and the outcome were about the same if the expenditure had not been greater. His summation was, "Well, at least we had something to do." Boys were kept busy.

I frankly admit that farming never appealed to me. Perhaps had I seen it from some other viewpoint than the end of a hoe handle or from dragging a cotton sack, it might have been more attractive. We had one team of mules, and he could more skillfully plow than inexperienced boys. The only plowing I ever did was with my donkey and with the flat-breaker during the last summer or so of high school. I was never strong enough to make a hand at shoveling grain. My work at threshing was filling sacks at the threshing machine, which was the dustiest thing one could do. We had no protectors; one's eyes watered, and he spit dirt.

The late summer brought picking cotton. A boy could take pride when he got big enough to pick 100 pounds a day. I think I made that goal once. Farmers rivaled each other in who could produce the first bale in the area. The community provided a small prize. When a farmer was striving for the first bale, the whole community turned out to pick; and it was done in one day. We picked for a neighbor; and at the end of the day, all who had picked gathered in front of his house and were paid on the spot. We were especially proud the one year when we had the first bale ourselves. I never had to stay out of school to pick cotton though that practice was common in our area. Neither did the school close for a season for cotton picking.

After cotton picking, there was gathering of pecans, and that lasted until Thanksgiving. We did ours in the afternoon after school and on weekends. I will always be amazed at my father's ability to climb a pecan tree and flail the pecans off the limbs. There were no mechanical shakers. Now that gas lawnmowers are in abundance, I continue to dream of what a blessing it would have been to have a mower under a pecan tree so that one did not have to search through tall grass for fallen pecans. On winter nights, my mother and father shelled pecans for selling. The pecan crop was an important part of their income. We took shelled and unshelled pecans door to door for sale.

The pecan trees we had were native with small nuts. We had one or more trees that had especially small nuts. A popular guessing game was to fill one's hands with nuts and have the other person to guess how many there were. If he was right, he got the nuts; if he was wrong, you got his. The opponent was always shocked when one opened his clasped hands to reveal these small nuts. My father learned the art of grafting and was in the process of developing a grove of larger nuts with soft shells. However, the pecan industry came to an end for us with his death. The renters never found any nuts to pay rent on.

Generous and Sacrificial People

My father and mother were generous, sacrificial people with what they had. Money was not theirs, but the products of the garden were for distribution. They invited the preacher to gather roasting ears from the corn field for canning. When a possum was caught in the chicken house, it was given to those who would eat it. At Christmas time, toys were taken to families who were suspected not to be anticipating any Christmas.

The Hollands grew old and decided to sell out on their long-time shoe store in town. Many of the items had long been in stock and were badly out of date, but bidding was vigorous. My father began bidding on lots of shoes which had been thrown together. I had never seen so many shoes of all sizes and designs as those he acquired. Some were even button shoes, though no one wore buttons any longer. Out of the whole lot, one pair was found which was wide enough for my triple-E foot. However, in order to be wide enough, the shoe was much too long. Shortly, the toes had turned up from the point where my toes ended, giving me the appearance and feeling of a big-footed elf. Despite the appearance, the shoes had to be worn out. Most of the shoes my father had purchased were sent off to the orphanage, the purpose he had in mind for them to start with.

Hospitals and medical services were not then what they are now. Roads were not paved, and illnesses required that one sit at night with the ill. Pneumonia was common every winter. The high-wheeled Model T Ford could go where lower cars could not. My father would take the doctor to the nearest place that could be reached by car, and then they would walk in across the creek and through the mud. Sitting at night was common for him. When a farmer was ill at planting time, my father and others plowed the land and planted the crop. This was the Social Security program of the community.

When my maternal grandmother's holdings were divided, Aunt Claudia received farm land to be rented out. But rented land had to be overseen, and this was my father's volunteer task. Equipment like the windmill was the landowner's problem, not the renter's. Repair work had to be done when farmers who had mechanical ability were willing to be out of their fields. On a particular Sunday, my father was helping repair a windmill. One of the workmen at the top of the tower dropped a wrench and grazed my father's head cutting a deep gash. Fortunately, it was only a glancing blow. I do not recall his missing worship for work any later time.

Unlike many farm wives, my mother did not have to do work in the fields. Her tasks were with the chickens, guineas, turkeys, pigs, garden and in the house. My father and the boys milked the cows and looked after farm animals. But with five children, housework was no picnic. Clothes had to be washed. Monday usually saw the wash pot heated up to supply hot water. The boys had the chore of doing that, but then there was the washing. Fairly early, we got an electric washing machine, and that ended duty on the rub board. The clothes were put through the machine and the ringer, rinsed and then hung on the barbed-wire fence for drying. The sun, not machines, did the drying whether summer or winter. In sub-freezing weather, the clothes froze on the line and had to be left there until they thawed. In an emergency, necessary things were dried in the house.

It was the custom at noon to feed hired workers on the farm. That meal had to be prepared. My sister was my mother's helper in the housework. She also never had to do outside farm work other than in emergency assisting in covering a loaded wagon that might get wet. On one such occasion, the wind got under the tarpaulin, blew her off the wagon, and she cracked a hip. She had many days in recovering. Threshing season was a time of especially hard work with extra mouths to feed and long hours to endure. The threshing crew worked from daylight until dark.

Canning in the hot summer was necessary in order to preserve fruit and vegetables for winter consumption. There was no air-conditioning. About everything – meat and vegetables – could be canned and, if done skillfully, could be preserved. Carelessly done, not only was the work wasted but also the supplies were wasted. With the coming of frost, tomatoes not yet ripe had to be gathered, wrapped in newspaper and stored until they ripened, which could be even up until Christmas.

Potatoes could be stored in the cool under the house and kept until needed later in the year. One season, it was rumored that Singleton farm, which was one of the luxury showplaces in our area, had a surplus of onions and had opened their fields to the community to help themselves. My father took us out to the field. We filled up sacks until the car was loaded down to capacity. My father cut a hole in the floor of the north porch through which we could put the onions, stored in the cool air under the house. We had an ample supply of onions for all purposes for a long time. There are many ways to fix onions!

Memories of Childhood

One has to be amazed at how far back into childhood one's memories go. Mine begin with playing Indian with my brother and sister and with a pedal car which belonged to my brother and was always recognized as his; but all of us as we came along rode in it. We all had kiddy cars of our own. Since my next youngest brother Clyde was only three years younger than I, it must have been at his birth that my uncles entertained us by playing thrasher on the remote end of the north porch while their wives attended my mother in the bedroom on the southwest corner of the house. Our game was preparing meals for the thresher at the cook shack, and there were raw potato strips to eat.

Airplanes were very sparse in the days before I started to school. At night, the flashing lights of airway beacons (the navigation system prior to radio) could be traced across the sky to the west of us. On one visit to Dallas, my mother suddenly told me that my father was going to look at cattle near Love Field. I could hardly believe my ears; I joined him, and we made a stop at the airfield after looking at the cattle. I could hardly believe my eyes.

When I was in Abilene, the government started a flying program. But war was threatening, and I knew where those being trained were heading. After I had been at Harvard, Lynell and I took John, who was under a year old, by air from Providence, R.I., to Meridian, Miss., to visit Lois and Joe Sellars. I finally got off the ground. I wondered at the time, "Is it possible that I will ever fly again?" Now, I have flown all over the world, but not with less enthusiasm for it. I earned my private pilot's license and racked up about 500 hours before I gave it up. It proved to be an expensive, though delightful, hobby which I could not justify.

I barely escaped a round with scarlet fever. A spring bubbled out of the ground at the root of a hollow cottonwood tree just opposite Rutledge's rock pit. It was on our south fence row. We never gave thought to the fact that it was only a couple of hundred yards below the cemetery. Springs are attractive to boys on hot days. Shortly afterward, I came down with fever; Dr. Harris diagnosed it, quarantined my family and ordered the well ones to take inoculations. I was so sick that I did not really care what happened. Dr. Harris suggested that the illness came from drinking out of the spring. I suppose the diagnosis was wrong; I recovered in a reasonable time. Or was it the fact that my brother LeMoine won a small sized bicycle at a city-wide drawing at the theater from tickets merchants gave with grocery purchases that made me well? LeMoine came wagging the bicycle home from the drawing while I was still in bed. It is the only thing I remember our family ever winning. I was already far too big for the bicycle; but it was a beauty, and my smaller brothers and I rode it around town for years.

Farming is a precarious livelihood. My father and his brother Don rented land to sow in wheat trying to increase their income. The wheat developed nicely and was harvested. Then it set in raining, and the grain rotted in the shocks. Another year, the outlook was good. The grain had done well and was ready to cut, but a hailstorm developed in the afternoon. In a few minutes, the ground was as white as if it had snowed. The wheat was beaten to the ground. The year was lost. We gathered up the hailstones and used them to freeze ice cream. That was better than crying.

Midlothian was subject to occasional windstorms. An old house like ours creaked and groaned in the wind. My mother could only gather us under the dining table and pray that the Lord would spare us. My father always sang "Jesus is a Rock in a weary land, a shelter in the time of storm"[1] during such storms. One such spring, the wind took all the sheet iron off the barn and scattered it over the field. The barn had to be re-covered; fortunately, there was some insurance. The wind also took the shingles off the house, and we all learned about shingling a house.

My brother Roy proved to be sickly as a baby, unable to survive on mother's milk or cow's milk. The doctor recommended a goat. None were in our area. My father learned that milk goats were available in the Pecos, Texas, area and ordered one which was shipped by train. She came in a crate and proved to be what was needed. Keeping goats was a new experience for us. In time, there were kids, and kids are something else, even in milk goats. A beautiful pair got into the fruit that we had drying in the sun. They bloated and died.

Sheep offered their problems. The fences around the farm had to be strengthened to make them sheep-proof. Then the sheep got cockleburs in their wool in the pasture. Before they could be sheared and the wool sold, the burrs had to be removed. That furnished a winter's work. One by one, they had to be taken and searched for burrs. The burrs stick the fingers, and the oil in the wool is smelly and dirty. However, it was work that could be done in a shed rather than out in the weather. Rams fight, and they get worms in their heads. The rams have to be caught and treated. Sheep lamb in the winter and often have difficulty, especially in cold, rainy winter. Dogs from town like to chase sheep and can kill them. The sheep have to be counted in the evening, and the ones missing have to be hunted in the darkness, likely to be found dead. I last hunted (after years away from home) in the evening after my father's funeral; it was an especially bitter experience.

The Depression brought tragedy to the Lewis family. In the division of my grandmother's estate, my mother and her sister received half each of a valley farm. Times were booming, and the future looked very bright. My parents wished either to sell or buy to have the whole and ended up buying the half they did not already have. The loan was for 10 years. But the economy collapsed, and in 10 years they had not been able to pay the interest, not to mention repaying the loan. The insurance company from which they had borrowed foreclosed, and they felt fortunate to be able to save the farm on which the home was. The inheritance was gone.

Along with that came the birth of brother James, who was a blue baby and died after five days. My mother was devastated. Shortly after, she was diagnosed as a diabetes patient and had to be hospitalized in Dallas for long periods of time. Doctors knew little about treating diabetes at that time. There were superstitions, one of which was that if one drank the water off of soaked prickly pear leaves, it would help. We had plenty of prickly pear plants in the pasture, and that was tried. Aunts, uncles, Grandmother and church members came in to care for the children while my father stayed at the hospital. There was no hospitalization insurance. As we worked in the fields, he commented that it would cost all that he could hope to make. We became acquainted with the hospital for the first time in visiting her.

She survived and was an insulin patient for the remainder of her life, which extended to 74 years. We learned about food weighing and special diet. We learned about insulin shock and saw how difficult it is to persuade a patient to take the orange juice required to bring her out. In the early years, she was always asking, as anyone with a like problem would ask, "Why me? What have I done?" But she cooked for her family what she could not eat. She adjusted and in the end probably knew more about her condition than those who treated her.

Farm life in the 20s and 30s offered its pleasures as well as its labor. We had a series of beautiful collie dogs and a series of cats for pets. The cats were valuable for controlling the mouse and rat population. The dogs ran rabbits in the fields, and that was fun. We often ate rabbits until we learned the danger of tularemia.

Families from church visited each other for meals which gave children pleasurable opportunities for play together. At the top of pleasure was the freezing of ice cream; almost any event was stimulus for that. The gallon and a half freezer supplied an abundance.

It seems a marvel that boys on a farm ever survive the various hazards a farm offers. Clyde and I received the chore of taking a mule to the valley farm five miles away. Being too lazy to want to walk and lead the mule, we came up with the idea of hitching the mule to our little red wagon in which we would ride. We never thought of what the mule would do if she looked back and saw what was following her. The blinders on the bridle probably saved us from that. But then there was the problem of how to keep the wagon off her heels when going downhill. We had seen our father tie a wheel and slide his wagon down the mountain, and so holding the wheel seemed the logical way to solve the problem. We were hardly past the house when Clyde decided to try the wheel. He grabbed it, and it whirled around putting his finger under it and taking the skin off the finger. He did not tell me or anyone else what had happened. With his wound, we made our journey, hitched our mule up with the other mule at the farm, and then brought the large wagon home as we were supposed to do. Clyde could show you his scar.

One of my worst experiences was in John Milton's shop where we were having the car or some farm machinery repaired. The shop was full of all sorts of machinery, and there were no signs forbidding a curious, barefoot boy from trying them all. A heavy jack fell and split open my big toe. I was ashamed to tell my father on the spot that I needed help. It bled profusely; the scar is still there, but I escaped bleeding to death and also blood poisoning.

The one vacation my family ever took was a trip to Glen Rose. There the mineral water tasted and smelled like rotten eggs; but swimming and hiking could be done. We rented a cabin with one room where all could sleep. The curtains could be let down for dressing but raised for sleeping. Before the week was out, rain set in, the creek rose to flood conditions, it was cold, and so we went home early.

My father had stories of his earlier experience as a streetcar conductor in Galveston. My mother had a relative who had visited Galveston after a disastrous flood. We dreamed and talked of taking a trip to Galveston and of gathering shells on the beach, but it never came about. He also talked of the summer he had spent as a guide in Yellowstone Park. To visit there seemed to be something that we just had to do, but it never came about. The Emory Hollands with their mail-carrying job had regular summer vacations with trips to places; but the farm with its animals had to be cared for the year around. It left one wondering whether we owned the animals or they owned us.

If You Have an Education

Fortune smiled on us when Ada Terril (Mother's cousin in Dallas) decided to dispose of her *National Geographic* collection and gave them to us. She was closing the private school for boys she and her husband had operated. There was also an unabridged dictionary and other book treasures. Untold hours spent in the *Geographic* opened to me a world I never previously knew existed.

Even earlier than that, a lady came to school as a representative of Southern Methodist who had traveled and made a collection of dolls from around the world. Her pitch was, "How would you like to go around the world?" But the next sentence was, "How much more would you enjoy it if you had an education?" Though I had never been out of Texas, the fever caught me; and I have no hope of recovering.

Worship was a regular part of our lives from my earliest years. There was never any question about going to church. In memory's eye, I can see at the left front of the auditorium at the first row of pews a special armchair where Uncle Isaac Holland sat. He was one of the elders.

Now and then, he would rise on his cane and give an admonition. One of his admonitions was for the young to memorize Scripture. Learning so many verses a week would give one a certain amount in a year; and if persistent, one could in a reasonable time memorize the New Testament. The admonition made sense to me. While the mules rested from flat-breaking land in the August sun, I took my New Testament out of my pocket and memorized. I never finished Uncle Isaac's program, but the Scripture learned has been valuable to me across an entire lifetime.

In my late years, my people had the custom of going by to bring the Hollands to services. They could no longer walk the about three blocks they were from church. We would arrive, and Aunt Vic would put her head out the door and say, "Pappy is not ready yet!" In a few minutes, Uncle Isaac would come out on his cane and sit in the swing; and in five or 10 minutes, Aunt Vic would appear. It is a standing joke between my wife and me when we are getting ready to go somewhere, "Pappy is not ready yet!"

Through most of my youth, the Midlothian church did not have regular preaching. Various brothers took turns of being responsible for teaching on Sundays of the month. Summers brought meetings conducted by visiting preachers. The visiting preacher was fed from house to house, and our home was always on the schedule. Fried chicken, vegetables from the garden and homemade ice cream always made for a sumptuous feast. My father was always a participant in work days of the congregation.

The congregation always contributed regularly to the work done among the Mexicans by John Wolfe. It also had an interest in a Brother Jelley, who worked in India. It regularly supported the Boles Orphans Home. When Barney Morehead came out with his picture of missionaries, a copy was posted in the vestibule of the congregation and remained there until after I left Midlothian.

My father was a self-taught Bible student, and he took his understanding of Scripture seriously. The demands of farming left only limited time for studying. His tools were his Bible, his concordance and B.W. Johnson's *New Testament with Notes*.[2] The *Firm Foundation* was read. Ultimately, he was appointed a deacon of the congregation. Midlothian, dependent on an agricultural economy, was more stable in population than most areas have been since World War II. One did not rise to leadership quickly where everyone knew everyone else intimately. My father had his Sunday in which he led the congregation, and at times he was the teacher of the younger adult group which must have included people until they reached about their fifties. During my college years, he was designated an elder and served in that role until his death at age 64.

It was the summer when I was age 10 that G.A. Dunn was conducting the summer meeting that I decided it was time to be baptized. There had never been any question in my mind about the need. One of my earliest memories at church is that of awakening after the service. The baptistery, which was under the pulpit stand, was open, and Mack Witherspoon was being baptized. I got my parents' permission, and as the congregation sang the first phrases of "All Things Are Ready,"[3] I came forward and confessed Christ. Loreta was also baptized that night.

Education was valued in the Lewis home. My father, even in his late years, dreamed of returning to college. He often said that he had never intended to farm, but he was disappointed when none of his sons chose to follow him in farming. School was perhaps a mile away, and regularly we walked as did most of the other children of the town. In rainy weather, we were taken and picked up. Grades were valued in students' reports, and each "A" earned a reward. After the loss of the inherited farm, my mother often admonished, "Get an education. No one can take that away from you." Time for study came ahead of farm work when work was not urgent.

When my brother LeMoine was ready for college in 1932, the Depression was in its depths. Uncle Bob and Aunt Louise were concerned that unaccredited Abilene Christian had no educational standing. A distant cousin Ada Terrill in Dallas, who with her husband had operated a private school for boys, thought that Southern Methodist University would be good for him. Others suggested North Texas State at Denton because a trusted brother operated a Bible chair there. But Abilene was the choice, and Ada Terrill loaned him $100 without interest to make it possible. We traveled in the summer to Abilene to get him a place to stay, and in the fall my parents supplied canned food from the farm for him to live on. Later, the rest of us followed his steps to Abilene. Five children through college on the income from a small white-rock farm during and just after the Depression represented great sacrifice on the part of parents – no small gift.

Chapter 2

HOW DEAR TO MY HEART

I left Midlothian in September 1936 to go to Abilene Christian College. I was back for the summer of 1937, but after that time I have been in Midlothian only for brief holidays. Even these visits came to an end with the death of my mother, Mrs. Pearl G. (Anna Elizabeth Holland) Lewis in 1962. Since then, it has been my privilege to be back only once or twice. The town has advanced as it must, but changes in familiar scenes were heart-rending. Thomas Wolfe said, "You can't go home again," and how true that is. Where the years went, I will never know.

The Lewis Family

The Lewis clan, which moved into the Midlothian community from the coal fields of Sequatchie Valley, Tenn., via Grapevine, Texas, before the end of the last century, circulated around the matriarch, who, widowed in early life, survived her husband by at least 40 years. Her life centered in her farm, in her church, the Hard Shell Baptist of Mountain Peak, and in her children and grandchildren. Her comment about me was always, "Little Jack looks kind of peaked."

Two of her sons had returned from World War I with mementos of the experiences they had had. She displayed the picture of one, a pilot, helmet and all, in a frame shaped as a portion of an airplane propeller. He had become a school teacher-farmer looking after his mother's farm until he married and rented land of his own. Another had been an ensign in the Navy. The picture of his ship was prominently displayed on the wall. He rented land, then bought a farm in the Depression and lost it. His family cared for his mother and her farm in her declining years. During World War II, he worked in a war plant in Dallas; I asked him how he was doing, and he remarked that if he had two jobs like that, he could afford to operate his farm. He was ultimately elected to a term in the state legislature, and after that he sold insurance.

The daughter taught school until marriage. Her husband tried a number of occupations, including farming. At one time, they lived with her mother and cared for her while he sold J.R. Watkins products. Ultimately, he became a peace officer and was killed in the depths of the Depression in the line of duty. There was no insurance. His wife was forced to place her children in the Masonic home. She was later a social worker and still later a hostess at an orphanage supported by the Eastern Star organization.

Another son was a bank employee in Waxahachie until the oil refinery there closed, greatly to the damage of the city's economy. He then took up insurance sales. Yet another son and his wife taught school outside the Midlothian area.

My father farmed on the east edge of Midlothian; and then there was the youngest son of the family, Bob, who sought his fortune in the Berkeley area of California making only periodic visits home. Family conversations always got around to the latest letter and to the question of when Bob would come next. The coming of a king could not have been anticipated more.

The Lewis home, located about two and a half miles southeast of Midlothian, was the clan-gathering place on Sunday afternoons. There one met uncles, aunts and cousins. The adults talked, and the children played week after week. There was farm machinery to investigate, including an old Ford tractor with steel wheels. It was too early for rubber tires. The shop had a hand-cranked drill press and other teasers. Then there was the barn – just right for hide and seek. Here and there ran kids big and small. The games were not exactly fair to the small, but they were never shut out.

The trip to Grandmother's house started out on the Mountain Peak road and then turned east at the south end of the Rice farm at Hillie Mahaney's place. It passed the Hawkinses', the McDonalds', the Mundans' and the Suddeths'. There were also a couple of Negro families living in poverty along the way. Joe Suddeth was a capable worker in the fields, but he had been born with a cleft palate which had never been repaired, making Joe difficult to understand. Offered ice cream at a Lewis gathering, Joe spooned the frozen delight down too rapidly and while eating and rubbing his head said, "My head hurts."

In wet weather, it was better to head down the Waxahachie Pike which was rocked, to cross the railroad at Dorsetts', and to continue to Rocky Shoals where at one period someone operated a swimming place. There one crossed the railroad again and turned west by Zion Cemetery and DeWitt McDonald's farm. There was less mud road this way; but once we did get mired up, spent the afternoon spinning wheels, and finally had to be pulled out by mules. The driver of the mules sat straddle the hood of the car, and the car engine and the mules got us out.

Christmas was clan-gathering time. Following earlier gift opening around trees in each family home, the whole group gathered at Grandmother Lewis's home for exchange of presents and for the family dinner. The ladies not only had worked long on handcrafted presents to exchange, but there were all the tasty dishes that go with Christmas to prepare. Candy was in abundance. I was never in the home of Uncle Jay when he did not pass candy. When he was old and in the nursing home, his sister-in-law, who was somewhat responsible for him, worried about his spending his entire retirement check on candy. The doctor calmed her, "He has lived 85 years. So he does like candy!"

True, we later went our separate ways, but family had a different meaning in that world than in the one in which I reared my sons – one in which they saw relatives only once a year, if that often; one in which uncles and aunts were almost strangers and in which cousins were only names.

Childhood Memories

Midlothian never had an air strip; however, my interest in flying was kindled before I went to school. Boyd Tindell, having returned from the war, had acquired an old biplane which he kept in the pasture on the Stephenson place southwest of town. Around and around our then white house on the east edge of town I ran following his circling long before I started to school.

One day, Tindell made a forced landing in the wheat field toward town south of our house. People flocked out through the unripe wheat to see the plane, much to the damage of my father's crop. I was taken out to see what the thing I had been chasing looked like on the ground and to see where the pilot and passenger sat. The episode touched off a spark in me which has never burned out.

The plane stood many years along the Mountain Peak road in the corner of a field on the Stiles place, surrounded by a barbed-wire fence. Later, the plane was no longer flown, and Tindell stored the frame, with all the covering gone and with the wings off, in the garage at the east side of the south end of the main street. I passed by it on the way to school every day. Later, it was in the garage that was on the main corner of town just north of the water tower. I saw it from the door many times when passing by and finally got up the courage one Saturday night to ask permission to get into it and sit a few minutes.

The barnstormers on occasion made Midlothian, using cow pastures for their landing field. Once a group came to a pasture out past Stephenson's place, and we went out and watched them, including the parachute jump. I can still hear the public relations man pleading with the crowd for contributions for the lady who had endangered her life by jumping. I was far too small to know anything about flying, but the side-slipping of the pilots as they lost altitude in order to make the short area of the pasture amazed me. They chased the cows out of the area with the planes.

It was a great day when D. Harold Bird, an oil man formerly of Midlothian, on two occasions brought his plane unannounced to Midlothian and used the Lloyd Rice and the Paul Rice cut-over grain fields on the Waxahachie road for a Sunday afternoon of rides for chosen friends. By then, Charles Lindberg had flown the ocean. Byrd's plane was a monoplane, not the biplanes we had seen before. The community turned out to watch. People came down telling my father how small his cotton looked from the air. He would have seen for himself had the offer come, but he was not in the circle to get a ride. He never rode in a plane. Byrd's father from time to time stuck a few children of about my age who belonged to family friends into the plane. There were many of us who wanted to fly, but even D. Harold Byrd could not give a free ride to every person in town.

Another group of barnstormers during the depths of the Depression used the cut-over field on the Stiles place beside the Mountain Peak road. By that time, I was about high school age and was working in the fields at 50 cents to a dollar for the longest day. It cost 50 cents to ride. Being tight by nature, I could not bring myself to spend the money for what I felt like I would have given almost anything to do. My brother Roy spent his money, took the ride and then when getting out of the plane saw 50 cents lying in the dirt. With such luck, his ride had not cost him anything.

It was not until after college and beginning graduate school that in the post-war period I finally got into the air in an old DC-3 of Eastern Airlines, which made nine stops between Providence, R.I., and Meridian, Miss.; but it was still a great experience. The thrill has not dulled after hundreds of flights, the gaining of a private pilot's license, and several hundred hours on my own in the air. It is a bit like the man who, concerned with the wickedness in the world, wondered why the Lord had not destroyed the whole. After his first plane ride and his seeing the beauties of the landscape from above, he came down to say, "I understand now! He has a better view of it than we."

A good portion of us in Midlothian walked to school except in bad weather. A lot about life was to be learned along the way. The sidewalk for us only began when we got to the Loves' house on the south side of the street. It was a quarter- to a half-mile from my house to the Santa Fe railroad. At that time, there were two sidings and the main track to cross. The passenger train made a round trip from Cleburne to Dallas each day. It was just at school crossing time that it made its morning stop going toward Dallas. If we were not ahead of time, we did not make it across until the train pulled out, so we got to see the mail and passengers unloaded or loaded. The night train going the other direction just about marked the time to go to bed in the evening, except in those times when one had to put someone on the train. My parents did that for visiting preachers on occasions. I never rode the train out of

Midlothian until after college when I started north to go to Harvard. On that occasion, I took the train to Fort Worth on the other track that ran from Ennis to Fort Worth beside our farm. From there, I went to Oklahoma City to visit my father-in-law where my wife was waiting.

In Midlothian, once one crossed the railroad going west, on the left-hand side was Cowart's lumberyard where Mr. McEldowney worked. I knew him because Caroline, his daughter, was in my class, and his wife was known over town for her Baptist church activities. She regularly was asked to lead in prayer at public functions of school and city, the only woman in our community to do so. At the lumber yard, one could sell for a dime each the whisky bottles he had picked up on the city dump. The lumber yard sold turpentine in them. On the right-hand side of the street, just west of the railroad, a factory was built at an early time on land that had previously served for a wagon yard. The factory building had a colorful history but proved to be the graveyard for many enterprises. I have long since forgotten the list of them.

One next came to McElroy's filling station and garage which was on the main corner. The route to school led straight across the main street here. At that time, this south street westward from the corner had not become a highway beyond this corner. Going from north to south, the highway ran down the main street, and one turned east at the south end if he were going to Waxahachie. Cities had not bogged down with traffic. There was even a parking area down the center of the main street as well as along the sides. Merchants would have fought any suggestion that the main highway bypass the business district. It would have ruined business. The pavement ended short of the intersection at the south end of the business block. It was the custom to U-turn here and head back north on the east side of the main street.

If one had occasion to turn up the main street, on the east side, he came (in my late years, but not the early ones) to Henry Spearman's shoe shop. At one period, a business ladies' lounge was on the east side of the street. Then there was the post office. Next was Pat Martin's furniture and hardware store. Martin was also the undertaker for the city and was aided by Mr. Clifford Patton. A part of the store was taken over during my years and made into a medical office for Dr. Harris. In early years, Harris's office had been in the upstairs on the west side of the street. Like many others, I hollered "Ouch" many times in Dr. Harris's office, and I was greatly distressed when his life was taken in a car accident after I had left for college.

The Bentleys, who had a son named Benson, had their variety store along this eastern row, and I did a lot of wishful thinking going through its aisles. Mr. Maggard had his butcher shop. The community was shocked when Thad Brown was shot on its rear steps by Mr. McGrew. Then there were grocery stores; at one time, one was owned by Mr. Copeland. Hamby Taylor clerked there. Clarence Saunders, originator of the supermarket idea, tried a store which was short-lived in Midlothian. It was advertised by the phrase, "Sole owner of my name." Saunders's Pink Palace houses the city museum in Memphis, Tenn., where I have lived for more than 50 years.

Around the corner from the grocery was the water tower and the fire station with the city lock-up above the fire station. Across the street from the grocery, still going north, was the garage at one time operated by Wave Few, and then there was a restaurant and then True's blacksmith shop. After a vacant space used as a wagon yard, on the next corner was Allmon's establishment which was a combination filling station and veterinarian's place. I did not make many stops there, but once we did take a bull for dehorning. Dr. Allmon used bolt cutters to remove the horns; the blood spurted from each horn like a geyser, but it did not seem to bother the doctor any. The walls were sprinkled down before we got the animal out into the open. I think that nothing was done to staunch the flow, but the animal survived anyway. After that time, we tied the head of future victims between the crouch of a low-hanging tree and sawed the horns off with a saw.

Doc Allmon himself, who served on the draft board when the war came, lived across the street to the north of his establishment; he had his garden along the street, but I have long since forgotten who lived in the houses after that. The highway made a sharp right turn at Doc's corner, passed a gin, and then either crossed the railroad to continue on to Ovilla or more prominently made another sharp turn after one block, this time to the left, to continue on to Dallas.

The locker plant on the right at the turn was built only after I went off to college. One soon came to the oil mill and the ice plant. At the ice plant, one could pick up ice for the old ice boxes which almost everyone used at home before the war. There were a few electric refrigerators with a queer round contraption on top for the freezing machinery. At the ice plant, the 300-pound blocks were made in molds that were lowered into the chilled brine for freezing. Then they were stored until needed. It was exciting for a boy when the family purchase of ice happened to correspond with the pulling of the molds and the dumping of the blocks of ice. It was also thrilling to see them pull from storage a 300-pound block and run it through the saws to score it for chipping into 100-pound or 50-pound blocks. With tongs, a strong man could put a 100-pound block into his refrigerator. What a thrill to be permitted to get the saw shavings off the machine for cold eating or to make snow cones. For those who wanted it, there was door-to-door delivery of ice, and the ice man was a significant member of the community. For delivery, one put his ice card outside his door or in his window showing the number of pounds he wanted. When I went east, I discovered that the ice man refused to carry ice to third-floor apartments. I bought the first gas refrigerator I could get in the post-war period and have had little to do with the ice men since.

The oil mill dealt in ginning cotton, in selling cotton, and in making oil out of cotton seed. For a farm boy, weighing the loaded wagon, watching the cotton being suctioned off the wagon, seeing it go through the ginning process, weighing the empty wagon and collecting the seed if one wanted to keep it was all a part of rural education. The hulls of the cotton seed and the meal from them were valuable for cow feed. In such circles, my identity was "Pearl Lewis's boy."

At one period, the oil mill was active in shipping cotton by truck to Houston. Men vied with each other for the fastest round-trip run to Houston over roads far less suitable than anything around today. Reputations for daring were built up, and on occasion one saw around town on crutches those who had survived some accident with their truck.

Still ringing in my ears are the screams which awakened me in the night when Furman and Dorman Sewell's mother (whose house was a half-mile or more from ours) received the news of her husband's fatal accident, leaving her a widow with a house of small children. She supported them by working. Tragedy again struck that family when Dorman lost an eye in a childhood accident with a BB gun. The wreckage of Sewell's pickup truck was hauled home on one of the company trucks and was left for a long time on the oil mill lot, a sad reminder to the community of what had happened in its midst.

Life in Midlothian had some aspects of which we are now deeply ashamed. The one Mexican family lived on the south side of the Ovilla road, some of its members not able to speak English. Jose, Lidion and perhaps some sisters were in school with the rest of us. They were fairly accepted in the community. The Mexican ladies pierced the ears of some other ladies who requested it. The men worked in the fields. Perhaps the greatest prejudice that was shown was in the feeling one should not trust them too far. My task was in weighing the cotton to make sure that there was no cheating on weights. On the occasion that a big rock was thrown off the wagon when someone was emptying sacks (whose sack I did not know), I was convinced that the suspicion was likely well founded. The Mexicans were good workers.

We also had one Jewish family who opened a shoe store on the main street near the southwest corner. As new immigrants, their English was broken, and the community knew that they were different. Being in need, they did a hard sell; the shoes did not always fit and did not always hold up. A daughter, Ann Rosenberg, was in my second- and perhaps third-grade class. Though not at all unattractive, she was the only girl with long black curls; and she was taunted with "Ann, Ann washed her feet in the dishpan." This family lived in the back of their store and complained that they were harassed by noise made by the band which occupied the floor above them.

The days when blacks were forbidden to stay overnight in Midlothian was earlier than my time; however, I was told that such days had existed. There had been a sign on the edge of the city warning the black man not to let dark find him in town. I was also told that it was the oil mill which imported blacks for labor and protected them until they were accepted.

I do remember one occasion when at night we went to town to see a march of the Ku Klux Klan. With their white robes and hoods and torches, they marched down the main street at night in a frightening way. Then they burned a cross on the Waxahachie highway in the pasture that belonged to Mr. Dorsett. I never knew what touched off the march.

Most of the blacks were housed across the street from the oil mill along the Dallas highway before one reached the railroad. Though the state paid $16 per student (as it did for white students), the black students went to class in the black Baptist church in their area – a one-room situation. Integration had not been dreamed of; facilities were separate but in no sense equal. Professor Mills, superintendent of schools, even then commented adversely on the inequality. Occasional black families lived in poverty quarters adjacent to families by whose names they were generally designated, like "Bell's Negroes." Some worked in seasonal labor on the farm for us.

In the summer when revival time came, it was the custom of the Church of Christ to set up its benches in the open air at the back of its building. The open air was a great help in the era before air-conditioning. Some blacks attended, but seating was provided for them on the west side of the area in a separate section. The practice of segregation was the same in the churches that it was in the culture in general.

Coming into Midlothian from Dallas, after one passed the black section and then passed Doc Allman's corner, he saw a garage on the right opposite Allman's which was operated at some period by the Brundages. Then he came to Jennings' Chicken Shack. Since we furnished milk to the Chicken Shack, I was in it many times. It was a period before sanitation was what it is now. The bottles were scalded, but the caps were pressed in from the top leaving the rims to collect whatever they would. In Midlothian, at least, pasteurization was unheard of.

The big office building on the northwest of the main corner housed offices for insurance and real estate persons. The names of Rea and Dees were encountered there. The corner itself was occupied by the bank. In the days of Floyd Hamilton, one night the bank was robbed. The robbers used torches to cut into the vault. On the way home from school the next day, we all had to stop by to see the sight. The bankers were busy trying to arrive at an estimate of their loss. The big holes were there in the vault door where the robbers had cut their way in.

In my early years, D.B. Holland had a dry-goods store on the north side of the street west of the bank corner. The Hollands had a Mongoloid (now called Down Syndrome) son who was the town personality.

Because both his mother and father worked in the store, he was always on the streets of downtown. Max seemed to be able to understand some of what was said to him; he was loved by everybody. He could make noises, but he could not talk and make himself understood. He was passed along in school to about the fifth grade – which happened to be the one I had arrived at – before the teachers brought an end to his school days. Max was very prominent in the downtown area. On parade days, he was always out in the mock pretense of directing traffic.

It was in the Hollands' store that I saw the first effort at air-conditioning. I think it was one of the Byrds that had on display an electric fan of the desk type with a wet cloth over it for the air to blow through and with a pan fixed so that the cloth would suck up needed moisture. The idea was sound for the evaporative cooler, even if the cooling at that stage was minimal.

The store had the old trolley wires by which the payments were sent up to the cashier's office and the change was sent back down. For a kid, it was a show. The Hollands had the old cloth sample books by which one picked out material for a suit from small samples and then had it ordered. My family used discarded sample books for scrap books in my childhood years. My scrap book, of which I have memories of many fond hours, is still in the possession of my sister. One of its paste-ins was a scene of a mother coming into a room to see her small child playing in the coal scuttle. He was covered with blackness but was pointing to the cat, and the title of the scene was "Kitty did it."

At times, there was a grocery store along the north side of the street as one went west. Then there was the hardware store. I remember Sam Martin and Ed Cooper in the hardware store. And there was another filling station and garage, and at one period Wave Few was there.

North of the highway, on the street which ran north and south, just west of the business buildings of Midlothian, on the west side of the street and almost a block off the highway, was located Caldwell's blacksmith shop. Caldwell's house was just south of the Santa Fe station on the west of the road to Waxahachie. His son Charles was in my class at one time. Broken farm tools and wagon tires needing shrinking required the arts of the blacksmith. He heated his fire with a hand-cranked bellows and quenched the metal in a wooden tub filled with water. Caldwell swung the hammer with a mighty arm during the week but found his second calling on Sundays and at public functions as usher at the Methodist church. He had a knack of packing people in. One of the tricks was to make two children occupy the same chair. Baccalaureates were often held at the Methodist church and, being in the summer, were very warm occasions. Added to the misery was that Midlothian was subject at that season to infestations of what we called "oat mites" – small black crawling insects which made church very uncomfortable. In fact, one of my uncles called them "church mites." People fanned themselves with fans furnished by the town undertaker. I thought I had gotten large enough to occupy a seat by myself. Caldwell came looking for space and saw my younger brother and me side by side. He asked if we could not sit together. I said boldly, "No sir!" Caldwell backed off, but the people around me roared until I was so embarrassed I could have died. I think it was one of the McDonalds who was either a late teenager or in his twenties who said aloud to me, "If they wanted to sit, they could have come early like you did, couldn't they?"

Various stores occupied the south side of the Fort Worth highway. Another part of the Holland clan had a dry-goods store. At one time, a theater, a dry goods store and a grocery were there. Back on the main north-south street at the corner was a bank where Mr. Alderdice was a cashier. One put his check in the window; Mr. Alderdice looked at the signature on the check and asked abruptly, "What is your name?" When the bank folded, this area became the A&P store. On the west side of the street, south of the bank or grocery, was the constable's office. Mr. Hayes (called "Handlebar Hayes") rendered that service many years. The theater moved around onto this main street. There was also an insurance office, and Mr. Sewell held forth in it. There was Lloyd's drug store where Mr. Beddow was one of the employees. His son Bob was in my class, and so I knew them well. They lived in the house north of the bandstand at Kimbell Park and built before my time by my parents as their first residence when they married. Haggards had another drug store on the main street. There was also a bakery.

I think we had only one zero spell in the winter during my childhood. At that time, my mother was in the hospital in Dallas, and my Uncle

Jay had spent the night at our place looking after us. In the morning, he took me to Lloyd's and bought me an ice cream cone. I have never questioned since that day that cold weather was the perfect weather for ice cream. In fact, any weather is perfect weather for ice cream. Someone commented in my presence not too far back that humans are the only mammals that drink milk after infancy. My retort was, "It is easy to explain why. Monkeys have not yet learned to make ice cream!"

Mr. Bennett had his barbershop in the row near Lloyd's Drug Store on the west side of the street. Here, Bennett himself, Ben Merrill and Curly DeGrande tried to keep the men of the town presentable. The old ceiling fans made the place bearable in the summer, and the spittoons on the floor gave a semblance of sanitation. Nothing is so itchy as getting a haircut when one is sweating. The barbers would take men straight from the thresher without a bath if the fellow wanted a haircut. A boy could sit out his turn and listen to a lot of things he needed to know and, perhaps, a few that he did not need to know. Excluding a few suggestive jokes now and then, most of the talk was reasonably clean. Bennett was a good Methodist, but gossip as well as truth was included in the exchange.

This was just the period when ladies began to cut their hair. So a beauty parlor was in this area also. Naturally, I never had any occasion to know what went on there. If my mother ever went to a beauty parlor, I never had any hint of it. As many other ladies of the time, she did her hair in a knot at the back of her head, and that did not require a hair dresser.

Once one turned the corner westward at the south end of the main street, he at one period was at the feed store; then at another just beyond the corner was the location of Burrett Byrd's operation for Sinclair Oil. Byrd at one time gave out rubber dinosaurs advertising Sinclair Oil. When the town was filled with small blown up rubber dinosaurs, it would have been hard to convince any kid that Byrd was anything but the best of characters. Sinclair Oil had also made a life-long impression. At another time, this area became Teddlie's book bindery, and for a time a half-dozen or so of my friends worked there. Still later, this area became an express office and a bus stop.

In my early days, Midlothian had a volunteer community band, and part of our entertainment was to go to Kimbell Park and listen to them play there in the bandstand in front of Beddow's house. People could park their cars on the street and sit around to listen. But on Saturday nights, the band also played in the filling station on the northeast corner of the main intersection near the water tower and fire station. Opposite was the bank.

On Saturday nights, people from the farms drove into town and parked. Some promenaded the street, and one could see who was with whom. It cast some light on local romantic attachments. Other people, like my mother, sat in the car for an hour or so to observe the people go by. Friends stopped to speak. It was the widest contact with the community. Everyone came to town. The band and its concert were a part of the whole.

The band, led by Mr. A.T. Baggett, decided to become a part of a reserve military unit out of Fort Worth. We all went to the auditorium at Dell Mason Dees Hall at school to listen to the concert with military officials there for an audition. The effort proved successful. The band was accepted and then had better equipment than before. After that, they did a lot of drilling in the park. The band now made its headquarters uptown in the upstairs over the Jewish shoe store and the Teddlie Bindery area. In the summer, the band went to Palacios for maneuvers. The community turned out to see them load on the train on the Fort Worth-Ennis line. Year after year, we saw them ride off on the train for camp. It is this program which determined the role of many when the war came on.

Other than the main streets, the streets of Midlothian were not paved in my early years. In some cases, one just had to wait for the ground to dry to get through. However, Model T Fords were built with higher clearance than modern cars are. There was no natural gas for cooking and heating at first, and there was no sewer. Everyone had his outhouse, and the alleys permitted the garbage man to clean them out.

Finally, the sewer was put in. It was a major project, taking many months. A special crew (not too complimentarily called "sewer rats") came in for it, and one might as well admit that some romantic affairs went on.

Putting in the line down the street which separated my father's farm and town was quite a feat since there is a great rise from the cemetery up to the crest of the hill. The line was almost on ground-surface level at the cemetery but had to have deep shafts and tunnels as it went north through the hill toward the railroad. There was a lot of blasting and rock accumulation. There must be a guardian angel who protects boys growing up. The shafts and tunnels were left open with no guards for boys on the prowl to go through. Had there been a cave-in, first, no one would have known that the boy had ventured in there, and second, there would have been no equipment to attempt a rescue after it was decided that was where he was.

In the early days, the west approach to Midlothian was up Sharkey Hill. The present route of the highway from west to east had not been set until I left Midlothian. The north approach was by the train station and the oil mill, Allman's place and the main street. At the south end of the main street, one turned east, crossed the railroad tracks, made an abrupt turn south, and went to Rice's corner before turning east to Waxahachie. Back in those days, Sharkey Hill was a good test of a car's stamina. To make it without having to shift into low was a feat to try for.

My Grandmother Holland's house stood on the crest of Sharkey Hill, on the south side of the road, back up a lane. Kimbell's was on a projection of the hill somewhat to the north of the highway. It was a prominent looking place, but I was never there. Since Grandmother died before I started to school, these days were long ago. At her death, the house passed to one of her sons who did not live in Midlothian, was occupied for a time by the Emory Holland family who were my cousins twice removed, and then ultimately sold out of the Holland family.

The rocking of some of the rural roads around Midlothian came fairly early in my memory. Rutledge's pit east of the cemetery was the source of supply. The wagons had a special bed for hauling rock and gravel. The driver brought his wagon to the dumping location, took off its sides and then one by one moved out the boards of the bottom while dropping the rock or gravel off. The boards and sides were then replaced, and the driver went for another load. The rock had to be shoveled in by hand at the pit. As very small children, my sister and I stood by the side of the road at noontime with our father's lunch waiting for the passing of the line of wagons until he came.

The first real road improvement I remember well is when it was decided to run the highway from Cleburne and Alvarado along the Santa Fe railroad and to come in from the south on the street that crossed the older highway where the Baptist church was located. There was talk of its continuing on to Dallas, bypassing the main business section; but the north section never got built. We kids coming from school found it interesting to watch the road crew lay the rock base on which the highway was to be built. At this time, there were new dump trucks, and we were amazed at their power and capacity. The road furnished employment for a lot of locals who had not done that type of work before; one was surprised at how many young men not accustomed to manual labor dropped their dignity and in the Depression were glad to work at hard labor. This road made going to Venus and Alvarado easier; the slope was gentler than Sharkey Hill. The test of the road came later when a bicycle contest was held between Harland Hicks and Charles Caldwell, two powerful cyclers, to see who could come from about Reeves's house, five miles away, up the hill to the school ground in the shortest time.

Children were born at home in those days, and the practical nurse was in attendance for at least a couple of weeks. Miss Mattie Pegram was used by a lot of people in Midlothian; in addition to her nursing and housekeeping, she had a way of telling stories to children. At her visit about the time I was six, after two weeks of her stories and her promise of a pony and other enticing things, it was a hard decision to make whether to go with her or to stay with my parents. I was not old enough to realize that it was all a game.

At an early age, I had been with my father to the gin, and then we stopped by the side of the house before going on to the field. I was big enough to climb over the back of the wagon but not big enough to hold on. Glen Price and one of the young ladies were disputing over the reins to determine who would get to drive on to the field. I am not sure of how much of the squabble I remember and how much I was told. Anyway, the team started, and off on my head on the hard ground I went. I only remember waking up in my mother's arms as she sat in the swing on the porch while others were standing around looking mighty penitent. I have always had a valid excuse for strange behavior. I fell on my head when I was a baby.

We had trees to climb, and two box elders at the front of the house had limbs just right for children. Unfortunately, they died, and much later a live oak was persuaded to grow on the south; but it was too late for play. The old cedar tree on the south of the house and the hackberries also made great play places until the worms killed the best of them. We had no storm cellar. Following one big storm when the wind had passed, the tin was gone from the barn, scattered across the field, and the roof of the house was ruined. The cedar lay flat on the ground, and the other hackberry had blown over partly on the house. We got new coverings on all our buildings. Ladders were around, and boys could climb even when too young to do any driving of nails.

People must not have thought about liability and lawsuits back in those days. When the Emory Holland family moved off the hill into their in-town home, we acquired a large rope from them which came from an oil derrick. We entwined it into the limbs of a tree on the north of the house. The rope was at least two inches in diameter and was perfect for climbing hand over hand. Up and down we raced. My brother Roy was behind in one contest and took the fast way down, only to peal all the skin off his arm with rope burn. There were also swings hung from limbs of trees.

We strung a steel cable from that tree to one at least 100 feet to the west, putting a length of pipe over the cable before fastening its ends. The cable was then greased. The pipe was long enough for two hands to grip. By climbing up the ladder and grasping the pipe, one could push off for a thrilling ride through the air until he contacted the ground near the next tree. No question that we had an attractive nuisance; the kids flocked to it; but as far as I know, no one was ever hurt.

From the Hollands, I also acquired the largest mouse-colored female donkey I have ever seen – almost as big as a mule. The cost was a total of $2, with harness and hack included. The Holland boys had outgrown the donkey, and there was no place to keep her in town. She could pull a plow, but most of all she could be ridden and could be driven to the hack in perfect safety. I do not suppose anybody could have made her run. I never detected a tendency on her part to kick. About that time, I went to the fair in Dallas and through the fence saw the horse race. The horses had their tails all trimmed nicely. I came home and tried to trim my donkey's tail the same way. It never grew back again. She was stub tail.

In my earliest school years, Mr. Taggart was superintendent of schools; but later, that task was taken over by Mr. L.A. Mills. My classes started in the first grade with Miss Alta Byers, who later married one of the Bennetts. Dell Mason Dees Hall held the classrooms for the first four grades. The entrance hall carried a list of names of the Midlothian men who lost their lives in World War I. None dreamed that we were preparing for World War II and that it would be the major event in our young adulthood. The auditorium in the building served for school and community gatherings. The flag was regularly saluted, there was chapel, and there were prayers. Those practices bothered no one back at that period.

I have no way of knowing the year, but a speaker came to make a chalk talk in chapel. He sang "The Holy City" while creating a picture of Jerusalem with pastels on paper. Few people from our area went to Jerusalem then – I know none. It never dawned on me that Jerusalem was one of the places that I would ever see. It was a long way from the cotton rows of Ellis County to Jerusalem. But the more than 30 visits I have made to Jerusalem in part had their stimulus by that man whose name I do not suppose I ever knew. He gave the picture he drew to one student chosen by a method I have forgotten. But I would have given just about anything at that time to have been that fortunate student.

Small things make deep impressions on children. A gigantic fire uncontrollable by the departments of Midlothian, Waxahachie, Venus and other surrounding towns called in for the emergency destroyed one of the large, fine old houses across from where Teddlie's Bindery was later to be. Working in the field about a half-mile away, we watched the flames from a distance. The house burned to the ground, and the lot remained open for the rest of my youth.

School graduations always brought the appearance of the president of the school board. Mr. Alderdice filled this function many times; but he had the trait, very embarrassing to him, of invariably forgetting his speech once he got on his feet. I doubt that anyone ever saw him when he did not.

Back in those days, the grammar school building was one of the oldest buildings, and it had no restrooms in it. It was customary to make the classes line up at recess as they filed out of the building, and then the line was dismissed for the grand stampede toward the restrooms in Dell Mason Dees Hall. It was thought less likely that we would corrupt the lower level boys than that the high school boys would corrupt us. Besides, the hours of use with the lower grades did not correspond.

On one particular day, I thought I was in too great a hurry to wait the line and the stampede. There was an incinerator about mid-way between the buildings. I was first out of the building; and instead of waiting the line, I dashed behind the incinerator so that when the line was dismissed, I would have a head start. It would all have been well had not my nearest friend followed me, and then another boy followed him. Mr. Coffee saw the third. When asked why we broke line, my friend insisted that he did not know we had not been dismissed – an obvious falsehood. The teacher quickly replied, "Why then did you hide?" Coffee let it go at that without asking me why I did it, but he grounded all of us for the recess period. I was floating by the time class took up again and had to ask special permission to go. I never tried that trick again.

A bout with scarlet fever nearly took the life of Pearson Hainey one summer. After a long quarantine, people were able to see him again. For some reason, I called at his house and as a child was shocked to see his shaved head and debilitated look. He recovered. Years later, after we were grown and the war was over, I was preaching in Providence, R.I. What a surprise when Pearson and his family turned up for worship! He was in the Navy and was stationed at Newport. However, after an initial visit, Pearson proved to be as irregular in worship as his father had been in Midlothian.

It was the Pegram boys, Robert Spearman, Person Hainey and one of the Hinton boys who kindled in me the interest in constructing models. I found their model airplanes, automobiles with toothpaste-top hubcaps, handmade tools and other things something that I had to undertake. Farming seen from the end of a hoe handle or when hitched to a cotton sack never touched me off. Midlothian then had no 4-H club to teach boys farming; it had no shop training for boys. Apple and orange crates furnished soft wood for working. I still carry a half-inch scar on the right wrist where a butcher knife split the wood too fast in my mother's hand and caught my wrist when she was helping me with the preliminary steps of making an airplane, before I learned to saw.

When I was about 14 or 15, the Fisher Body Corporation announced a contest to build a model of the coach in which Napoleon rode to his marriage to Marie Louise. They offered four-year college scholarships to national winners and lesser prizes to others. The coach is the emblem of Fisher Body Corporation which can be seen on the plate on all their cars.

With the crudest equipment, I undertook making a coach. My mother let me have the corner of her kitchen for my shop. The first year, I did not succeed in making the deadline, though I did make many of the parts of the coach. The second year, I purchased flat materials from a company which offered them. I carved the rope decorations out of all-day sucker sticks. One day the keeper of the study hall at school let me get by with carving in the study hall; but the next day, she suggested that I would be better off studying. Little wonder! Spelling at that point was not one of the things I saw relevant to life.

I shipped the coach off in its box on the deadline day; unfortunately, it suffered some damage in shipping; but it was far too crude to win any of the prizes anyway. I later saw some of the better ones on display at the fair in Dallas. I did get a master craftsman's certificate as did all boys who completed models. Later, the railroad freight offered to settle by paying for the materials it would take to repair the damage done in shipping. They said that a boy's time was not worth anything. I dropped the question and never asked further for a settlement.

Some years later, I met in college the boy who had won the Arizona state competition. I still had my model displayed in my living room until about 1987 when a car crashed into my house and demolished it. When I tried to get the rubble appraised, an antique dealer directed me to a goldsmith in Memphis who had himself built a model in the older boys' category in the contest. He had been a state winner. He had been older than I, had had a father who was a craftsman and had shop training before he built his coach. He evaluated his own model at more than $20,000 after all these years. He volunteered to come out and look at what I had left. I thought he was a little unkind in pointing out the defects in my work. I knew about them already. A boy without training is a little out of his element in a Fisher Body Corporation competition. In exchange for an exorbitant fee, the man gave me a very low appraisal for the insurance company. The company rejected the appraisal as being unreasonably high and chose their professional appraiser. Her figure was five times higher, and her fee, which the insurance company paid, was five times lower.

It was an exciting day in Midlothian when the Singleton farm near Mountain Peak was opened. Here were steel posts and net wire fences as well as new barns of mammoth size with steel stalls and steel gates. We were accustomed to barbed wire strung on wooden posts along fence rows which either grew up in weeds or had to have a lot of work to keep them clean. Barns were old structures that periodically had to be cleaned out. If one had chickens, he was plagued with mites, a condition that had to be treated.

My brother and I drew the task of creosoting the interior of the barn while fighting the mites. Hands and necks were covered with mites; periodically, a swipe of the creosote cleaned the hands of the crawling creatures. No one had suggested that the dip would burn the skin, and it did not feel like it did at the time; but the next day, the skin peeled off, and the sun was merciless in making the hands and neck burn.

Midlothian of 70 to 90 years ago was a very diverse community, extending from those apparently very well off to those with practically nothing. The Jake Sewells, with their fine brick home south of the Santa Fe station and of the cemetery on the east side of the Waxahachie road, gave the impression of having the most affluent standard of living. I was never in the house, but there were house servants and a large automobile when others were driving Model T Fords. The Depression changed all of that. The Sewells experienced reverses and moved to more modest quarters to lead a more restricted life.

At the opposite end of the spectrum must have been Mrs. English, who lived along the railroad track and took in washing to support herself and her daughters. When the Baptists got a young unmarried minister, one of the daughters set her cap for him and was successful. It showed the community that money did not determine everything.

The Roarks moved into town, and the boys did day labor in the fields. Euless made a lot of noise around town with his yodeling. With no pasture of their own, they took their cow daily to the railroad right of way for grazing. It was a sad morning when the cow though staked somehow got on the track and was hit by the passenger train. The Roarks had chased rabbits with their greyhounds, but I still wonder with the cow gone how they had anything to eat.

Jim and Sally Dorton were colorful in their own way. This unmarried brother and sister lived in a small house just west of Kimbell Park. Jim did day labor when it was available. They had no indoor bath. When Sally wanted a bath in a washtub, Jim had to go out back and sit on a stump; and when he wanted one, she did likewise. Jim developed the habit of talking to himself. When asked why, he said that there were two reasons: First, he liked to hear a smart man talk, and second, he liked to talk to a smart man. I understand that Jim, cheated out of his burial insurance payment, was ultimately buried in the pauper area of the cemetery.

The newspaper was run in my day by the Usurys, who had their office on the west side of the main street. That was long before Pen Jones came. The paper was the Midlothian Argus back at that time. The paper was acquired by Noll Sewell, who in his early days shocked Midlothian puritans with a gossip column which hinted at unconfirmed rumors about citizens.

To me, Tom Newton was the personality of our town. Tom worked in filling stations. At first, the Model T had its gas tank under the driver's seat. To fill it, the cushion had to be removed. The cushion was then replaced when the tank was full. The attendant had to pump the gas up by the old hand pump. One could see in the glass tank at the top of the pump how many gallons were being put in by gravity feed. When I was quite small, someone did not get the hose right; and as I stood inside the car for the filling, I got a good showering of gasoline. It was only later that tanks were filled from the outside.

Tom was a likeable character who had a good appreciation for a joke. He liked to talk, and he liked people; but his life was very tragic. His lovely wife had suffered a near fatal automobile accident which left her with motor if not brain damage. Tom took care of her. My mother, late in her life, remarked about how she was impressed with Tom's loyalty to his invalid wife.

Like most of the rest of the town, Tom turned out for the school football games. At first, the playing field was north of the railroad which ran from Fort Worth to Ennis; but eventually, the ground was graded off to make a field back of the school buildings. There were no bleachers. The spectators stretched out along the side lines. At one game, Tom was dissatisfied with some of the calls made by the referee. He kept heckling the referee, and the referee became annoyed. After another heckle, the referee said, "Who is calling this game?" Tom was on the field like a shot and took a swing at the referee. Though he missed, he was quickly pulled off. The referee penalized the Midlothian team heavily. The constable came around to tell Tom to behave himself and that he would be under arrest after the game was over. I heard business men, Tom's friends, quietly telling Tom not to worry; they would take care of his fine.

Another of our personalities was Mr. Nailor, who lived on the north extension from the main street before one came to the cotton yard. Nailor had lost some fingers in some sort of accident. He had a large household which included Talmage (popularly called "Crip"), who had suffered polio but who could blow a trumpet better than anyone else in the community. Public functions always had Talmage to play "My Rosary." Another son, R.L. (but popularly called "Sonny Boy"), was one class below mine. Sonny Boy was a mischievous, energetic boy. We all could have cheerfully killed him the year he pulled his ribbon down on the May Pole dance, making it impossible to unwind the pole. A lot of tears were shed over that. The other pole went through its entire performance without an error.

Mr. Nailor always had a cigar in his mouth and had a habit of rubbing his hands together when in the store and saying, "I want a cigar." He must have had some sort of occupation, but I never knew what he did other than seasonal work in the cotton yard where he cut samples. When the WPA came along, he became chief of a work crew. His health would not have let him do any hard work.

Mr. Spears was the city garbage man. He had the slowest team to pull his wagon that I have ever seen. It was about two miles from the city back to the garbage dump at the east extremity of my father's farm. The Waxahachie Creek, the railroad, the land owned by Mr. Dorsett and that of my father formed its boundaries. The road to the dump ran along the north side of the railroad. Just before one got to the dump, he passed Maggard's slaughter house, and there he crossed back to the south side of the railroad. Both the dump and the slaughter house were far enough away from the city not to pollute the air except when the wind came out of the east.

The slow mules were tempting to idle farm boys who were day-dreaming when they should have been chopping or picking cotton. I am ashamed to admit that one of the Pegram boys and I hid in the tall Johnson grass along the railroad and made noise just as Spears came dragging along with his old team. The frightened mules took off farther than anyone had ever seen them go in one direction with Spears struggling to control them while we took off in the other lest we should be detected. We were relieved when it was over that he was not hurt. We had not even thought about that possibility.

As I said earlier, walking to school is a good education. One came to know who lived in every house, a lot about their traits and what sort of dog they had. One also learned about those with whom he walked.

By the time I got to high school, the bell tower of the school had rotted, and the old school bell which previously could be heard all over town to hasten reluctant children had to be taken down. For a few years, it was rung on the ground to mark the beginning of classes. Then Robert Spearman came up with an automatic bell which he had made by putting a wheel on the winding stem of an alarm clock over which a tape ran that had been cut at proper places so that when the tape got to a point, contact with a bell circuit was made. By carefully setting the clock at the beginning of the day, the janitor could sound the bells at the proper time without being present. Jeff Rickets, the janitor, could be found in the mornings at the bell clock with watch in hand trying to see that the bells would indeed be on time.

Mr. Mills then decided to dispose of the old bell and let some of the boys tie into it with a sledge hammer. They had already broken a chunk out of it before I got my plea in to save it. Mills gave it to me, and we hauled it home and made a chicken coop out of it. It finally went to the scrap metal drive during the war. My pack-rat tendency to save old things goes way back.

When in high school, I volunteered to back Miss Ora Driscoll's car out of her driveway for her on Fridays so that she could go to her home in Mansfield. She furnished a ticket to the football games in exchange. I was proud to do it and had never attended games regularly before. Among other things, she taught some mathematics classes. After her class, I got into trigonometry with Mr. Mills.

Along the way in trigonometry, we came on a problem which I could not solve, and no one in the class succeeded in solving it. We took it to class for several days and kept asking Mr. Mills for help. He kept putting us off until I became convinced that he could not solve it himself. I went to Miss Ora Driskoll and asked her for help, telling her that I did not think that Mr. Mills could work the problem. I assumed that I was speaking in confidence.

She worked the problem out, and I went back to class the next day for a demonstration to the class but was embarrassed to death to learn that she had told Mr. Mills what I had said to her about not believing he could work the problem. I never knew whether he could or not; but I still believe that he could not. Mr. Mills was a good administrator. At the close of my father's funeral in 1952, Mr. Mills came by before we left the cemetery, put his hand on my shoulder, and said, "Jack, if your father could speak to you now, he would say, 'Carry on!'"

Professor Carter taught science and made me the laboratory assistant. My duties were to get out the equipment from the storage room and to return it after the class was over. I was delighted with the task. One day, however, as I was replacing material in the storage room, time for recess came. While I was at the back of the storage room, I heard the door close, the lock snap, and the closing of the classroom door as Carter left for recess. There was no way out. Shouting would have been futile. Fortunately, it was not the end of the day. Half an hour later after recess, the next class convened. I knocked on the door. Carter opened it, and in chagrin I sneaked out, picked up my books, and hit the door as fast as I could. I do not think anyone else was ever locked in the storage room.

Tragedy

Life in Midlothian in the 20s and 30s had ample reminders that people are only a breath. Our street was the scene of its number of tragedies.

Little Cathey Bennett in her second or third year of school suffered a compound fracture of an arm in a fall in the barn and died of lockjaw. Mr. Wesson, the old patriarch with his chest-length beard, lived near downtown in the last house on the north side of the street. Only the electric transformers and some open space separated his house and the Santa Fe railroad. He was regularly seen sitting on his porch until one day when he was walking along the tracks a train backed over him.

One of the Merrill boys, of high school age, was accidentally shot as he talked on the telephone when a friend handed him a handgun with which they had been hunting. It was a crushing tragedy for his parents.

Dave Maggard, star athlete of the high school, made a mighty throw of the javelin at the county Interscholastic League meet at Waxahachie. Unfortunately, a young man, unauthorized to be on the field, crossed just in time to be hit by the descending javelin. Following this fatality, the javelin throw was banned from competition in succeeding years.

Aubrey Springer, trying to kill rats in his barn by shooting them, had the misfortune to shoot just at the moment his young son Dalton looked under the barn from the other side. After great anxiety on the part of the whole community, Dalton recovered to carry a scar on the front part of his head for the rest of his life. He developed into the fastest sprinter in town in my high school days, winning the county and advancing to the district meet.

The box factory came to town and was located on the north side of the Ovilla road just east of the railroad. Strong-armed men working there after setting a nail could drive it completely with one blow. The community burned the waste slabs of the factory for fuel. One sad day, one of the factory's employees, who rented the Woodall house at the end of our lane, stooped to pull a sliver from the saw, slipped and fell into the saw. After this fatality, the box factory did not last long. With the factory closing, my father acquired some of their sheds and re-erected them around our barn, giving shelter to farm animals which previously had been in the open even in the worst of weather.

The one-way bridges on the highway were death traps, and that one between the Rice and Rutledge places on the Waxahachie highway proved to be the Waterloo of more than one unsuspecting traveler. The grade railroad crossings also claimed their victims. One of the Lawsons with two passengers got to a crossing on the way to Dallas at just the same time the passenger train did.

With un-insulated houses largely heated by coal-burning fire places, each winter brought its cases of dreaded pneumonia and the even more dreaded chance of relapse in a pre-penicillin age. Its history is written in the headstones in the family plots in the cemetery. The town had no hospital. The well took turns sitting with the stricken and then buried those who did not make it through. In our end of town one winter, one of the ladies thought she was sufficiently recovered from a bout with pneumonia to scrub the floor in her house. Seized by relapse, she only had time and strength to gasp, "Let me see my baby."

At an engagement announcement, the prospective groom said, "Someone shoot me while I am happy!" A guest grabbed the shotgun, which he assumed was not loaded. He fired, and that ended the celebration.

Farming was hazardous enough without the calamity of the Depression when men who could not afford to raise cotton for 30 cents a pound held it to finally sell at six cents. The radio sang, "Seven cent cotton and forty cent meat, How in the world can a poor man eat?" [1] People were glad to work 10 hours for a dollar a day and then some for 50 cents.

If a farmer planted his cotton and the rains set in, the grass grew faster than the cotton. If he plowed too closely, he buried the cotton with the grass. If he did not, it was a toss-up whether the crop would be worth what it would cost him to get the cotton hoed. A cotton plant dug out of the surrounding grass was stunted. If it did not rain, there was a question of whether there would be a crop. Midlothian farmers did not irrigate with sprinkler systems, and the ground was too unlevel for other types of irrigation. One season, it rained after planting just enough to sprout the seed and bring it up. It did not rain another drop until picking time. Believe it or not, there was some cotton to be picked which had grown without rain!

Someone commented that an infidel is a person who lives a long way from the source of his food supply. Midlothian in the Depression was close enough to bare existence to keep one conscious of his dependence on a higher power and the need to have a treasure which poor seasons, accidents, robbers and grasshoppers could not touch.

Church

Religion was always a vital part of life in Midlothian. The Methodists, Baptists, Presbyterians, Church of Christ and First Christians always had buildings along prominent streets. Families were divided up among these groups. There was some visitation back and forth at revivals, but I cannot claim to know much of what went on other than in the Church of Christ. The preachers of all the groups periodically appeared at school functions. Everyone in the community knew when there was a change of preachers; when a man who had been in town a long time, as the Presbyterian preacher, had been discharged, some suggested that his treatment had not been entirely fair.

There are stories that have been handed down which illustrate something of the zeal of my home congregation in early days – things that happened before my time. It was a point of pride with the congregation that from the day of its beginning the Lord's Supper had been observed every Sunday without regard to weather or other hindrance. World War I intervened with its horrible influenza epidemic. To try to stem the epidemic, the government prohibited public assemblies for a time. The congregation met on the lawn in the open for worship at that period, thereby abiding by the law while also being faithful to the Lord. They rendered to Caesar what is Caesar's and to the Lord what is the Lord's.

My older brother, LeMoine, who has gone to his reward, passed another story to me. It was a time when cars were not as universal as they are now. I well remember the family who came in their wagon from the country and hitched their team to the fence at the back of the building. All others walked or came in cars. The issue confronting the congregation at that time was the introduction of individual communion cups. It seems that all in the congregation except that one family accepted the individual cups. Congregations all over the country split over the question, and the effect of that division a century later still exists. What did the church in Midlothian do? They put a large container in the middle of the tray for those who wanted one container, and they surrounded it with individual cups for those who preferred them. I am proud to have in my spiritual heritage a people who loved the Lord enough and loved each other enough to work out their differences in a way to have peace with each other. I have seen tensions in congregations since that time where people did not manifest that sort of love and toleration. Our history as a people has not always been characterized by that kind of love.

My brother had his own chapter to add to this story, which I learned from him. Years later, he was in a meeting at the Village Congregation in Oklahoma City. A woman obviously very active in the preparation for the service and in the activities of the congregation said to him, "You don't remember me, but I was the little girl with the long brown curls who came to church in Midlothian in the wagon after everyone had cars." I reflected when I heard the story that Midlothian could have driven those people out of the congregation. I have seen it happen in other places. But with the passage of time, the point of dispute was no longer an issue.

The church in Midlothian during my childhood never had a fancy building with a lot of classroom space. It was basically a small vestibule and an auditorium. The exterior was painted white. The once attractive steeple with weather vane had to be taken down when it needed repairs. At the front of the auditorium on the right, a part of the pulpit platform had been cordoned off by a partition higher than one's head to serve as a small classroom as well as a dressing room for men when there was a baptism. Women of the congregation started the children out in Bible study in that space. Their teaching materials were the Gospel Advocate picture cards with a Scripture text on the card. It took a lot of skill to teach children with no more equipment than that. The class seldom lasted for the entire Bible study period. The Rutledge girls, Sister Reaves and others did some of the teaching while I was at that level.

On the left side of the platform was a similar dressing room for women that also served as the next level class in Bible study. Here also various ladies taught. By that level the students could read, and quarterlies from the *Firm Foundation* or *Gospel Advocate* served as material.

Junior high and high school students had a couple of rows of seats at the back of the auditorium. During my time, Brother Emory Holland was the teacher of that level. There was no formal grading or promotion. One just promoted himself when he felt the need.

At the right front of the auditorium was a class for young adult couples.

Various brothers taught it. At one time, my father was the teacher. On the left side of the auditorium was the class for older adults. Brother Lon Reeves was the teacher. Johnson's *The Peoples' New Testament*[2] with notes served as teaching material in some of these adult classes. It was a read-a-verse-and-comment sort of teaching.

All of this confusion was going on at the same time in one auditorium. The congregation did not have resources to build classrooms until after I went off to college.

The Albert Thompson family had five or six children. The older ones of us will remember Sister Maggie Thompson's red hair and her alto voice in the singing. Brother Thompson assumed responsibility for any young people's program that we had. It was a great blessing to us.

At the left front of the auditorium at the first row of pews was a special armchair where Uncle Isaac Holland sat. He was one of the elders. On the right hand at the front of the auditorium was a special armchair for Brother Sam Martin, who was another of the elders. Some people in town called the congregation Sam Martin's church. Ed Cooper with his tuning fork was our song leader. He also took care of the contribution and paid the bills. Periodically, he gave an oral accounting of income and expenditures. In our family, we were trained to give by receiving a nickel each week for the collection plate. Brother Cooper wanted to train younger men to lead singing. Hershel Reeves was the best prospect and developed into a capable leader. One Sunday without previous arrangement, Cooper called on me to lead a song. He really meant my brother Clyde, who had studied some music for the band. I had had none, but Cooper got the names mixed. Forward I went, announced a number, and tried. Sister Witherspoon sitting on about the second row picked up the tune and pitch and carried the song to keep me from falling completely on my face. I will never forget that. When working in the mission field, I often had to lead the songs despite not knowing a note of music. There was no one else to do it.

In my early days, there was no regular preacher; sometimes there was preaching once a month; at other times, various men of the congregation had responsibility for presenting a lesson. There was also some spontaneous speaking. Uncle Bob Reeves often arose to say a few words. Usually, the remarks went longer than impertinent kids' patience lasted. A silent moan went up when Uncle Bob arose. His favorite thought was how eternity went "on and on and on." Identical gestures were always used to give the impression of extended duration. That is what the young people felt that Uncle Bob was doing – going on and on and on.

We were simple rural people doing the best that we understood of what the Lord wanted in worship. Draped across the front of the pulpit was the white hand-worked drape that Sister Reeves had spent many hours making. The drape reminded us of the date of the founding of the congregation. My mother had been present on the first Sunday as a teenage girl. The Lord's Table was covered with a white cloth that had been carefully washed, starched and ironed. At the proper time, the one presiding reverently removed it, folded it and placed it aside. The under cloth had worked on it the words, "In Memory of Me."

Various sisters took special pains in preparing the bread before coming to service. They passed the recipe for unleavened bread from sister to sister. There were no matzos in those days. The bread dough was carefully and lovingly scored so that it was easy to break into the portions needed for the four plates for distribution. If one broke the bread before he said the prayer, he was thought uninformed. The bread was also marked so that each person could break off a one-quarter inch square. At the end of the service, the white cover cloth was unfolded and again placed over the whole.

In these simple ways, we were taught that this world is not our home. We are just passing through. We had stamped in our minds that if we gain the whole world and lose our souls, all has been in vain. With Brother Teddlie, we enthusiastically sang, "Earth holds no treasures but perish with using, ... Heaven holds all to me."[3]

At different periods, we had men coming from Dallas for Sunday appointments. Tillit Teddlie, whose songs we sing, and the Jewish Brother Eckstein, whose book *From Sinai to Calvary*[4] is still around, were among them. Brother Shelton came from Waxahachie; there were others I would not like to slight, but the names escape me now.

The Church of Christ had revivals every summer, and they were great events with preachers like Horace Busby, Cled Wallace, Foy E. Wallace, Jr., Roy Lanier, Gus Dunn, Athens Clay Pullias and G.K. Wallace being among the favorites. There were no amplifiers. A strong voice was needed for preaching. The meeting also brought a chosen song leader. C.R. Nichol, Tolbert Stovall and Tillit S. Teddlie were among them. The preacher was always a guest for meals in various homes during the meeting. It was a delightful experience to have them in our homes.

As we all know, summer is hot in Midlothian. Air-conditioning had not yet appeared. We had the summer meeting outside on the lawn back of the church building. Funeral home fans were a part of the necessary equipment. For a revival, benches which had been stored in the upstairs of the grammar school building were brought out and set up on the back lawn. After a revival, they had to be returned to their storage. No one worried about the separation of school and religion. After I went off to college, the congregation built classrooms, and there was no more space for outdoor meetings.

As the years went along, Harry Reeves became one of the elders of the congregation. Albert Thompson, who lived in the Onward community, did a lot in the direction of work with young people. While all the other families had open touring cars on which one had to put up curtains when it rained, Thompson already had an enclosed hardtop car. My father's family and the Thompsons visited back and forth a lot.

While I was away in college, my own father became an elder, and later Emory Holland did. Emory had been Bible school teacher in the high school class during my years at that level. Also during my high school years, the congregation finally got into a position of having preaching every Sunday. Horace Teddlie moved to town to spend part of his time preaching and part of it binding books. It was a blessing and a step forward for us.

It was not the little brown church in the wild wood or in the dale; rather, it was the white church near Kimbell Park on the main highway. It was a sad day for us when the steeple had come to such condition that it had to be taken down, never to be replaced. The building was enlarged as the needs of the congregation grew, but the architecture was never the same. It was here that the funerals of both my mother and father were held and, fittingly enough, conducted by Horace Busby, who had baptized my father in his early life and then had married my father and mother at the beginning of their life together.

Change

In retrospect, the changes in life since the 20s and 30s are both shocking and marvelous. From Tindell's biplane, we passed to Lindbergh's crossing of the Atlantic through the Tin Goose and on to modern jets. At night, we followed with our eyes the sequence of flashing navigation lights to the west of Midlothian for the early mail planes, but these gave way to radio beams.

We moved from Model T Fords, Darts and Reos to Model A's and Chevrolets. Hand cranks which often broke arms when the engine backfired gave way to self-starters. Kerosene lamps hung on the outside of the car gave way to electric head and tail lights. From these early days, cars moved on to today's burners of unleaded gas. From mud roads which went along property lines and turned abrupt corners to avoid fields, we moved into rocked roads and then to asphalt. Highways came to be laid out on convenient routes, taking choice property. One-way bridges disappeared. Super highways in most areas are post World War II.

Rural schools with multiple grades in one room taught by one teacher disappeared with consolidation and school busing. Before busing, one young man bicycled seven miles each way each day to attend high school in Midlothian.

In Midlothian, someone damned up the spring on the Ovilla road north of the Rea place and made a swimming pool. Town young people with no work to do could ride out on their bicycles for a swim on summer days. A drive-in theater with black and white film but no sound was tried. Captions on the screen told of the plot and the conversations. There I saw my first movie. In time, the silent movies gave way to sound and later to color with a theater on the main street of town.

The past eight decades have been a period which began with mules on every farm to do the plowing. Tractors were rare indeed. When World War II was over, almost as if by magic the mules and horses had vanished. With them went forever the way of life represented by trade days in Waxahachie and Alvarado. King Cotton had given way to diversified farming. Cattle grazed where men had plowed and where men, women and children had pulled cotton sacks before. Mechanical pickers and welfare checks took the place of day labor in the fields.

There was no rural electrification until the Roosevelt era. Filling the kerosene lamp, polishing the chimney and trimming the wick were daily tasks in preparation for coming darkness. Then came some experimentation with wind-driven and gasoline-driven generators. The windmill pumped water into a storage tank from which it flowed to house and to cattle trough. For many houses, drawing water hand over hand with chain and pulley was the only source of supply. Rabbits or other small animals fell into the wells and contaminated the water.

Washday involved drawing an abundance of water. Fires about the old black wash pot heated the water. Rims of automobile tires, when available, though making a lot of black smoke, became a considerable improvement in fuel over wood. The rub board was a part of the equipment of every household. Water was wrung from the clothes by twisting them, or in some cases they were put through a hand-powered wringer. Lines for drying strung in the yard were never adequate, and the barbed wire fence served as a supplemental clothesline for drying. Eventually, Maytag came out with a gasoline-driven washer which agitated the clothes and then powered the wringer. Those people with electric power had the same sort of machines powered with electric motors with less noise. Starch made from powder was used in dipping collars and cuffs and other objects needing stiffening. Lye soap came from grease acquired in the early winter when hogs were killed.

Permanent press was yet 40 years in the future, and ironing always followed washday. After being moistened by sprinkling, the clothes, including innumerable pleats in skirts, were smoothed by hot irons warmed in the fireplace or on the cook stove. People on the electric line in town had electric irons and were regularly visited by their rural relatives who came to do the family ironing. It all led farm wife Lulabelle Pledger at the end of a long day to remark, "I'm tared like I been ornin."

The Watkins man who sold everything from vanilla flavoring to cattle dip has disappeared from the landscape. I am continually reminded of his passing by my school's occupying the estate of Leroy King, who was president of the company. His multi-room mansion with its marble baths and walk-in safes makes up our administration building, and my office was once one of its guest rooms. Gone is the mail-order business represented by the Sears Roebuck catalogue in every home. Gone are the pleasant hours spent day dreaming through its pages about things one had no hopes of being able to order.

On the farm, vegetables were ready for canning at the hottest season of the year. Beans, corn and tomatoes went into cans or jars. Corn had to be pulled at the proper ripeness, shucked, cut off the cob, cooked and placed in sterilized cans. In the early days, the hot cans were sealed by soldering them with the soldering iron; but later there was the rotary sealing machine which made them airtight. If the seal was not proper, the percentage of loss was high. A can with swelled ends had spoiled contents. After a coating was developed which retarded rusting, cans could be cut and flanged for reuse. In the hardest years of the Depression, men searched the garbage dump for discarded, re-useable cans. Peaches, plums, dewberries, blackberries and grapes were preserved in jars.

In the Depression years, most people were "pore," but others were "plum pore." If this requires any explanation, then you did not go through it. Ancient rural rent houses infested with bed bugs were treated by their occupants with periodic burning of sulfur. The advent of DDT was yet a generation in the future. To avoid the heat of the houses, many rural people moved their beds into the yard in the summer. Crime was no major problem.

One highlight of the summer around Midlothian was threshing time. The Miltons, Mundons, Wards and others had their threshing crews which went from farm to farm until the harvest was finished. Farmers traded work with each other and hired special labor. The women prepared tasty meals for their husbands' farmhands. The threshing crew ate at the cook shack which went with the thresher; they slept in the fields in order to begin work at daylight. The workday was over only at dark.

The separation point between men and boys came when one was mature enough to make a season with the thresher. The "pitchers" in the fields with their pitchforks put the bundles from the shocks of grain onto the wagons. The man on the wagon stacked his load until it would hold no more. And then at the machine with his pitchfork, he threw it off bundle by bundle into the threshing machine. Good men "burned out" in the hot Texas summer sun and had to call it off and go home. Harland Pearson set a record for our area by making a threshing season on a bundle wagon minus shirt and hat, becoming browner by the day.

Younger boys could sack the grain as it came from the thresher. The loaded wagons were taken to the barn, and those strong enough shoveled it off into the storage bins. Grain to be sold went on wagons to the public scales and then to the railroad siding where augers lifted it into the waiting train cars.

Threshing lost some of its glamour when the old steam engines were replaced by tractors. The threshers gave way to combines, and an age had passed.

At the end of the Depression, Midlothian seemed to offer only limited opportunities for its crop of young people arriving at adulthood and especially for those who had not caught the urge to farm. The exodus was continuous. Unable to see the "Acres of Diamonds" about which Russell Conwell spoke, we followed the lead of the fairytales we had been brought up on and set forth to seek our fortunes. The grass over the fence may not have been greener, but it looked greener to a lot of us. Sir Edmund Hilary said he climbed Mount Everest because the mountain was there. We had no quarrel then, and have none now, with those who stayed; but there was a mountain we had to climb!

Chapter 3

GET AN EDUCATION

There was never much question about whether I would go to Abilene Christian College or not. My brother LeMoine had been there four years and my sister Loreta one year. My problem was that I thought I wanted to study engineering of some sort. I loved making things but had little concept of what engineering might lead me to. I only knew that ACC did not offer a pre-engineering program. The recruiters from Southern Methodist University who came to Midlothian High School made their program sound exciting. But they did not get me to SMU.

It was heart-breaking when on the night of the senior banquet, Superintendent Mills announced that Dorothy Reese had beat me in grades by a few hundredths of a point. I had worked like a dog that last year to beat her, though I admit that in previous years I had other interests than making top grades. She had been a top student all through high school. I thought I was ahead of Dorothy. The next morning I was in the superintendent's office asking to see the record. As I suspected, a crucial grade had been changed on the permanent record. It was in an English class where the teacher had assigned me the task of keeping the roll, using her grade book for the list. I knew what the grade for Dorothy had been in the first month of the year, and now it was changed to a higher grade, without which she could not have beaten me. Dorothy was really a first-rate student and must have been humiliated at what this new teacher who did not know her record had given her. I told the superintendent that the record had been changed. He did not know anything about it but called the teacher and suggested that I talk to her. The teacher only said that it was her mistake to have a student keeping the roll out of her grade book. No rectification was made.

Off to Abilene

As salutatorian, I still had a smaller scholarship which made college possible. My mother and father canned vegetables and meat during the summer and, with the approaching school year, loaded them into their trailer with my sister and me in their car. Off to Abilene (which was 180 miles away) we went. My housing was to be the room LeMoine had occupied with Arthur Davis for four years, and he, doing a post-graduate year, was to be my roommate; but he was going to be a week late in finishing his summer preaching assignment.

Sister Crockett lived on Cedar Crest and rented space to boys. The Thompson brothers occupied a room in the house, smoked and left the place like a rat's nest when they moved out. They were planning to preach. Irvin Driscol and another student, whose name I have forgotten, also lived in the house; but LeMoine and I had a room off the garage. It had a bed and a gas stove but no washbasin or bath. The creek bank back of it served for an outdoor toilet; there were bushes enough to hide behind. Water had to be carried in a bucket from a faucet on the back steps of the house, and a wash pan served for cleanliness. Bathing was done in the showers at the school gymnasium. The cost of these facilities was $4 a month.

Sister Crockett let the students use her washing machine for an added cost. On my first turn to do the washing, although I had often heated the water at home for washing, had wrung out the clothes and had hung them up, I had no experience in determining what went with what. Socks washed with underwear gave me a set of peculiarly colored underwear, much to LeMoine's amusement as well as of the other occupants of the house whom he made sure knew about it. I wanted to hide.

I was the only student at the Crocketts' who was not planning to preach. As they ranted about the scholarships of the athletes when they thought preachers ought to have the advantage, I was on the negative side. The next house to the north at that time was Bradshaw's. Bradshaw had built on to his house in order to have space for boys. A lot of aspiring preachers lived there – Nick Craig, Arnold Watson, Vernon Hollingsworth, the Waller brothers, Eugene D. Smith, Claude Guild and who knows who else. Back of Bradshaw's, the creek was wide enough and deep enough to swim in, and the boys made use of it without regard to sanitation problems. The school had no swimming pool; college boys find ways to amuse themselves.

Upon arrival in Abilene in the fall, my parents unloaded their trailer, saw that Loreta and I were in our places and then set off for home. The winter's supply of food was stored in boxes under the bed. No feeling of loneliness known to me is comparable to that of being left at college except that of coming to realize that the home-going of a loved one (father, mother, wife or brother) means that they will never be back. Such self-pity will destroy one in the one case as well as in the other, and the only cure for the disease is busy activity. Fortunately, activities for freshmen got under way the first evening.

I had been charged by LeMoine that I should go out for cross-country track. He ran cross country in the fall, and he had won the district meet mile the previous spring. I had never participated in athletics in high school; but I made my way to the gymnasium and asked Sunny Cowan, who was in charge of supplies, for the equipment I needed. Then I set off down the hard gravel road leading south in order to begin getting myself in shape. I discovered that one did not run very far before he gave out. I also learned quickly that inexperienced legs on a hard surface can do a lot of damage. In fact, in a short time, I developed a first-rate problem of shin splints. The shins became so sore that I could hardly make the five-block walk to and from classes, and climbing the administration building steps to class was done only by pulling on the rails and by sheer determination. One afternoon, the gun fired for a practice run of a group of us around the track; by the time I had made the first turn, Coach Weems was yelling, "If you have a limp, don't run."

In Depression days, money was scarce, and we never carried any in the fields. My first week at college, I decided that a quarter was ample riches to carry so that one would never be in want. Years later at a family gathering, I mentioned my quarter, and my father cried, which made me awfully ashamed for having mentioned it.

Freshman activities were exciting for a country boy. I volunteered for a contest in the gymnasium in which a girl fed a boy a banana, and Jaxie Lewis (no relative of mine), later Mrs. Roy Palmer, stuffed me. We did not win but did get rid of the banana in a hurry. In another contest in which one paid a forfeit if he said the word "yes," upperclassman Batsell Baxter sucked me in by asking if I were LeMoine's brother. College publicity literature had described some persons expected to be freshmen that year; and in the evening exchanged on the lawn, it was interesting to meet them. One girl's father was a military pilot, and because I was bugs about airplanes, the story about her had gotten my attention. With the first norther, her father flew up from San Antonio bringing her fur coat, and he landed his plane in the field east of the college.

LeMoine had a crush on a girl which seems to have ended up being pretty one-sided; but his demand of me was that I promptly get a date. I had never taken a girl out in high school. When LeMoine arrived after a week of college and found that I still had not taken one out, I was threatened with no food unless I did. I picked one I had never spoken to, met her at the door of the gymnasium at the end of the evening's activities, and asked to walk her home only to get a flat turndown. A later effort with one in the dormitory who knew Loreta got me one date but refusals after that. Later in the year, I took a girl named Doris out numerous times; meanwhile, LeMoine had gotten over his despair and was dating Doris's roommate. The four of us had some picnics. However, it had all run aground before the year was out.

C.A. Norred was preaching for the College Church. Now and then he came into the pulpit with a frock tail coat. His mannerisms were such that I used to be able to mimic him; but I have long ago forgotten the idiosyncrasies. Freshmen had their own Bible school class in the administration building on Sunday mornings, and the congregation met in Sewell auditorium. W.R. Yowell, psychology teacher, and Lawrence Smith, business manager, were the teachers of freshmen. Yowell was dry; Smith outside of class was known for his yarns about Johnson County with which he entertained at school gatherings. One was of the fellow whose land was so fertile that it wore his watermelons flat, dragging them as the vines grew so rapidly. He solved the problem by putting the melons in little red wagons, but he went broke buying axle grease for the wagons. Bible school lessons may not have been particularly deep, but they were more than freshmen knew.

LeMoine had persuaded me that I should take two speech classes the first semester. I had been in speech contests in high school. I filled out my cards at registration with two classes and got to Professor Schug. He asked me what I intended to major in; when I told him I was heading for engineering, he called the whole registration line to attention and spoke about wasting time with a student signing up for two speech classes. There was no place to hide.

Don Morris, vice president and freshman speech teacher, was genuinely interested in students and from his recruiting efforts knew every one of them. As he called the role, it was something like, "Mr. Malcolm Smith," and when Malcolm answered, Morris would give a million-dollar smile and say, "Mr. Smith from Grosbeck, Texas." There was more smiling as though Grosbeck was the most important place in the world despite the fact that it was a crossroads. One could see Smith swelling. And so it was with every student. Another class member was James Sanders, who was blind; he also got special introductions, as did everyone else.

We struggled through the techniques of speech with stress on various sorts of pauses as well as on other things. I remember the "pause for applause," though I did not expect to get much of it. I worked on freshman debate, and Louie Welch (later mayor of Houston for four terms) and I teamed up to take on high school teams at such places as Baird to which we hitched our way. Louie took me home with him to Post one weekend, and we had a round with the Post High School team. In Morris's class, I spoke once on George Washington Carver but got the location of Tuskegee wrong. Another time, I told of building a coach in the Fisher Body contest. Morris seemed to enjoy that speech and told me of another student named Walter Dougherty who had ranked high in the contest in the Arizona competition. I never saw

Doughtery's coach, but he was around ACC for several years.

English was taught by the track coach, J. Eddie Weems, who had a precise method of speech. He had a lot of stories of his great relay teams of the past and of their winning at the Drake relays. He was particularly fond of one runner who had come from behind and had won.

I saw a lot of Weems when trying to run, and I was really sorry when at the end of the year he moved to Pepperdine College, which was just beginning in California. He took his choice runners along with him.

Weems assigned the English class the task of writing an invitation. Spelling had never been one of the subjects that I put attention to in grammar or high school. I wrote, "I invite your presents … ." Weems read my paper to the class and announced that he would not come. I have had no problem with that word since. I can still hear him dwelling on the word "vocation" which he called our attention to as being in the Bible. I felt like I had sort of evened things out when I came out with an "A" in English for the second semester. The examination trap which caught most of the class was whether to say that a thing is unique or more unique.

My mathematics course was taught by Hosea Lewis (no kinsman of mine). I had done pretty well in mathematics back in high school with courses in both algebra and trigonometry. But I failed Lewis's first examination. In the post-examination interview, I confessed I did not know why I was not getting it, and he said it was too early to drop the course. I had not thought about that possibility. As time went along, it proved that Coach Weems' sister was having trouble in the course, and on the side he wanted me to tutor her. I finally ended up with an "A" in that course also, despite the slow beginning. I later did work with Professor Mullins, who was known to the students from his initials as "Mind Muddler." I guess the work was not too bad. He proposed to me that I major in mathematics, which I had no ambition to do. Do not ask me now what eight times nine and a few other combinations along in that group would equal.

Homer Hailey was at the peak of his Bible-teaching career at Abilene Christian. He quoted Scripture without end, always was reverent in all things and preached at the Fifth and Highland Church, which at that time was meeting in the basement of their uncompleted building.

Hailey had the power to kindle a spark in a boy. Aspiring preachers flocked around him. He loaded up his car when he went out to hold meetings at Albany and other adjacent towns. He was enthusiastic; he thought about preaching, and he talked about debating. His influence and that of others made a future career in engineering less certain than it had been before. However, the way still was not clear. John Early Arceneaux (a well-known Texas preacher and debater) in addressing the preachers admonished them that if they wanted to preach they had to plan to be students all their lives. My reaction was, if there is any one thing I do not want to do, that is it.

The fall ran on rapidly. The football team had not won a game all season. Finally, they did win one, I think against Howard Paine, by one touchdown, and the ACC crowd promptly made it to town to snake parade the streets. We had not gone more than a block or two when Doris wanted out of it, and so we quit.

Homecoming was celebrated by the freshmen building a bonfire. Telephone poles were set on the corners to contain the trash which was stacked high. The goal of the rivalry between ACC and McMurry was to try to burn each other's bonfire. No telling what would have happened to a person had he been caught in the effort. Our bonfire was kept safely for its purpose.

One Spanish teacher in ACC at that time was Fern Hollar, who was a distant cousin of mine and whose grandmother and grandfather lived in Midlothian. She had a car and on one weekend recruited a group of students including Loreta and me to go to Fort Worth and Midlothian. But by the time we delivered the girls to their homes in Fort Worth, it was a late arrival in Midlothian. Fern learned to transport students only to the train station, not door-to-door delivery. At Christmas, I hitchhiked home and made it to Midlothian to learn that the church was having a meeting with Horace Busby as the speaker. This time, it was not in the summer as ordinary but just before Christmas. Noticing the crowd as we passed the building, I asked my benefactor who had given me a ride from Fort Worth to let me out. When the service broke up, people greeted me. My father was behind them. Someone noticed a tear and asked him what was wrong. "My boy is here," he said. It was during this meeting, if my memory is correct, that it was announced that he was to be an elder. He had served many years as a deacon.

I had studied a couple of years of Spanish in high school, but I tackled Latin in college with Dr. Howard Schug (one of the about four men on the faculty with such a title). Schug was a German linguist who had eye problems, had certain mannerisms, but was the essence of courtesy; even when he ran into a chair, he would back off and apologize to the chair. It was the last year that Latin was offered in the college. When I discussed with Dean Adams the fact that I would not be able to go on in Latin with Schug; he assured me that I would never need Latin. For his work as a dean, I am sure that his advice was sound; but for my work as a biblical student, a competent knowledge of Latin would have been one of the most useful tools I could have acquired. After we had struggled for most of the year together, Dr. and Mrs. Schug had his Latin students over for an evening in his home. A Hispanic couple came with their baby during the evening for a wedding which Schug performed while some of the girls held the baby. The students played Monopoly much past the student curfew; when we delivered student Dora back to Chambers Hall in another student's car, she was in real trouble. I understood that she got off by telling the hostess that she had been at Schug's house and that I had seen her home.

On Monday evenings at Abilene, the students had what was called "Mission Study." Visiting missionaries were invited to speak, including both students who had come from areas where the church was not strong and those aiming to go to the mission field when they graduated. Dr. J.W. Treat and Schug were the sponsors and regularly traveled across town for Monday night meetings. I never understood how they had any time for home life at all, seeing how many school functions they participated in. Both were interested in Hispanic evangelism and regularly preached for Hispanics.

Across the street from where LeMoine and I lived were the Bennetts, who had made a fortune from striking oil on their ranch land they had earlier homesteaded while living in a dirt dugout. The Bennetts were caught by the Depression; but the day the bank was to foreclose, oil was discovered. They had given the college more money than any other couple up to that time, and the gymnasium was named for them. Oil had not turned their head; they moved to Abilene to put their children in school, had a cow and sold milk to us at 10 cents a quart. Imagine wealthy people milking a cow and selling milk! Nearby also was education teacher Dr. Grover Moreland. When his regular student was away, he needed his cow milked; my farm experience qualified me, and the remuneration was milk.

LeMoine and I divided the housework. He prepared breakfast; we snacked at noon because of afternoon classes as well as track practice; and then it was my task to fix supper. The basics came from opening cans of vegetables and meat which had come from home. Occasionally, I shopped for fresh vegetables and fruits. I still have a notebook of recipes with which I worked though I have not used them since college days. Cornbread and biscuits usually turned out edible to hungry boys. Vegetable stew with bits of ham for the meat tasted mighty good. And at times, there was fried chicken which LeMoine brought back from his visits home.

I learned to make pie crusts, and the plums my mother canned the previous summer tasted mighty good in a fruit pie properly thickened with the right amount of flour. As the year rolled on, the vegetables slowly were exhausted; the quantity had not been balanced, and there was more canned corn than anything else. Our fields furnished an abundant supply. That abundance of corn left me with a lifetime aversion to canned corn and not much desire even for roasting ears.

The Struggle and Call to Preach

Along in the fall, as student preachers played musical chairs moving up to more desirable places, LeMoine was invited to preach at Olden, which was considered one of the more choice places for student preaching. That meant he had to give up his appointment at Hamby where he had been going for some time. Hamby had trained (and continued to train) many generations of Abilene student preachers, among them Reuel Lemmons. It was LeMoine's idea that I ought to try to go to Hamby, even though I was not at that time planning to preach. I only went to Friday night Preacher Training Class when they had a special speaker whom I thought I ought to hear. I prepared some sort of lesson, made the half-mile walk out to Albany highway, and started walking the nine miles to Hamby with my thumb stuck up at every car which passed. I was inexperienced at hitchhiking. It was the morning of the first cold norther of the fall and was plenty cold. Someone picked me up, and I made it on time. I explained that LeMoine had sent me. They were courteous enough to let me make an effort, and, as I recall, it lasted about 10 minutes. The Estes family, who attended but did not live in the Hamby area, insisted that LeMoine had been in their home many times; and they were kind enough to transport me back to school.

Hamby may have had a half-dozen houses. One of them belonged to Brother Boley, an elder whose wife had died. I was his guest several times at the sparse table he set. The people at Hamby were generous enough to let me make an effort. They had another student they were trying to encourage who also came once a month. Farmers in the area were poor. I got $3 a Sunday for the time I went there. I was a frequent guest of another of the elders, Brother Jennings, and of his son who had recently married. The homes were sparse indeed, but the hospitality was warm. Before I stopped going to Hamby, Brother Jennings developed throat cancer from his smoking and died. Still another family in the congregation was the Sharniks, who were German and who seemed to be prosperous. They went deer hunting near San Antonio, were successful and knew how to cook the meat. That was my first introduction to venison. Sunday dinners were delicious to a batching student.

The Hamby church building was one of those in which the potbellied stove sat in the middle, and the pews were on two sides of the center isle. Two small glasses (no doubt snuff glasses) served for holding the fruit of the vine. I (accustomed as a child to individual glasses) was very thankful that the preacher sat at the front and was served early in the communion. A visiting lady from Abilene, after one of my efforts at preaching, confronted me and asked me why it was that all the preachers preached on the same subjects. I do not remember what I told her. I was very embarrassed, but I knew why they all preached on the same subjects. It was because they all borrowed their sermons from the same outline books, if not from the books from the same speakers whom they heard. We were diligent in getting down the outlines of the preachers we listened to. A preacher's effort was evaluated by whether or not it was an outline that would preach. Hailey ranked high; and when Paul Southern came to teach at the college, his outlines were easy to get down.

Brother Jennings had a daughter named Johnnie, who was a country alto. Sunday afternoon once each month was community singing at the Methodist church building. Johnnie was always in demand for the Stamps-Baxter song quartets. All the singing was of that beat. The song leader from the Northside congregation in Abilene always made it out to the singing in Hamby. He and Johnnie sang on many quartets. He had the tragic misfortune that his gun discharged when he was cleaning it after a hunting trip, killing his wife. In due time, he and Johnnie married, despite the considerable discrepancy in ages. I encountered her once in downtown Abilene after that, but I never knew how the marriage worked out.

The lectureship theme my first year in college was "Missions." An impressive list of men and women from all over the world came. Hettie Lee Ewing from Japan was in the college that year and was in some of the classes I took. Dr. George Benson was just back from China, and he spoke thrillingly of his experiences. It was the first time I had ever seen him. Dow Merritt from Africa told his lion-hunting stories, among more serious matters. The millennial question was heated in the churches at that time; and when the college allowed a brother from Japan, rumored to have such leanings, to model Japanese clothing before the audience, some strong adverse feelings were stirred, even though that person had made no speech. Problems of support of the churches for missions were discussed at length. One was that of the congregation who sent a man to the field and then did not continue his support until he returned home. Someone proposed that there was a need to send the Africans to convert such congregations instead of their sending Americans to Africa. However, Schug jumped up and brought the house down by saying, "If they will not hear Moses and the prophets, they would not hear an African." The lectureship marked the beginning of a new day in emphasis on missions, and many students who heard those speakers later headed for the mission fields.

R.H. Boll came to Abilene for a meeting at a congregation known to be premillennial. LeMoine suggested that we go and hear him, though we certainly did not want anyone to know that we went. Our social standing among ACC student preachers would have dived to zero had it been known. Boll was a capable preacher, but he impressed me as being somewhat mystical. I do not remember the topic, but I think it was, "Is the Coming of Christ Premillennial and Imminent?" I shook hands with him after the service and told him where I was in school. He made no comment. I never saw him again.

It was widely advertised that Foy E. Wallace, Jr., would speak on Sunday afternoon at the Northside congregation's building. I hurried back from Hamby that Sunday in order to hear him. Homer Hailey had given us a lot of material in his Bible class on the millennial question, and, after all, students are impressionable. Wallace was a master with an audience. He spoke for two hours, and no one seemed to mind the length of the presentation. My father had gone each day to Fort Worth to hear the Wallace-Norris debate when I was a high school boy. He had told us of his various impressions of that exchange when he came home each day. I expect that I could not have spelled the word and likely understood little of what it meant, but I was impressed with the fact that it was something one should oppose.

Clinton Davidson came for a speech in chapel. It was rumored among the student preachers that his position on the millennial question was not clear. He told of his success in the insurance business, stressing what seemed to be his proof-text for success, "I can do all things in him who strengthens me" (Philippians 4:13). The preaching students felt called on to get a commitment out of him. I will not comment on their lack of courtesy. Although he was a luncheon guest at the home of W.R. Smith, a group of us led by Woodie Holdon, who was older than most of us, turned up at Smith's house before the lunch was finished and had to wait until he came from the table. I listened as they grilled him. He was equal to the test; no clear statement was made. Finally, Holdon apologized for the "little dog attack on the big dog," and the group left.

I spent the summer after my first year in college at home working on the farm and speaking almost every Sunday for the Midlothian congregation. Along in the summer, Don H. Morris, vice president of the college, sent me a letter asking if I would like to milk his cow for my room rent the next year. I hitchhiked to Abilene to talk to him about it. His house and cowshed stood about where the Family Life Center of the University Church now stands. It was a lot closer to school than the Crockett place was. I took the job. Morris's garage also had a room attached to it, much smaller than the Crockett one but with the same facilities. The window of the room opened on the cow lot. The cow had to be taken out and staked each day and then brought back in to be milked.

At my first effort at milking her in the fall, I discovered that she was like no cow I had ever met. Milking her must have been extremely painful to her. She kicked wildly. The problem had to be solved by tying her, hobbling her, milking her into a quart cup, and then pouring the milk into the bucket. Seeing my problem, my father acquired hobbles for me before he left me with her. The cow gave about six gallons a day; so apart from the milking problem, she was considered valuable. The milk then had to be taken to Mrs. Morris's kitchen, strained and prepared for use. Mrs. Morris had definite ideas about wearing cow lot shoes into her kitchen.

Because the cow was expecting a calf, along during the winter she dried up; then there was the question of what I would do for my rent. That was worked out by my doing the washing for the Morris family. Daily chapel attendance was required of all students. But the washing had to be done in the morning in order to let the clothes dry on the line. I went to Dean Adams and told him that Mrs. Morris wanted me excused from chapel one day a week to do the washing. He did not see how he could fight it, so he granted the request.

The cow broke loose from her stake a few times and had to be hunted over the neighborhood. I was trying to participate in debate and oratory, and there were meets to go to. What little preaching I was doing was at places which could be reached after the cow was milked and before she had to be milked again. When out of town, I got substitutes to do the milking; but they did not seem to please Mr. and Mrs. Morris. I came back from a speech meet late one night and awoke the next morning with a cold rain falling. In the night, the cow had calved in the lot. I was awakened by Mr. Allen, Mrs. Morris's father who was visiting her. He was in the lot trying to get the new calf into the dry. Before the year was out, they decided it was not worth worrying with keeping the cow and someone to milk her. Years later, when Morris had become president of the school and invited me to become a teacher in ACC,

I told him that after the cow experience, I had never expected to live long enough that he would offer me another job.

The room attached to the garage was large enough for only one person; so this year when I cooked, it was only for myself. On occasion, Bill McCowan, who was batching in another such place, and I would exchange meals with each other. On a few occasions, Mardell Lynch and John Stevens came over, and we worked on debate together. The rest of us worked our heads off; John entered the contests without preparation and won over all of us. Fred Barton entered but always forgot his speech.

The second year put me into Charles Roberson's Bible class. His method was to write his class notes on the board which the student copied into his notebook, and then Roberson went over them. The notes had a lot in common with his book *What Jesus Taught*.[1] Roberson was a dignified person of whom students stood in awe; but at the same time, he touched a spark for desire of learning in a number of students. They would all say that they owed their later academic careers to him. He offered the student the choice of taking final examination or of memorizing a list of passages from the New Testament. It was not hard for me to make that choice. Those passages have been very useful to me over my career. Roberson entrusted me with the task of seeing that the students learned their passages. I was to sit and listen to them recite one by one. I discovered right off that a lot of students – including some preaching students – were really out to bluff their way through, pretending that they knew what they really did not know. It was hard to hold them to the line. I later graded Greek papers for Roberson.

I did a lot of struggling with myself during that year with the question of whether I would try preaching, go on with the engineering or do something else that I had no clear idea about. A winter with the cow and the washing persuaded me that another summer on the farm was not the way I should go. James Reynolds was recruiting students to sell Bibles. He took me down to the hotel to meet the representatives of the Southwestern Company of Nashville, Tenn. A person would have had a lot of resistance not to sign up when Mr. Henderson got hold of him. Students who had sold the previous summer had fabulous tales about their success; those who had failed did not say much about that, so one got a very one-sided picture. But selling books got me out of the cow lot and out of the batching business and put me in the dormitory for the rest of my school career.

Denominational preachers talk about their struggle and call to preach. If they struggled more than I did, they have had quite a struggle. I finally convinced myself that the training I had in speaking, the pleasure I got out of it, the love for study of the Bible, and the need were ample reasons for undertaking it. Before the second year was out, engineering had passed out of my head for keeps. I was ready to accept the reduction in tuition offered by the college for preaching students. A wealthy lady in Houston had set up a fund out of which partial tuition would be paid if one promised to refund the money if he did not preach after college.

Finishing at ACC

Early in my career, I had an encounter with Kendal Jones, who, though of small stature, was a star athlete in tennis and basketball. Some of the athletes who lived in Abilene (of whom Jones was one) showered, shook themselves free of water, and put their clothes on. Seeing me with a towel, Jones demanded that he be permitted to use it. I flatly declined. He replied, “You are a freshman, aren’t you?” Though hazing was against the rules, ACC had not completely ridded itself of hazing. I did not know what to expect next but was not about to be second in using a towel or to take licks from the belt. The incident passed. The second year, when I signed up for Earl Brown’s course in American History, I discovered that Jones was the paper grader. It was the only college course that Loreta and I were both in at the same time. After two examinations in which she made “A” and I got “B” without a mark on my papers, I scribbled a note at the end of the next one which said, “If you are going to mark the paper down, mark what is wrong with it.” The rest of my papers were marked “A.” Student graders are not always as objective as teachers would be.

First Aid under Dr. John Paul Gibson, college physician, could be counted for physical education credit. We learned how to handle various emergencies. The memorable point of the course for me was when I had the task of getting a hypothetical object out of the eye of a fellow student. We were taught to roll the upper eyelid over a matchstick in order to reveal the object. I just could not get the fellow's eyelid to roll. After I had sufficiently tortured the student, Dr. Gibson said to him of me, "Now it is your turn to work on him."

Admission to Alpha Chi, the honor society, was chiefly by grade points and character. Those requirements came as a matter of course, and I participated in the state meetings held different years at Kingsville, San Marcos and Nacogdoches. I had not seen any of these places before but had a burning desire to see the world. Paul Witt, chemistry teacher, was faculty sponsor; by means of those occasions, I became well acquainted with him. He secured a place on the program for my oration "The Gulf Stream," which was an appeal to save German Jews from Hitler's pogroms.

Admission to the A Club was another matter. Grades, character and leadership ability were the requirements. Its stated goal was service. I encountered an upper classman whom I knew from a chemistry class and his having whispered to me on examination, "You have the equation upside down" when I did not know he was looking at my paper. I reversed the equation and missed the question. I learned to be more guarded about who was looking over my shoulder. This student told me that I was being considered for the club; but a few days later, he came back to report that the club had decided that I did not have "leadership ability." Judging from the number of things I have been entrusted to have charge of across life, they probably were right. However, there is always the question of what one is leading and what methods are to be recognized. Snobbery sometimes plays a role in judgments.

The following year, the opinion was different. Induction into the club took the form of a bit of intellectual hazing. It was the custom at the initiation to make the candidate think that his candidacy was still in question and that a few things had to be clarified. Most candidates were anxious to be admitted, so the pressure created by the doubt was extremely strong. On Sadie Hawkins' Day, someone passed the word around that all were supposed to go barefoot to class. It seemed harmless fun enough, but then someone got out of hand and decided that Paul Southern should also be barefoot. Then they tried to take his shoes off; that brought an end to Sadie Hawkins' Day for that year. That I had come to class barefoot was raised as a doubt about my qualifying for the club. Today, I feel certain that I would have said, "Gentlemen, I have better things to do. Good day! You can keep your club!" But with me barely out of my teens, the pressure of the delayed year and the disgrace that both brother and sister had made honor societies pretty well got me down.

Membership in social clubs in ACC was by invitation. It was not a situation where every student was invited to some club; but the select group already in selected the candidates for admission. So money, social activities, popularity and the like formed the lists. It is perhaps "sour grapes" to say that I never cared for membership in any of them – and I was never invited to any. The rumors were that the initiations to some were pretty raw; and at least some students questioned that the activities were really Christian. I never tried to find out what they did. Some fine students were in all of them.

Though with proper planning I would have easily finished college in the regular four years, I decided to spend five years in order to get a double major in Greek and Bible with a minor in speech. I am sure the fact that LeMoine went five years played a role in the decision; but he had been in a post-graduate course, and I was determined to remain eligible for speech contests, track and other things I liked to do. I had been financially independent of my parents after I began selling books or they likely (and rightly so) would have vetoed the idea.

The students were kind enough to elect me forensic manager, which gave me leadership in speech activities and also a seat on the student council. Kelley Lewis (son of Hosea) and I teamed up for debate. It was a Mutt and Jeff combination, for Kelley was barely five feet tall. I was also selected to be leader of Evangelistic Forum for the fall semester, leader of Mission Study, scribe of Philo Koine, vice president of the A Club and also vice president of Alpha Chi. I participated in Pickwickian Club, which was for creative writers, and in Melponinean Players, which was the drama group. In fact, I woke up at one point to the fact that I did not have a single free night in the week.

War was threatening, and the draft law had been passed. All the men of the college had to register, and the lines were set up in Sewell auditorium. Though in my opinion as a preaching student, I was entitled to a 4-D classification, the Ellis County draft board was determined to make it otherwise. It was part my own fault, for in addition to filling out the questionnaire that I was a preacher, I had indicated that I was a conscientious objector. Had I left the last part off, I probably would have had no trouble. I was called to appear before the board several times, which interrupted my attendance in class. Certain draft boards defined their authority wider than the law gave them, and that was all the more so when they met a reluctance to serve on conscientious grounds. The call-ups continued to come through my stay as preacher in Throckmorton and Huntsville, making appeals to the state board necessary more than once.

During the year, the army camp at Abilene opened, and the Oklahoma unit which was to occupy it moved in. The long lines of trucks passed by the college campus. The reality of approaching war was brought home. A drunk soldier climbed through a window in the girls' dormitory one night; after that, prominent football players patrolled the campus at night with night sticks. The mascot of the army unit was a large Saint Bernard dog. A rancher caught the dog chasing his sheep and did what any sheep rancher would have done with dog or wolf – he shot him. There was almost a private war between the army and the rancher.

Since childhood, I had been wild about airplanes. The college this year offered flying as a course; but I could see where those taking it were headed, and so I forewent the privilege. Without a car, I did not see how I could get back and forth to the airport for practice anyway. The one girl in the class married one of the fellows who after the course served as a ferry pilot during the war and then made a career with Delta Airlines.

LeMoine was now preaching in Snyder, northwest of Abilene. I would hitch a ride to Snyder, borrow his car and go out from Snyder to small rural churches to preach. One of these places was Hermilee.

After a summer of book selling in Evansville, Ind., Clyde and I were to room together in the dormitory. He had been less successful than I in selling, so he had immediately to look for work. Luck would have it that he promptly found a place in Helvey's Café, which was across the street from campus. That gave him his meals. I was eating in the school cafeteria. It was not many weeks until he was completely enamored with a redhead who also worked there. In a couple of years, they were married before finishing school. The fact that they completed 50 years together through war and peace, through many vicissitudes of sickness and health, one must admit that it was a fine choice.

I came back from Evansville with a corresponding relation with a girl there named Kathyrn, whose family had been extremely kind to my brothers and me. The Catherine of Nashville, who the previous year ate at the same table with me and on occasions went out with me, was not returning to school for the fall. She had taken me to the movies on Sadie Hawkins' Day, and we had been to the banquets together. One Sunday afternoon when I was in town, I went with the group which regularly went to the county jail to preach to the prisoners. The students stood in a walkway outside the bars and sang, and the speaker delivered his lesson. The audience was a captive one with no option but to either listen or shut the noise out as best they could. One of them asked the speaker if he had to be baptized to be saved. Instead of citing a Scripture or giving a forthright answer, the speaker hedged. On the way home, I was fussing on the bus because of the answer; two freshman girls whom I had never seen before asked me, "Why did you not answer him?" One was an attractive blond with a green plaid jacket.

I suppose Lynell Carpenter was flattered shortly after when I, a senior, asked her for a date. She and her sister Lois were living in Chambers Hall, which was the light-housekeeping dormitory. With the Depression not yet over, with two girls in school at the same time, and with four children at home, a preacher was doing well to send them even on the tightest scale.

One heard from Lois, who was quite talkative, a lot about Joe; before the year was out, Lois had decided to drop out of school at Easter and go to Meridian, Miss., to marry Joe. I think the plan never got her father's blessing, nor did he ever completely forgive Joe. However, two children, numerous grandchildren and nearly 50 years together despite grave sickness would suggest that it was not as foolish as it appeared to some at the time.

One of the activities I attempted each year was the Cox Extemporary Speaking contest. LeMoine had insisted on that during my freshman year. About a month before the contest each year, the topics for that year were posted so that one could make preparation if his schedule permitted it. There were usually about 30 topics so that only surface preparation was possible. On the day of the contest, one drew a topic out of the hat, went off for an hour to get ready, and then delivered his speech. The experienced student preachers usually came off winners. I have long since forgotten the topics I drew. In my final year, T.B. Underwood, Jr., came out in first place receiving the gold medal. I came out second receiving a nice copy of the American Standard Version Bible furnished and personally inscribed by F.B. Shepherd, who had earlier preached for the College Church and at that time was preaching at Sweetwater. Later, I had association with Shepherd in New England when he came to hold meetings and then visited him in Hawaii when I was on my way back from Japan. Shepherd was an Englishman who, though long in this country, had not dropped all of his English accent; but he was a prince of a fellow and a very capable preacher. I do not know what Underwood did with the medal, but I still treasure the Bible. The inscription reads:

The World is Wide
In Time and Tide
And God is Guide
So do not Hurry.

The Man is Blest
Who does his Best
And leaves the Rest
So do not Worry.

To
Jack Lewis
Compliments of F.B. Shepherd
Use on your Study Table.

The time I dreaded drew near. The delightful experience of college was coming to a close. It was time to graduate. The senior trip was to Monterey, Mexico, and was my first experience out of the country. The group climbed to the top of the cathedral in Saltilo. I was the first in line, and the guide held out his hand for a tip. I gave him some coins expecting others to do their part. He threw them on the ground. Among other things, riding the horse-drawn carriages was pleasant. I have in the attic the bull's horns I acquired. No one wants them displayed.

Two graduating preachers were invited to speak at the College Church on the last Sunday of the school year. My turn was at the evening service, and I came back to school for it rather than preaching at Throckmorton where I was going regularly. I chose "The Seven Wonders of the Bible" as my topic. When I got up to speak, I noticed that Dr. Mullins was operating the recording equipment which he did not usually do at a worship service. My brother Clyde, without telling me, had arranged for them to record the sermon. Radio studios then used large 16-inch disks for recording for which now there would be no equipment. I eventually gave the record to the Harding Graduate School Library without ever having had a chance to listen to it.

President Cox had the seniors over to his house for an afternoon party. The quartet made up of Wayland James, Earl T. Moore, Leon Locke and James Black sang "Going Home." It aroused a bittersweet feeling.

When the graduation programs came out, I saw *summa cum laude* by my name. As the various distinctions were announced, I heard it said that I had the highest grades for the entire college years of anyone in the class. When my mother later was telling my Uncle Jay about it, he stuck out a hand and said, "Put her there!"

Chapter 4

CAN YOU COUNT?

What can make a man dream, after 40 years have gone by, an all-too-vivid dream of undelivered book orders? Five seasons in the book field with the Southwestern Company. That is what can!

Perhaps one year in college batching in a garage apartment with a hot plate, no running water and no bath, a summer working at home on the farm and a second year in another apartment of the same facilities but adjoining a cow pen with a cow to milk in exchange for rent – all that persuaded me to sell books. Stories of the successes of Don Morris, Walter Adams and Dr. John Paul Gibson did not hurt in the effort to persuade. An uncle of mine, Fred Lewis, had been a Southwestern man a generation before me; however, I did not know that when I made my decision, and his experiences played no role in my choice. My mother and father, whom I had told rather than asked permission for my plans, took me to Dallas to meet my ride. My father bade me farewell with the question, "What are you going to do if you have a crop failure?"

Port Arthur, Texas, 1938

James Reynolds, my crew chief, took us all to Nashville to sales school on a non-stop run from Dallas in his green Plymouth. We arrived in the early morning on Saturday and acquired a sleeping room in the basement of the Central Church of Christ building, across from a garage whose loud speaker blared "The Yellow Rose of Texas" at very early hours in the morning. While the others caught up on sleep, I took a preview of sales school, listening to the send-off on Saturday afternoon of the graduating group.

Reynolds had the idea of picking up some expense money by preaching on Sunday. With nothing better to do, with only $20 or $30 in my pocket to get me through sales school and with the prospects of a free lunch, I went with him and the others. His information on what small church might not have a preacher that day was in error, and after learning the facts by going to about three places in succession, the hour of worship had arrived. We did get the invitation to lunch from a hospitable family; boys don't think about the work a hostess has put to it; but Reynolds and the others did not get to preach as they hoped they would.

Monday morning found us in sales school held in a vacant store adjacent to the Southwestern offices. In 1938, the Depression was not yet over. With its coal soot, downtown Nashville looked to me on my first trip out of the open spaces of Texas more suitable for filming gangster movies than anything else. The poverty restaurants in the downtown area offered a plate with a green vegetable, mashed potatoes and ground meat for about 25 cents. Free catsup was on the table, and a whole bottle poured over a plate made the meat edible for that void which is a teenage appetite.

First, sales talks were memorized and practiced. Mr. Faulkner instructed on the *Dictionary* and *Safe Counsel.* There was a cookbook for someone to work on. The name of the instructor on the various Bibles escapes me. Then Mr. W.E. Henderson gave his famous speech on "Can You Count?" stressing the need of keeping accurate records. His chief story was of the salesman who came back through Nashville at the end of the season to be told that his balance was $100. His reply was, "You owe me, or I owe you?" The school closed out with instruction on how to get a place to spend the night, how to get meals and even how to handle details like bathing and using deodorants.

Another non-stop run, lasting a day and most of two nights, put us about 3:00 a.m. in Beaumont, Texas, where Reynolds, Irwin Driskill and Paul Woods were to spend the summer. The area had been selected, I am persuaded, not because it was especially promising for bookselling but because Reynolds had a summer job preaching there in the place of his uncle who served the church regularly but had revival meetings to hold. Buren Carr and I were to take Port Arthur. While the others slept off their travel fatigue, I bought a hat, got out on the highway and caught a ride on to Port Arthur where Buren was supposed to show up in due time. I had a school friend, Kenneth Badgett, who had been alerted that we were coming and whom I called. He picked me up and took me to his house to stay until other quarters were found. Almost as soon as Buren arrived, Kenneth had arranged for us to stay on Proctor Street over a café run by a Brother Coons, who himself lived in the back of the café. Despite the cockroaches that plague port cities, it was livable for bookmen. Breakfast and dinner could be had in the café; and furthermore, Coons and a few others had withdrawn from the Sixth Street congregation and were operating a storefront church/mission a few doors away from the café. They were glad to have Buren and me to preach, sing and teach classes for them. Proctor Street was pretty well a row of taverns and was the street separating white and black town. Before the summer was out, Mrs. Coons died in childbirth, leaving her infant and a preschool boy for her distraught husband to try to provide for.

On my first afternoon in Port Arthur, I canvassed the two sides of a short street which Kenneth lived on without any success; but the next morning, I headed out to the east edge of town in the direction of Orange to go at the task seriously. Taking the instructions of the sales school literally, that no houses should be skipped, every house, including bars and filling stations, was canvassed. By mid-morning, orders for a Bible reader, a family Bible and a teacher's Bible had been taken. The teacher's Bible was purchased by a Texaco filling station attendant who was willing to put down a deposit of $5. He feared he would never get the book; to my great surprise when delivery day came, he paid without hesitation.

Port Arthur was a port and refinery town. The smell of the several refineries penetrated the whole area. The ships passing on the ship channel were the first ocean-going ships I had seen, and they were very fascinating. The humidity was high; it rained some every afternoon, and the mosquitoes were fierce. In fast order, I learned from sleepy-eyed men speaking sharply that the sign "Shift worker; do not knock" meant what it said and that yards with the sign "Dangerous Dog" were exceptions to the rule "Do not skip any house!"

The population of Port Arthur had a sizeable Catholic representation at a time when Catholic Bible reading was not what it is now. Though we had a Catholic Bible to offer, I do not recall ever having found anyone who wanted one. Once one had detected that the customer was Catholic, the best thing seemed to shift to the cookbook or the dictionary. However, having mentioned the Bible seemed to be like waving a red flag before a bull, and any effort after that was largely futile. A man stopped me in one of the subdivisions to inquire what I was selling. When I told him, he said, "Why don't you go down to the WPA and apply? I understand that they are taking on fellows there."

The suburbs of Port Arthur had been recovered from the swamps by fill and by dredging shells out of the bay; once out of the subdivisions, one was in the swamps again. Carr and I in canvassing ran through them like rabbits devouring a cabbage patch. Then there was nothing to do except tackle the main city itself – Carr on one side of the street and I on the other. The sample case had been designed for sitting, and we had been taught to use it for that when making a presentation in order to have the book right in front of the customer. Carr, a school teacher who was older than I by a few years, would rest in the shade periodically and say, "If my Mommy could see me now!" Though we were taught to keep a record of calls made, that practice for me proved impossible, and the figures reported were only wild guesses. There was no loafing; I was going from house to house from early morning to late night. The police stopped me for canvassing twice but after questioning me decided not to arrest me. The magazine salesmen who had beaten the customers had made the people suspicious of salesmen. The Hertel Bible salesmen were our chief enemies. The Hertel men must have made a mint of money judging by the Bibles they had left behind.

By the Fourth of July, all the city and suburbs except black town had been covered. We tackled black town because the company offered prizes for sales on the Fourth of July and because there was no other place to go. I qualified for a prize for the day. Sales in black town were easier, but deposit money was more difficult to get. I learned that black people in that area bought and paid for burial insurance; but if that collector beat you to them on payday, you just waited until the next one and hoped to be faster on the draw.

What could we do after covering the black area? The company suggested re-covering the territory we had already covered; that might have been fruitful, but it did not seem like it at the time. We crossed the Natches River by ferry (the high bridge was under construction but not yet open) to try the poverty-stricken villages on the road to Orange and then Orange itself. We extended ourselves on into Lake Charles, La., without much success. My only two memories of Lake Charles are the hot nights where one tried in vain to sleep in cheap rooming houses under electric fans and the effort to preach to a black congregation which interrupted all the time with their "amen."

We took a turn at the suburbs of Houston, 80 miles west of Beaumont, with only enough sales to have to go back for deliveries of what we had taken deposits on. Buren went home early to start to school. I did a run down to High Island, which was land's end but which had a few houses. There I was almost eaten alive by mosquitoes. I covered the villages from there on the road back to Beaumont. It took almost as much time to hitchhike from one to the other as it did to canvass all the houses when one arrived. Again, there were hardly enough sales to deliver; my chief benefit was that the road ran along the beach, and I got to stop and pick up a few sea shells. That was a "first" for me. I took a turn at the sawmill town of Woodville. The sawmill towns were poverty-stricken and yielded poor sales. I finally ended up re-canvassing sections of Beaumont which the crew there had earlier covered.

At one time during the summer on Sundays, I was taking the morning bus 40 miles on the Beaumont-Houston highway. There I was met and carried 22 more miles to Sour Lake to preach for a congregation meeting in a home. After night service, I was delivered back to the café to catch the bus back to Beaumont, arriving at midnight. One weekend, there was a hurricane warning out. I was not then conscious of the destruction hurricanes can do and the danger I faced. I waited in the café many hours until the danger passed and the bus ran.

My friends at the Proctor Street church loaned me cars with which to do my deliveries. I made the mistake of ordering out too many books which were expensive to pay the freight on both ways – out and back – when deliveries turned out at only 50 percent of the orders. It was a bitter disappointment. The black orders were particularly low on deliveries. Had one been able to collect a few dollars a week, he could probably have delivered a good portion of them. But I had to return to school.

With deliveries over, I had to hitchhike home. I caught a ride to Houston with a man who was going on to Dallas the next morning. I spent the afternoon delivering my orders there, and the next morning I rode with him. Mr. Henderson's "Can You Count?" now came home. With the quantity of books returned, I was not really sure I was going to be able to stay in school. Nevertheless, I moved into the dormitory that fall, forgot about batching in garage apartments and ate in the school dining hall. The summer had been a turning point in my life. I was never home again except for brief vacations; I never had to ask for financial aid from my parents again. It had not been a crop failure!

Portsmouth, Ohio, 1939

With prospects of being a crew chief, I recruited fellow students during the winter. Mr. W.E. Henderson came by on his annual trip to help get them signed, and we all went down to the hotel to see him. With the close of school, two of us rode to Nashville to sales school with Clifton Inman who, also as crew chief, had two of his men with him. When we made a stop in Bonham, Texas, one of those boys announced in horror that his billfold containing all his money to get him to the field was missing. A hurried trip to the police relieved our minds. It had already been turned in by an honest finder; otherwise, a book career would have been wiped out before it started.

We chose this year, and in all the following years, to stay in the YMCA. Sales school was easier for me on the second time around. Dortch Oldham and Fred Landers were only crew chiefs at this stage of their book careers and were going through the same sales school. Mr. Faulkner, Mr. Netterville and Mr. Henderson conducted the school. This year, Frank Driver and I were assigned to Portsmouth, Ohio, and two other members of my crew to Greenup, Ky. Inman dropped the three of us off at a rooming house on Sunday afternoon; we went to the Grant and Summit congregation that night and asked the minister Harris Dark to help us find a place for the summer. A family named Rheinfrank offered us a sleeping room. Next door was the Rheinfranks' brother who had a son home from college spending the summer doing nothing. The Rheinfranks also had a girl of about our age named Florence staying with them. Though attractive and available, she did not get much attention out of the book salesmen. On one Saturday afternoon, young Rheinfrank, Driver, Florence and I had an interesting discussion over whether one should kiss his wife out of duty or because he loved her. Rheinfrank and I argued for love; Driver argued that it was out of duty; and Florence was non-committal. After she was gone, Rheinfrank informed us that no girl was going to admit she liked to be kissed. I did not know about such matters.

Ohio was quite different from Port Arthur. The clang of the Catholic church bells rang in my ears for years. The steel mills were working only part shifts; poverty was everywhere. One could take an order in early summer in what looked like a prosperous home and come back in September to find poverty because the man had been laid off just after the order was placed. Rather than swamps, there were hills and hollows, all full of houses within walking distance of each other. The rural area had prosperous farms. I canvassed Sciotoville late in the summer but never got around to needing to tackle Portsmouth itself. Frank went one way in the country, and I went another. Portsmouth was stretched along the Ohio River. I tried to walk to the edge of town – two hours away, though I did not know it – covering what would have been covered for a nickel bus fare. The game was not only to see how much you could sell but also how little you could spend. Here, however, I knew that I had practiced poor economy before I got to work that morning. My selling philosophy was to send to the company on Saturday all money not needed for the weekend so that on Monday morning one had the options of selling and collecting or of begging if he ate. Hunger is quite a work motivation!

Shortly, Frank had established contact with a small rural congregation with which he spent a lot of time during the summer; I also was preaching at Lily Chapel each Sunday about 15 miles out of Sciotoville once I had sold through that area. The people were very cordial and surprised me with a "pounding" at the end of the summer. They were particularly fond of George DeHoff in that area, and I heard his name many times.

One encountered every sort of religious belief on the book field. One lady ordered a Bible though insisting that the Lord would come before delivery date. I was willing to take the chance. I delivered the book as scheduled but thought it not wise to remind her that she had been wrong. The Cadle Tabernacle in Indianapolis had an early morning religious program on the radio that Mrs. Rheinfrank listened to. I left the house many mornings with the tabernacle music and themes in my ears. The radio gave regular reports on how tall the corn in Indiana was.

One rainy evening, I was accepted into a home to spend the night. After the lady had gone to bed, the man who was a well digger unburdened his soul. Though older than she, he had married the woman hoping for a child; but some time back, her periods had stopped without explanation and his hope was blasted. A month or two later, I was walking down the road and he passed with his rig and stopped to tell me the good news that his wife had presented him with a new child. At that time of life, I did not know anything about women; but I did think a fellow who did not know that his wife was nine months pregnant was not quite "with it."

People in Ohio were out of work, working in small coal mines or working part shifts in the steel mills. In the hills, I encountered the man who wanted a book but who had no money. He wanted to trade a large biscuit-sized watch which was running when he showed it to me but which hardly ran until I was out of his sight. I needed a watch and was unduly proud of having it even if it did not run. I was confident that it could be repaired. I left it for repairs in the shop in Midlothian when I got home; but there was a burnout, and the owner had no insurance.

In the rural homes at night on frequent occasions, I encountered my first bed bugs. They also could bite when one sat in an armchair in the middle of the day on sparse occasions. A meal in a home might be cream peas cooked and served in abundance of milk, hulls and all. Then there were those places where supper was entirely of biscuits and flour gravy that had never seen meat. Breakfast could be dry cereal alone – adequate for an office worker but not much for a teenage boy walking all morning. These good people shared the best they had. People who had been out of work for years had hardships that we had not known on the farm in Texas. On a week-long trip through the country west and north of Portsmouth, a supper at a small town restaurant gave me food poisoning. After a miserable night, it was embarrassing to have to go from outhouse to outhouse along the road the next day.

The elements of privation were quite offset when one worked in the prosperous farm areas. I came late in the evening upon the Turner farm. Mrs. Turner was no longer living, and Brother Turner and Ralph, a grown son, were living in the house. Daughters that worked in Portsmouth were home on occasions. One of the Turner girls later married George DeHoff. I was at that home several times during the summer. If one came upon a family gathering, the family always insisted that he eat from the bounteous table before he went on his way. I met the Lemmon family who had eight children. Ralph later sold books with me in Pennsylvania. Years later, when my son John arrived in Miami, Fla., as a graduate student, the first person he encountered at church was Ralph. The Lemmons took him in, just as Ralph's parents had befriended me, until he found an apartment.

The church people persuaded Frank and me to go to an area gathering on the Fourth of July instead of selling that day. It was a pleasant outing; the food was wonderful; many people were there who we hoped would look at our books. As I recall, I won either the sack race or the boiled egg in a spoon race; but there was no interest in books – not a single sale for the day. There were other church dinners during the summer; some family always adopted Frank and me on those days and insisted that we eat what they had provided. Bob Prince, who was just a little boy then in a family who was especially friendly to us, later came to the graduate program in Searcy and took an M.S. with us.

In Portsmouth, as in Port Arthur, the church people loaned me their cars to make my deliveries. The volume of sales had been comparable to the preceding year; but now I knew to make allowance for non-delivery and not order too many books. However, the percentage was considerably improved over the previous year. Sister Rheinfrank bade me goodbye with the words, "I expect to hear great things from you!" It had been a pleasant summer; I would not have believed I would never be in Portsmouth again.

Clifton Inman, who with his crew had spent the summer in Huntington, W.Va, picked us up in his old Model A Ford for the trip home when deliveries were completed. Running across Indiana, I noticed that the choke wire was exposed just in front of my foot. Clifton was dreaming away at the wheel. I reached my toe over and lifted the wire. The engine promptly cut off. But before we slowed much, I released it. The motor caught on again. Clifton wondered what was wrong with his car. Later, I tried it again; he by now was really wondering if we were going to make it home. Enough of a prank is enough. I did not tell Clifton for 25 years what I had done. We made it back to Denton, his home, without mishap. I thumbed a ride on home to Midlothian and slept the fatigue of the summer off.

Evansville, Indiana, 1940

My older brother LeMoine, who was now four years out of college, decided that he wanted to try bookselling. He persuaded my younger brother Clyde, who had just finished high school, to come along. In addition, I had some other fellows in my crew. LeMoine had a car and took us to Nashville to sales school. Mr. Henderson had the crew chiefs out to his house for dinner. When area assignment time came, he had me in and asked another salesman in his office force about Evansville, Ind. He got the reply that if we could work the urban area, it offered possibilities. Mr. Henderson without hesitation assured him we could do it. I had never thought of Evansville before; so why not?

Evansville was near enough to Nashville that we were there by bedtime on Saturday. We got a motel room and then showed up for services on Sunday where Charles Campbell was preaching. The plan was for LeMoine, Clyde and me to take the Evansville area for our territory and for two others to take Princeton, which was the next city farther north. In the afternoon, we deposited them there and left them to their fate.

On Monday morning, we arranged with the motel to keep our luggage, and we split three ways. My sales volume for the week was pathetic compared with the previous years. On Saturday, feeling low, I traded a subscription for a Bible to a barber for a haircut. LeMoine had done better and was pleased as a kitten, but Clyde had done worse. LeMoine and I had a running battle all summer over sales volume. Clyde had come in on this Saturday earlier than the other two of us to the motel and had taken a bath. When we decided not to continue to stay there overnight, the owner charged him 15 cents for his bath. Bookselling was not Clyde's cup of tea. An elderly widow in the congregation agreed to let us live with her. She curtained off the double doors of her living room and let us have it for our quarters but also allowed us to have the use of the kitchen. In previous summers, I had not attempted batching. It was a very fine arrangement for all the four of us – her and the salesmen. She grew fond of us; she gave us sample rare coins her husband had collected. She corresponded with our mother after we were gone. LeMoine sent her holiday cards until he received her death notice.

The rural area north and west of Evansville had a large Catholic population. Work there was completely fruitless. One very rainy evening, I came to a house in the hills and asked the people (who were not Catholics) if I might spend the night. They gave me a bed, took a mattress off another, and put it on the porch for the other fellows in the household to sleep on. I was no sooner to bed than the bugs began to bite. I tried the bare springs; but one cannot sleep on springs. I crept out and thought I would sleep in a car out front, but it was locked. It was a sleepless night for me. I also spent a night with a kind Lutheran family and shared a bed with their son who claimed to have visions. I tried a week at New Harmony, west of Evansville, where early in the 19th century, Robert Owen, the atheist, had tried to found a communal colony.

Clyde was not doing well on his own, so I had to tackle the metropolitan area with him to see if he could be helped. Eventually, all of us were at it alternating streets or working on opposite sides of the street. Selling went hard in Evansville. For the first time in three years, I went a few days with no sales at all – a hard blow to the ego when it is the first time to be experienced. I was stopped by plain-clothes detectives and taken to the police station because I was selling without a permit. When I explained to the chief that the company had instructed us that permits were not needed, his retort was, "Your company does not run this town." He tried to make me say that taking orders and then delivering in September was not really an honorable way of doing business. I expect that they had had unfortunate experiences with the magazine boys. I invited him out to our house to see the books on hand ready to deliver which he was not interested in seeing. He then told me to deliver the books and to get out of town. I asked him who was going to take me back out to my territory which was quite a distance from the station. He made clear that it did not concern him and that I was to get there the best way I could.

We met in Evansville an unemployed factory worker who was very pro-labor and very anti-management but who wanted to try selling books. With Mr. Henderson's permission, he joined my crew, and we tried Henderson, Ky., and then Owensboro, Ky. LeMoine's car gave us a mobility I had never had before and gave the possibility of covering a wider area than would have otherwise been possible. Each night, we were back to our own room. About dark one evening, I arrived back at where we had parked the car in Owensboro to find the police waiting. Someone had reported that LeMoine's out-of-state car had been parked there all day. I explained our business. The patrolman said, "There is something wrong here. Salesmen usually cover a block or two and then come back and move the car." We always left ours all day and then sometime had evening calls to make where women had been interested but had to ask their husband. However, when the patrolman radioed his headquarters for instruction, the sergeant merely said, "If the car is obstructing traffic, move it." The car was legally parked and was actually bothering no one. The patrolman went his way and left us alone.

The Hunt family in Evansville particularly befriended us. Mr. Hunt was a wholesale grocer. He gave us a tour through his large establishment and then presented us with a box of canned goods of various types. I remember he told us that if you do not want peanut butter to stick to the roof of your mouth, you turn the cracker upside down to eat it. On a special day, he and his family took us on a ride on a paddle wheeler on the river. When delivery time came, the daughter Kathryn, who was a very attractive art student but who unfortunately had been born with hearing and speech defects, furnished me transportation in getting the books out. Book salesmen are on the receiving end of an awful lot of kindness.

Clyde finished his deliveries and hitchhiked home before LeMoine and I were through. LeMoine finished last, late at night; we then drove through to Nashville to be there when the company opened the next morning. We settled affairs with the company, returning all the leftover books we had hauled down with us. I called at the home of Catherine, who had eaten at my table in the dining hall at school but who was not returning. I also called at the home of Professor Boise, whose son Paul was supposed to ride to Texas with us but had turned up with a fever and could not go. Then we made a non-stop drive through the night, alternating driving, until we were back home again.

Harrisburg, Pennsylvania, 1941

Just out of college and obligated to begin preaching for the congregation at Throckmorton, Texas, in the fall, I had assembled my crew during the preceding winter. My brother LeMoine had recruited his crew out of teachers and high school students in Snyder, Texas, where he was preaching. They went in the car of the teacher Roy Lacy and in LeMoine's car via Nashville sales school to their territory. I found transportation for my group with a West Texas teacher who was going to Nashville to enter Peabody College and who was glad to have help with the driving. At the Dallas bus station, our assembly point, I was being paged to the telephone for a long-distance call. Two of my men had gotten cold feet and were canceling out. My brother Clyde and I went on. We were to meet others in Nashville.

LeMoine and his group were assigned to Cumberland, Md., and to Central Pennsylvania. Larnell Nichols and I were to go to Harrisburg and Clyde and Ralph Lemmon to Carlisle. Clyde and I were able to ride with Roy Lacy to Bedford, Pa. Thinking we would do better hitchhiking separately, we parted hoping to meet a week later. Not able to hitchhike on the new turnpike, I got a ride over the mountains to Chambersburg; then in the darkness, I got another ride on to Carlisle where I spent the remainder of the night in a motel. Next morning, I made it into Harrisburg and went to the post office to see if there was any word from Larnell Nichols, who had come up on the bus. There he was leaving me a card at General Delivery and amply glad to see me. With the aid of his bus driver, he had found a room where he was staying.

We chose different routes out of town to work. I took the city bus to the end of the line and started canvassing. I had never been that far north before. The second day, a cold rain came which made the teeth of a boy in a sport shirt chatter. To get out of the rain, I found an unfinished house whose roof made it dry enough but which did nothing for the cold. I finally found a hospitable farm renter with whom I spent two nights. I missed most of a day's work from the rain. At the end of the week, I had run up the lowest first week volume of my career. My pessimistic report to Mr. Henderson brought back a reply in which he pointed out that though the volume was low, the collections had been more than 50 percent of the total, and that it was not at all bad.

At the end of the week, Larnell and I found a sleeping room with kitchen privileges in the home of a Mrs. Yohe on Derry Street. We spent the summer there, awakened each morning at a hour earlier than we wanted to get up by Mrs. Yohe's hoarse awakening call from the lower floor to her husband still upstairs: "Ira, Ira."

Harrisburg was the only place I ever worked where there was not a congregation of the churches of Christ. By Saturday, we had a card from Clyde, who had arrived in Carlisle on the second day and had by some means located a Pontiac dealer where he would pick us up on Sunday morning. We took the bus over and were mutually glad to be together. Ray Eyster came by for us. The congregation met in a small rural village called Walnut Bottom in a very small but adequate building. As we parked, Ray said, "I understand that some of you preach. We want you to preach for us." As the oldest and the leader, I drew the task and preached each Sunday through the summer. The congregation of a handful of people, largely of the Eyster family and of his sister's family (the Hisers), had what I had never heard of before – two buildings. An old stone building that dated back to Alexander Campbell's day stood in the fields out in the country. The frame building had been purchased because some of the older members lived in the village and could get to it. The state law demanded that one service a year be held in a building to retain tax exemption for it. In August, the annual yearly all-day meeting was held in the stone building. It was a great day, and the bookmen in LeMoine's crew also came over for it. As the war progressed in the next few years and directories were needed for transient people, I saw that the Walnut Bottom congregation got a listing for the entire Harrisburg area so that others would not have the difficulty finding them that we had had. Servicemen did come, and the congregation grew. Now it is a large congregation with a fine brick building in a section of Carlisle. The old stone building has been renovated with some additions to it, and it now houses another congregation and is regularly used. In a display case, they have the old silver chalice used in the early days for the communion.

Ray and Rheba Eyster adopted the four of us who were working in the Carlisle-Harrisburg area for the weekends. Each week after church, they had something planned. They had a son and a daughter of about our ages. Rheba introduced me to a new dish, "corn soup," and to chilled Jello filled with mixed fruits. Second to ice cream, it has been my lifetime favorite. They showed us off in all the churches around the area: Martinsburg, Sunbury, Washington, D.C., and others. The weekend in Washington, D.C., was a first for us and was a highlight of the summer for all of us. It was arranged for us to stay in the home of the Mills family. Young Ray Eyster showed us all the monuments and buildings. Then on Sunday morning, I taught a class at the 14th (later 16th) Street church and listened to Hugo McCord preach.

Several years later, Brother Eyster asked me to look in on Bill Baldosser, who was dating the Eyster girl but was then in army camp at Abilene, Texas, and I looked him up. When we moved from Providence to Cincinnati, I arranged a night's stop at Carlisle so that I could say "Hello" to the Eysters. I exchanged cards with them until they both died – first Brother Eyster and then Sister Eyster. A number of years ago, I was greatly surprised one day to receive an inquiry from Bill Hiser of Carlisle about my Holy Land trips. I inquired and found that he was the Hiser boy who had undulant fever the summer of 1941 and had been unable to get out of the house. His chances did not look very good at that time. Bill and his wife went to the Holy Land and then had me up to Carlisle for a meeting. Bill Baldosser and Bill Hiser were elders at Carlisle. Young Ray Eyster was active in the congregation meeting at the rock church building. Somehow I felt that Ray and Rheba Eyster would have been proud.

In Pennsylvania, I learned terms like "you'uns" ("you ones") and "come here once" ("come here"). They laughed at my "you all." My benefactors who stopped to give me a ride would comment, "Listen to that southern boy talk!" New places like High Spire, Middletown and Hershey offered challenges for sales. As the summer wore on, the roads were lined with ripe blackberries and cherries that made tasty snacks. The farmers were thrifty, pious, conservative people who were hard to sell, but whose word was like cash in the pocket. I had a small summer volume but had the largest percentage of deliveries for my four seasons. So it all balanced out. I encountered for the first time the plain people whose men wore overalls to church and whose women wore only plain grey dresses with white aprons and with neat little white caps on their heads. I learned of people who prayed over their food both before and after they ate it.

On the Fourth of July, with eyes on a sales prize, Larnell and I headed for black town. However, it was a rainy day. After losing an hour trying to stay dry, I found an open drug store, and we purchased umbrellas and sold on in the rain. The volume was adequate for the prize and the collections adequate to make sure the time had not been wasted. I reported to Mr. Henderson that I was through losing time from rain, and he printed my letter in the weekly honor roll.

With deliveries staring us in the face and no close friends in Harrisburg to turn to, I asked Ray Eyster if he could rent us a car. He replied, "I dasn't." Evidently, sales were preferred to rentals in Pennsylvania. I had never owned a car, but the next alternative was to buy. At my insistence, he showed me a used blue Ford V-8 two-door and quoted a figure that I am sure was below the market. The next morning, he sent young Ray to meet me in the State House in Harrisburg to get the title fixed, and I drove away with the car to make deliveries. The following Sunday, I handed him a money order bought with my collections for about half the price of the car. He took one look at it and said, "That is big money!" When we finished our collections, I went by his agency and found that he was out; but I handed his secretary the balance for the car. She pulled the title out of the drawer and gave it to me. We went by the Eysters' house to say goodbye. Ray called while we were there and then came out to see us off. It made me feel good when they commented on the fact that they knew I would not leave the state without paying.

We went by Cumberland, Md., to pick up Clyde, who had gone down to be with LeMoine. LeMoine was at work. We were in a hurry and did not see him. LeMoine went on from there to Harvard when he had finished his selling. I did not see him again until 1944 when I went to enroll in Harvard. Clyde, Larnell and I made our way, via Nashville for settling with Southwestern, on home in my own car. One might say as Jacob said of himself that I had crossed the river with only a staff in hand but had returned with a paid-up college education, a car and money in the pocket for a start on my life's work.

Dallas, Texas, 1944

I likely would have called it quits with four seasons of book selling had it not been that I made a mistake in judgment in setting the termination date for my preaching in Huntsville, Texas. That left me with a month and a half before time to report to Harvard. Temporary jobs were not readily available. My thoughts had again been turned to book selling when Mr. Henderson wrote me asking if I could consider making deliveries for Fred Landers, who thought he would be drafted before he could complete them. I had to decline. I could not get away from my work with the church at that time. But with free time and no short-time job in view, I wrote Mr. Henderson inquiring about the possibility of selling in Grand Prairie, which was near my parents' home. It was taken, but he proposed Dallas. He had a Southwestern man there named Clarence, whom I had encountered in sales schools in earlier years. Clarence was from McMurry College, which is located on the opposite side of Abilene from ACC (now ACU) and was its most hated football opponent. Clarence was doing some selling while he attended the SMU School of Religion (later Perkins School of Theology), and he had an apartment just a few blocks from SMU that he was willing to share. With this arrangement, my wife was taken care of by visiting my parents where I could see her on weekends and then later by visiting her parents in Moore, Okla.

I came back from one of these weekends to find Clarence telling a wild story of having returned to the apartment which adjoined the garage on the back of the lot. He had to walk down the drive past the house to get there, but the young ladies occupying rooms there had not lowered the shades when dressing. They had heard his footsteps on the drive as he passed and had called the police to catch the "peeping Tom." The police searched the grounds, oblivious to the fact that the "peeping Tom" was safely in his apartment. I doubt that Clarence ever let the house know what had actually happened.

The wartime economy made book selling an entirely different game from what it had ever been before. Clarence pointed out an area of the city he thought would be fruitful. After I had a couple of $100 days in selling on city streets – about equal to a good week's business at the end of the Depression – Clarence decided that I would not need his coaching about selling. The four weeks accumulated a larger volume than I had seen in any of the four summers. Dallas had a large Church of Christ population and a lot of working-class homes. For the first time in selling, I was able to do a respectable business with the Church of Christ people.

The short period of canvassing and the one week allotted to delivery made it necessary to estimate delivery needs in advance so that the books could be shipped and be on hand on delivery day. My car had been sold in preparation for going back to school. My parents loaned me their car for making deliveries; but on delivery morning, no books had shown up. Nashville had assured me that they had been shipped. Had postal service been as unreliable then as now, one would not have dared depend on it. When I inquired at the postal substation, there in the middle of the floor stacked high were the boxes. Nashville had by mistake shipped them to General Delivery rather than to the apartment address. The post office did not know what to do with them but fortunately had not yet shipped them back to Nashville.

The booming wartime economy made the percentage of deliveries very good. The next week when my father-in-law asked about my success and I shared with him that I had cleared more than $18 a day after expenses, he could not believe it. It was more than he was making on his job in a war plant. The month furnished a nice nest egg with which to begin graduate school in Harvard.

A Trade to Follow

With full apologies to General Douglas McArthur, old Southwestern men never die. They just move on to new territory and entice unsuspecting students with their yarns of experiences they have had. Like Paul said of himself, they are debtors to all men – to those in whose beds they slept, to those whose food they ate, to those whose cars they drove, to those who treated them like they were their own sons and, not least, to those who bought their books.

Southwestern taught me to be self-reliant, independent of the finances of my parents. It gave me an education on a more secure economic level than I would have had otherwise. Mr. Henderson taught me how "to count." I learned to deal with all sorts of people and all sorts of situations. I saw places I would never had seen otherwise. I do not recall what became of my old sample case. Perhaps I turned it in to the company at the end of the fifth season. On occasions, I dream in the night of a sample case lacking current prospectuses, of prices that do not fit the current market, of selling in places where I never sold and of orders taken with deposits given that somehow I overlooked in delivery.

Mr. W.E. Henderson last visited me about 1949 in Providence, R.I., when he came to pick up the car of a relative who had been shipped overseas by the navy. As we talked about the progress of my graduate program and of the uncertainty of my finances, he commented in his smiling, winning way, "Remember that you always have a trade you can follow!" It is a trade that I have never again needed except in dreams – and one I never intend to need!

Chapter 5

THE COMPANY OF EDUCATED MEN

When I graduated from Abilene Christian College, I was at the end of the formal educational process afforded by the schools supported by our people. The general atmosphere in some circles at that time was that two years of college were adequate training for preaching, and in others it was four. After such schooling, one had the training he needed, and he ought to get out and get at it. A two-year trainee held a meeting at Phillips Brooks House in Harvard Yard and is reputed to have issued a challenge every night to the Harvard professors to debate him. Fortunately, no one accepted his challenge.

There were, of course, some few exceptions to the satisfaction with college training as being adequate. W.B. West, Jr., had been through a graduate program at the University of Chicago and the University of Southern California. J.P. Sanders had been in Vanderbilt; J.D. Thomas and Frank Pack were in graduate programs; but they were not then personally known to me. Homer Hailey had done a masters degree at SMU, and Carl Spain was seeking a B.D. there. J.W. Roberts had done some work at Butler University.

The general pattern at that time was to do graduate work in education, history, English or psychology, even if one intended to make a career of teaching Bible. In some cases, the coach, the chemistry teacher, the mathematics teacher or others were teaching the Bible courses without any graduate training. Anyone self-trained could teach Bible. The number of Ph.D.'s in the college in all fields was not many more than one department would now have. There were disturbing rumors about men who had gone into graduate studies in religion and had departed from the faith. Many people were convinced that such was the inevitable outcome for the student who went on for graduate studies.

I owe my own course of action to two factors. First, I am by nature a bookworm who had rather study than work. I found graduation day a sad day because a pattern of life which I loved was coming to an end. Graduate education offered an extension of what I enjoyed most. Second, there was my brother LeMoine, who opened my eyes to the possibility and need of continuing in school. Without him, the thought would have been completely beyond my mental horizon. My classmates thought I was foolish not to be satisfied with the degree I was obtaining. I talked to only two people who were actually encouraging about additional schooling. The one was Charles Roberson for whom I had graded Greek papers. Roberson seems to have kindled a desire in a number of students to learn. The other person was a preacher who, according to a rumor which reached me shortly, must later have had second thoughts about the matter.

I must confess that, being "thoroughly furnished" by having taken Roberson's course in "Bible Versus Modernism" out of which I got certain impressions about something I did not understand, I arrived on the Harvard campus not knowing whether to look for pitchforks and red suits or for milk and honey. There is no question that one felt that he was laying his hope of eternal life on the line and that his past associates were surer of that than was he.

To Harvard

We set out on a fall afternoon in 1944 from Lynell's parents' home in Moore, Okla., for Boston with a tight schedule. An overload of hand baggage as we walked to the electric car line, which would take us 15 miles into Oklahoma City, made Lynell want to leave the Indian blanket I had used on my bed in college in the ditch beside the way. I would not hear of it. We barely made the car and then in Oklahoma City caught the train to Saint Louis.

The next morning when we changed trains in Saint Louis, the conductor was standing beside the new train shouting "Boston! Boston!" (rhyming with "ah") in a New England accent that I had never heard before, but which all these years later still rings with magical memories.

The train was crowded with soldiers; I wore my cowboy boots I had acquired in my last year of college which I was so proud of, and I took several jibes from the soldiers about being a war shirker. After an overnight ride, a good portion of them disembarked at Worchester, Mass. Finally, we drew near Boston and stopped at the Back Bay Station. I had no concept of where to get off but rode on to the South Station, which was the end of the line and was the baggage claim.

I called Harold Thomas, who had preached for Brookline but was then preaching for the Natick church and who had been helpful to those of us who planned to come to Harvard. That brought the suggestion from his wife, Roxie, that we take a $3 taxi ride (an unheard of luxury for me) to his house. Henry Forgy, Richard Walker and W.B. Barton, Jr. – all from Abilene Christian College – were also entering Harvard Divinity School that fall. The Forgys and Walkers were already at the Thomas house while they looked for other accommodations. While running errands, Roxie Thomas took Lynell and me to the top of Brookline Hill and pointed in the direction of Cambridge. I could see in the distance the spires of what was for me a land of unknown adventure.

In preparation for our coming, a good Christian lady, Sister John Harper, had offered to keep us until we could find an apartment. John was not interested in the church but was cordial enough to us. They had come up from Port Arthur, Texas, for John to work in the Boston shipyard. Out of their large family, two children were still at home. They had an apartment in a government project in South Boston. John took me by taxi back to South Station to get our luggage. The *Queen Elizabeth* had just come into the shipyards to have repairs done for torpedo damage she had suffered in crossing the Atlantic. He insisted that we must see the ship. It was the largest thing on water I had ever seen.

Despite having friends on hand, finding an apartment in war-crowded

Boston was almost hopeless. Though I had found a student couple who would consider letting us share an apartment with them, this first effort at looking failed. Lynell and I had agreed to meet at the Harvard subway station for an afternoon of looking. Evidently, Lynell, on her first independent subway ride, stayed in the station, and I waited at the top outside. She despaired and returned to the Harpers. I waited in vain all afternoon. The couple offering to let us share their apartment felt they had to get the landlord's permission for their proposal. We never followed it up.

My brother LeMoine then came up with the idea that we could rent a room from the Alexander Suttie family with kitchen privileges. Their flat was near Central Station in Cambridge and was within quite a long walk from the Divinity School. The Sutties, who were among the mainstays of the Brookline congregation, had come over earlier from Scotland, and they were very generous, colorful Scots. Their daughter Buntie was married to O.H. Tallman, who preached in Manhattan, N.Y. We stayed there most of the winter but then in the spring found an apartment about three blocks from school.

Lynell went to an employment agency, paid their fee and got a secretarial job at Raytheon which could have been gotten by applying directly without the fee. But then we did not know Boston, the job market or job finding.

Before many weeks, the balmy weather we experienced on the day of our arrival had changed. It was snowing; for a southerner, that was a thrill. But it demanded rubber shoes, then rubber galoshes and a hat. Lynell needed warm clothes and at the first opportunity went looking for a warm coat. She came up with a fitted, sable-dyed coney coat at I.J. Fox Company. It was a beauty; but I took a lot of ribbing from my brother (then still a bachelor) about how much I had spent on rabbit fur. Furthermore, each year when I took it in for conditioning, I got some dirty digs from other furriers that Fox prices were exorbitant. But it helped Lynell through New England winters the seven years we were there. Since it was fitted, after one or two children, it had to be discarded.

Harvard Divinity School in 1944 had a student-aid program called "Compensated Church Work." The student had great liberty in choosing what sort of work he would do; and then after that, money left at the time of the American Revolution by philanthropist Edward Hopkins was supplied to help him with his school expenses.

Before my going to Cambridge, it had been worked out with the Providence, R.I., congregation and with the preachers already in New England that were carrying on various works that I would work with the struggling group at Providence. They met in Parlor A of the Biltmore Hotel on Sunday afternoon. The Biltmore was across the plaza from the train station and was a block from the bus station also. It was very convenient for people scattered at the Quonset Naval Air Station, the Newport Naval Base and other military installations.

I got off to a slow start at Harvard. By subway and city map, I found my way to Andover Hall in time for opening chapel. Then I saw my advisor. Classes were to meet after registration was completed. I was assigned for advising to Professor A.D. Nock. I also saw Hebrew instructor Edwin Broome and reported that I had studied some Hebrew but was uncertain where to place myself. He handed out a Hebrew book for me to read. I took it, looked at it and felt it needed turning right-side up; however, the book had been handed to me right-side up to start with. Broome said, "I think you should take beginning Hebrew." A few other preliminaries took longer than perhaps they should have; then it suddenly came to light that Professor Pfeiffer had given his opening lecture in "Introduction to the Old Testament," and I had missed it. LeMoine, standing by when the sad truth dawned on me, got a good laugh at the stupidity of his little brother, just at a time when little brother wanted very much to make a good impression.

Professor George LaPiana gave his opening lecture in "Early Church History" in the afternoon. At noon time, I had to go to Harvard Square for supplies; but in coming back, I took a wrong street branching off the Square. By the time I found my way back to Andover Hall, I had also missed half of that lecture. It just was not my day!

Students were required to pass an oral examination in English Bible knowledge, for which my Abilene Christian College Bible major and my preaching experience were good preparation. Unitarian students usually had to take the examination several times to pass it. The examination came in the spring of 1945. I was assigned to Professors Nock and McDonald. Nock was a classical scholar who had been diverted into History of Religions and into some sections of backgrounds of the biblical field. McDonald was an expert in Muslim studies. It was my first contact with either of them except for seeing Nock on registration day. They led off by asking me to tell the places where angels were mentioned in the Bible. I began with Abraham's visitors and did a run down on others. "But is there not an earlier case?" they asked. I could not think of any. "How about the Garden of Eden?" they inquired. I insisted that those were cherubim, and I had not mentioned them because they are not actually called angels. They said, "They are the same thing." They also knew about the seraphim in Isaiah's vision. At about this point, Professor Nock asked me if I were related to LeMoine. When I told him I was a brother, he turned to Professor McDonald and said of my Bible knowledge, "He comes by it honestly." Later in Hebrew class when a group of us were sharing with each other and with Edwin Broome our experiences on the examination, Broome laughed and said of my examiners, "You would know more about the Bible than those two old birds would." The transcript shows that the mark on the examination was "Excellent."

The Philosophy of Education

The philosophy of education at Harvard involved bringing the student into direct contact with the world scholar. There was less time devoted to what scholars had said than to wrestling with questions the significant text presented. It was an atmosphere in which scholarship was respected; one heard no slurs cast against the intellectuals; there was no magnifying of the glories of ignorance. To be in error was considered a cardinal sin. The greats of the past – George Foot Moore, Kirsopp Lake and others – looked down upon one from portraits on the walls, and their names were mentioned with respect. Somehow, the student came to feel that he was a participant in the battle of light against darkness and of information against ignorance. He felt that he was not in any sense wasting his time in "burning the midnight oil" and in applying his mind to the challenging questions with which he was confronted.

The approach to religious questions was, without apology, that which world scholarship calls "the historical approach." Few references, if any, were made to the opposing viewpoint. In fact, when Wilbur Smith's book *Therefore, Stand*[1] fell into my hands, I read it avidly and then wrote Smith a letter of appreciation for the new world it opened to me – a world contrary to that in which I had been immersed. What knowledge I have of Evangelical scholars and their works, I did not get at Harvard.

Edwin Broome, instructor in Hebrew, was the only really young man on the staff. Brilliant but egotistical, Broome is the only teacher I ever had that I did not consider treated students as gentlemen should have been treated. An avid evangelist for liberalism, Broome was in his last year of a non-tenure appointment. His Hebrew class had a mixture of undergraduate students (many Jewish) from the Yard and of Divinity students. The class was part Hebrew, part propaganda for higher criticism and part ridicule of the intellectual integrity of the student who did not accept higher criticism. One of the students bowed low and good naturedly bantered Broome in the hallway, "There is but one God, Channing, and Broome is his prophet!" Broome agreed that it was a well-put description. Near the end of the year, Broome laid in front of the students a petition to be signed requesting that he teach Biblical Archaeology the following year. We all signed; we wanted to pass the course. Later, Professor Cadbury commented on the fact that students had circulated a petition to keep Broome on the staff. It was nothing of the sort! Broome had circulated it himself and had put the students in a position where they had to sign.

Professor Robert Pfeiffer was a heavyset German American with a loud laugh who presented undiluted literal literary criticism in class of the sort for which he is known from his *Introduction to the Old Testament*.[2] The heavy plowing was enlivened by what I considered blasphemous stories when he was treating some biblical episodes, such as when he explained the death of Uzzah as a case where Uzzah reached to steady the ark but accidentally stepped into a pile of fresh bull manure, slipped and hit his head on a hard object. The people then said that God killed him. The story got a great laugh from the class.

On a personal level, Pfeiffer was very kind. He returned to students the royalty he made from their purchase of his book. I later took a seminar in Psalms with him which met in his study in his home. The study was about a block from Andover Hall. It was in its shelves that

I first saw the collection of Hebrew Union College annuals which I think played a part in turning my thought into paths I later followed. There was a large box on one shelf marked "Unpublished Papers." I was duly impressed. The seminar had several men and women who were teachers in the Jewish Teachers' College, and then there were several regular Harvard men. One was John Scammon, who was quite a bit older than I and who was then librarian at Andover-Newton Theological Seminary. He later became Old Testament professor with a career in the book of Psalms. John and I later were roommates on the New York University Summer Seminar in Israel – my first trip to the Holy Land.

Professor Pfeiffer was not one to bully students over their religious beliefs. At the end of his lectures on "Introduction to the Old Testament," he said, "There are some fundamentalist students in this class who think that everything I have said is a colossal lie. I do not require that you agree with me. I do require that you know what I have said." Harvard in those days was a free atmosphere in which men of widely divergent views could study. The historical approach was stressed in all classes, and the best job that was possible of persuading the student was done; but one was not required to subscribe to any particular belief. The number of Evangelical students who got degrees in those years is a witness to this freedom.

A Methodist by denominational affiliation, Professor Pfeiffer insisted that faith and scholarship are two different things that could not mix. When he prayed in chapel, it was with the most humble air to "Our dear heavenly Father." I heard him deliver in Divinity Chapel a most impressive homily on "You shall love your enemies." He raised the question how one can obey that demand. Taking the episode of David and Hanun, he pointed out that one often mistakes the motives of others and that the other person may not be the enemy that one thinks he is. He said that one can love an enemy because the enemy will tell you what your friends will not. He said that those people who had said that he was a jackass had made him look at himself to see if they were telling the truth, and then it made him work harder. They unintentionally had been his friends.

Professor Willard Sperry, dean of the school, had responsibility for freshman orientation; and he did a great deal in the way of explaining how to shift over from the American system of education to the British, heavily dependent on examinations, on which the Harvard program was patterned. He had interesting experiences to tell out of his own background in British schools. Sperry was not strong on language study. He openly said that the only thing he got out of Hebrew was weak eyes. One had a pretty good picture of how to get ready for comprehensive examinations when he got out of Sperry's orientation. I followed as explicitly as possible his suggestions with good results.

Sperry taught ministry. He was a Congregationalist with a great insight into the preaching problem. Harvard made no effort to teach denominational polity. Sperry confessed that the denominational seminaries probably had more to offer in "go getting" church methods; but he insisted that 10 years out of seminary, the Harvard men would be ahead. He had gone through quarrels over the school and the Congregational creed which set forth Calvinism. He told of being on the witness stand when he was asked if he believed the creed. He replied that if they were asking if he was a Congregationalist and the son of a Congregationalist, he was; but if they meant did he believe the creed under discussion, if he knew his own heart, he did not believe a word of it. The attorney then turned to the judge to say, "Your honor, this is our problem. We have a creed that no one believes."

Sperry insisted that he had learned from his mother that the preacher should be in the home of every family in his congregation at least twice a year so that when calamity struck he could go to them as an old friend and not as a stranger. He insisted that the preacher should have a fixed period of his day for study when he was not accessible to anyone. He cited the case of some of the better known figures in the Boston area who were inaccessible all morning.

Sperry had his code of ethics for preachers. One does not seek favors from his constituency or ask for clergy discounts in the stores. He does not speak derogatorily of his predecessor in the pulpit nor does he interfere with the congregation, making difficulty for his successor, after he is gone. He insisted that gratuities received for funerals should be acknowledged with a note thanking the family and kindly informing them that the gratuity was being given by him to a favorite charity which he knew they would be willing to have done.

Sperry also offered a course in devotional literature which I later took. The classics of Christian devotion were read. A student prepared an introduction to the document for the week to present to the group; then the treatise itself was discussed with Sperry pointing up special topics. I drew the introduction to Augustine's *Confessions* as my assignment. That course was rewarding; I think I realized it when I was called on to speak extemporarily on Augustine after 35 years had gone by, and I found that I still remembered the basic outlines.

Sperry was a heavy man who shook his jaws vigorously as he spoke. I can still hear Sperry with shaking jowls quoting B.H. Streeter saying, "The thing that impresses me most about Mark is the violence of the man." Had a cartoonist been drawing him or had a student been imitating him, his jaws would have been given special attention. I think I never met a man with as much insight per square inch into preacher's problems as Sperry had. He had written books on worship which are still widely read after he has long been gone. He had an appreciation for a well-turned phrase. When he cited a particularly apt one, he would say enviously, "I wish I had said that!" From him I learned of Streeter's definition of Christianity as "the religion that believes in going about doing good, particularly that kind of good that involves going about." At one time, Sperry had made a comparison between the emotion of a football crowd in a stadium on Saturday afternoon and the emotion of religion. A *Time Magazine* reporter had erroneously quoted him as saying, "The only religion left in America is football." The narrator of the sharp exchange over this matter saw it as his way of getting his point over that one must be accurate in quotation. He told of experiences where students had made compilations of devotional poetry for publication as handbooks in devotion without their having raised the copyright question or the royalty question. Thus, he stressed that one cannot borrow just anything that suits one's fancy. It is too bad the writers of church bulletins have never found this out!

Professor Sperry told of being asked to review a book on war-time prayers in which examples like those of men shot down over the sea who were in life rafts at the point of starvation were featured. They prayed, and it rained; or a gull or fish came near enough to be caught, and the men were saved from starvation. As he told it, he had written the prospective publisher that he thought it would be more interesting to have the author write about Johnny, who prayed and then got his head blown off. The editor wrote back that he did not think the author concerned was capable of writing that book. One would remark that not only was the author not that capable, neither was Sperry nor the rest of us. There are some things we cannot explain.

Professor Sperry was preacher for Memorial Church in Harvard Yard, and he put great stress on attendance at morning prayers with a group, most of whom never had any intention of going. Not many Harvard undergraduates came either – never enough to fill up even the choir, not to mention the auditorium. I was in a position to go only during the first year when I lived in Cambridge. I did not choose to sing with the organ, but there were readings, prayers and addresses. It was my first introduction to responsive reading. The churches I had come up through just did not do that.

One morning, something went wrong with the organ; it could not be shut off, and it wheezed through the whole service in a disconcerting way. I wondered if it was an aid to worship or an unnecessary innovation that we could well have done without.

I was not actually present when Sperry decided to close the library during chapel hour. Stories circulate when Harvard men get together. It is said that as he stood outside the door when the diehards filed out of their study carrels he said, "This kind only comes out by prayer."

Professor Henry Cadbury was a genteel, very kind Quaker who had been discharged from the faculty of a college during World War I for his pacifistic position but who lived long enough to be accepted back into the same college with honor after his retirement from Harvard. Internationally known for his humanitarian work at the head of the American Friends Service Committee, having received for them the Nobel Peace Prize, and for his research and his books dealing with Luke-Acts, Cadbury's writings are still a "must" for all who work in those areas.

Cadbury was capable of sharp barbs at positions with which he differed, such as when he made a takeoff on the New Deal agriculture program of Depression years and said that already by Franklin Roosevelt's Chicago speech, one could tell that Roosevelt had decided to "plow under every third American boy!" He facetiously characterized Harry Truman's "lend lease" program as the "lend lose" program. However, no student ever found him either unkind or personal. He commented on the fact that Evangelical students after graduation had not always manifested the same courtesy toward their former professors that they had experienced at the hands of those professors. He was greatly loved by his students. I have never heard a former student speak of his memory with the slightest disrespect.

Cadbury had the most withering way of deflating the most positively stated case by quietly saying with a puzzled look at its conclusion, "Now I wonder?" Discussion classes invite the vocal rather than the thoughtful to consume the time; and Cadbury's classes, though masterfully directed, were no exception. Students named Morey and Barker did most of the talking. After one of these periods, another student came into the Commons Room and said, "Barker is still barking." I am not convinced that expounding one's opinions is the best way to learn. Perhaps it was Cadbury's classes that persuaded me that "Discussion is the pooling of ignorance."

"Introduction to the New Testament" came in the spring of the first year; "Problems in the Gospels" and "Problems in the Apostolic Church" came in the second year. It was in the second year also that I tackled "Hellenistic Greek Readings" under Cadbury. Though I had taken many courses in "*Koine* Greek" in college and even had been paper grader for "Elementary Greek" for two years, like many students, I had let it go when I graduated. Under the circumstances, I would list "Hellenistic Greek Readings" as the most difficult course I ever attempted. On one occasion, I spent hours looking for a form in all the Greek tools known to me. I had the good fortune not to be called on to recite that sentence; the student who got it did not stumble. The form was part of a hyphenated word of two parts. The first part on the upper line was a good Greek word which made sense when taken alone; the word I could not find was a leftover part of it which also made sense when the two were put together, but not alone. I developed a first-class case of shingles before "Hellenistic Greek Readings" was complete.

Seminars with Cadbury in "Paul" and in "Second Century Literature" were really tutorials. One reported an hour bi-weekly on the reading he had been given. Cadbury asked questions on the reading, commented on special points and made suggestions for further reading.

Professor George LaPiana, an ex-Catholic priest, lectured on "Church History" in less than clear English at a favored hour in the afternoon. One of my brother's favorite stories was of coming out of LaPiana's lecture on "Abelard's *sic et non*" with lecture notes he had taken on "a sick nun." By my time, Ralph Lazaro, a graduate student, sat by the board to write on it proper names mentioned. A signal to Lazaro would put any term on the board one had not caught. The lectures were most challenging. After the first year, I audited LaPiana's "Social History of the Church," though it was not required in preparation for the S.T.B. degree. The grade of "A" was sparingly given by LaPiana. After the "A" for the year I was in "Beginning History" had been announced, Dean Sperry bent over to me in a friendly way and said, "I hear you did well with Professor LaPiana." A fellow student came into the Commons Room and asked, "Who is Jack Lewis?" When I confessed to it, he said in a friendly, jovial way, "We hate your guts!"

When Harvard men get together, stories about Arthur Darby Nock flow, each narrating his story of humiliation until one is not absolutely certain whether he actually experienced an episode or has lived it vicariously at Society of Biblical Literature meetings. Rising out of the slums of London, Nock, an undisputed genius, had become a world's authority in his field, though possessing only a master's degree. When asked why he did not do a doctorate, Nock's reply was, "Who would examine me?" He lived primarily for the articles and books he wrote. At registration the first year, the counselee was instructed to report to Nock at his apartment in Elliot House after six weeks to let him know how he was doing in his studies. Elliot House was at the far side of Harvard's buildings and had been taken over as housing by the military; that is, all had been vacated except Nock, who would not move. To see him, one had to get past the sentries. Once in the apartment, one found every chair and every inch of the table piled high with books dealing with whatever topics Nock was currently working on. Because there was no space on the desk, Nock had the drawer pulled out and was working on that. A few questions about one's classes and one's sermons were asked. One had the definite feeling that Nock did not really remember until you appeared that he was supposed to see you. His invitation at parting that you come back to see him carried no specific date – a fact that you and, probably, he also appreciated.

My experiences in his "History of Religions" class I have narrated elsewhere. I entered his "Seminar on the Gospel of John" under two handicaps. First, he had not forgotten that I did not attend his lectures, and second, he specifically said at registration that he wished I had had more preliminary work. It was my first seminar experience. He expected one (without preliminary thought) on the first meeting of the seminar to take one of the topics he suggested for study. Because I hesitated, I got assigned "Traditions of the Authorship of the Fourth Gospel" to be presented one week later at the next meeting of the seminar. Nock's method was to have one student read a paper each week. He interrupted with questions about points raised. Woe to the student who mentioned any point he had not thoroughly checked out and was uninformed about, including relevant dates. I made that mistake and got assigned a 15-minute paper on the relevant topic for the next meeting of the seminar; at that one, I also over-extended myself and got a third assignment. By that time, I got the message. One got smart fast under Nock.

Nock dealt particularly harshly with students who thought well of themselves. The seminar had in it a local Congregational preacher who had written a book or two on the Gospel of John and who did not have an inferiority complex. Nock guffawed at points in his paper as the student read it. He did all that he could to humiliate the preacher. Nock had a photographic memory and usually referred to material by chapter, page and "three-fourths of the way down the page." Glenn Barker was reading his paper in a seminar and gave a classical citation. Nock corrected him on the verse number. Barker looked down at his paper, thinking that he might have misread, and said, "No, it is verse six." Nock hit the floor and said, "What the … do you mean by contradicting me?" Barker withered.

By the time I got to Nock's "Seminar in Acts," I had already learned procedure. I volunteered promptly for a paper on *Praxeis*, the word in the title of the book; and I made sure I did not mention anything I did not have dates and full information on. With my paper out of the way by the second meeting of the seminar, I could enjoy the rest of the seminar.

Harvard men were shocked when Nock died in his early fifties. Though the gulf between the knowledge of the beginning student and Nock was great, if the student was ever able to climb up, Nock became extremely helpful. He was basically kind, and the bluff and bluster hid behind it a lonely man, genius in ability, who, like all gifted people, found one of lesser ability difficult to reckon with. He demanded that the student put forth his best. Sloppy work was a cardinal sin. Kermitt Schoonover told of having been asked by Nock about his grades. Schoonover admitted that he had some A's and some B's. Nock said, "Only A's. You will find it pays off." Schoonover, late in life, said, "For me it did." Nock was loved by his best students.

My first year, Professor Joel F. Auer was in Europe in the fall semester, and Elton Trueblood, a Quaker, came as visiting lecturer. Trueblood had already issued his *Logic of Belief*.[3] We were all interested in his effort to present evidences for belief, but I found his argument from religious experience unconvincing. He gave his lectures, and then he invited students to raise questions. I asked how experience could be an evidence when Mormon experience led one way, Quaker experience another, and Holiness experience led in yet a third way. He only replied that the young Mormons he had contact with openly admitted that Joseph Smith was a "jackass." Trueblood grasped clearly the issues between Henry Forgy, Richard Walker, me and himself. When another student followed with a question asking for an explanation of our disagreement with Trueblood, he replied kindly, "The problem is that they are trying to hold on to the infallibility of Scripture." I felt the emotional appeal when he asked if I was willing to contend that Augustine, Luther, Calvin and thousands of others who reported religious experience were deceived – an appeal like that when Luther's *Anfectung* kept making him ask himself, "Are you alone smart?" However, I did not then, nor do I now, consider that Trueblood's argument from religious experience is a valid proof.

Professor Auer, of Dutch ancestry, did not return from Europe until late in the spring semester of my first year. Dean Sperry made suggestions about readings in "Systematic Theology" – an area completely new to me. When Auer did arrive, his lectures were largely of the same content as his book *Humanism States Its Case*.[4] Auer was as much of a cue ball as anyone ever saw, and he felt of his head as he lectured. Auer had one chief target – Calvinism. He saw only two possible positions – Calvinism or Humanism; nothing between could claim logical and intellectual respect. He reviewed harshly in a periodical one of J.D. Bales's books and said that its chief merit was that it was brief. Near the end of the semester, at the special request of a few students, he lectured one class period on Karl Barth. I passed the comprehensive examination on "Systematic Theology," but I never learned much about it. I could never decide whether there was a black cat in the dark room, and certainly I never did find him. Those Evangelical students who went into "Systematic Theology" for a major insist that Professor Auer was very kind to them and was most helpful to them in getting study grants when they needed them.

Work with the church in Providence, attendance at midweek services both in Brookline and in Providence and school work left little time for social life. Harvard Divinity School must have had some functions I have now forgotten about. I never attended any and never met the wives of any of the professors. Those of us who worked with the various congregations got together now and then for an evening; and later in my stay, we had a periodic area meeting at which wives were included.

The Unitarian Association entertained all first-year men at a luncheon at the Boston Club. The old "saw" about the Unitarians was often repeated around the Divinity School – that they had four cardinal points in their belief: The Fatherhood of God, the Christhood of Jesus, the Brotherhood of Man and the Neighborhood of Boston. At the luncheon, I remember the topics of conversation moving around past Harvard personalities, the first Unitarian of whom had been Henry Ware. According to the story, Ware's favorite way of opening a topic was to say, "I am not aware … ." The national leader of the association informed all that he was not a graduate of the Divinity School because in his day Hebrew had been required and he chose not to graduate rather than to take it. Someone asked him if he had ever needed it in his career. Without hesitation, he replied, "Not in the slightest!" It was not strong encouragement to a beginner struggling with Hebrew.

The procedure at Harvard was to have the lectures, then to have a two-week reading period with special readings in preparation for examination, and then to conclude with the examinations themselves. The examinations were a new experience. One's mark depended entirely on what he did on them. My brother pointed out that past examinations were kept on file in Widener Library for anyone to consult who wished. I probably would have done very poorly had I not known that. The philosophy of examination was to see what the student could do in applying in a new situation what he knew. There was no single right answer to a question; the questions did not duplicate those used before. At first glance, one did not see how the question dealt with anything he had studied; but with further thought, he found that he could mold his information into an essay that answered the question; and if he touched all the relevant bases, he got a good mark. I have tried this sort of examination on my own students but have found that they are not conditioned for it and are only confused by it.

Examinations at Harvard were given in monitored halls in Harvard Yard with many classes assembled in one room at the same time. Examination booklets were given out in which to write the answers. No pages were to be torn out of the booklets. The questions for each course were printed out. The examinations were timed; and if one wanted to avoid a scolding, he only completed the sentence he was on when the timekeeper said, "Gentlemen, this examination is over!" One learned to look over the examination, to assign a certain number of minutes to each question, to outline his approach, to write and then to move on to the next question when he had exhausted the time allotted. There was often one major question such as, "The bishops of Rome, Ephesus, and Antioch met between sessions at the Council of Nicaea over a glass of wine and fell into a discussion of the apostolicity of their respective Sees. Give the conversation." After that question, there might be lesser items which checked one's knowledge on specific highlights of the material the course covered. If one wanted his grade quickly, he could insert an addressed postcard in the examination book, and the grader would send it to him.

When Christmas time came that first year at Harvard, those of us of the church who stayed in Cambridge rather than returning to our homes were treated to a festive dinner in the evening in the home of

Helen and Paul McNiel, pillars in the Brookline church. Paul over many years was father and chief stay to all workers in New England.

During the spring, I happened to be out for a brief walk in Cambridge on the afternoon General Patton came back from the war. I saw the crowds lining the streets near Harvard Square and joined them without knowing what the excitement was. Patton and his associates came by in open cars, parading like Roman generals in a triumphal march. It was only when I read the paper the next day that I knew what I had seen.

A student who came to Harvard Divinity School after my time stated on a college lectureship that the most serious problem he encountered was the one, "Where shall I park my car?" As far as I am concerned, this statement was a facetious remark, a falsehood, a statement of one who did not grasp the issues he was facing, or the school was entirely different in his time from what it was in mine. Though the professors at Harvard were mostly admirable personalities and were courteous and kind, the material they presented in their classes was largely new to me, raising issues that I had not had time to think of before. If accepted, it shook the foundations and made one search the inmost regions of his soul. It was an experience in which one learned new appreciation for John Henry Newman's "Lead, kindly Light, amid th' encircling gloom, Lead Thou me on; The night is dark, and I am far from home." [5]

Outside of Classes

What the professors did not accomplish in the classrooms in their presentation of the historical approach from a liberal viewpoint, a few of the Unitarian students led by Instructor Edwin Broome set out to accomplish in the "bull sessions" in the Commons Room. Broome had written an article psychoanalyzing Ezekiel and had found him sexually frustrated. He considered himself quite oriented in psychology, a great intellectual and an avid evangelist for the Unitarian cause. After the bankruptcy of the cooperative lunchroom which we have mentioned earlier, a group of us brought sack lunches, and lunch time was the occasion of dealing with what was going on in the churches. Broome set himself as chairman of the group to evaluate the sermons preached the previous Sunday as well as to expound his own. He always found those sermons which differed from his liberal outlook very defective and found the intellect back of them defective, if not lacking in integrity. At times, papers were read and seminary life given a going over in the light of his viewpoint. It was, of course, a give and take affair, but one in which one, no matter how determined, was always in a minority. Henry Forgy and his wife attempted more social contact with students than I did by having them to their apartment. He had shown one of them the *Twentieth-Century Christian Magazine*. This student took pleasure in heckling you in the hall with "A Twentieth-Century Christian!"

The Unitarians all smoked, told of social drinking parties in their churches, used coarse language and at least left the impression that their lives allowed great freedom. After our experiences in the Commons Room, we found it completely unbelievable when one week they told of the Uxbridge, Mass., church hiring a new preacher whom the congregation had chosen over another because he used so much Bible in his sermons. We could not think of anything that befitted a Unitarian church, as we knew of it, less than that. One week, one student came in reporting that he had had Broome and his wife over for an evening, and another student asked what seemed a very normal question in the light of the image Broome was projecting: "Did he get hold of your wife?"

Much later, one of the Unitarians confessed to me that the whole act from first to last had been a charade and that they were hazing. They knew that the conservatives thought Unitarians were short on Christianity, and they, acting as teenagers might do, were out to confirm them in their worst suspicions. He said of the group of us, "We have found that you are very capable and are not the religious snobs we took you to be."

I took it as a considerable compliment the day two of them got into a discussion over whether there was any book in literature that they knew as well as I knew the Bible. One, who had previously been an English literature teacher, thought it possible that he might know some of Shakespeare's plays that well; otherwise, it was no contest. I have not retained a memory of the same detail of the Bible I had then. Unitarian mores are quite different from those to which I subscribe; its theology has no appeal to me. But many of its men are admirable personalities and are very interested in the betterment of mankind.

Seminaries (whether Harvard, Hebrew Union College or Harding Graduate School) attract some emotional misfits. During the war, there was a manpower shortage, and some people doubtless got into the school who would be rejected in any other situation. One fellow was selected as student body president that first year I was there. The dean insisted that the students needed a closer organization and that there needed to be more student activity. Later, this poor fellow in New Haven, Conn., rang the doorbell of his counselor and then shot the counselor when he opened the door. There was Roy, the Greek Catholic deacon, who was headed for the priesthood but who was apparently homosexual. At the end of the year, Roy underwent emasculation and at the same time dropped out of school.

Despite the few misfits, there was a considerable majority of well-adjusted, fine fellows in the Harvard Divinity School during my time. There were probably as many Evangelicals as there were liberals. Many of these Evangelicals were headed to mold Evangelical thought since that time. I met Harold Greenlee, George Ladd, Edward Carnell, Samuel Schultz, Glen Barker, Louis Foster, Roger Nicole and many others.

Paul Jewett's wife, a very friendly and attractive person, worked in the library as assistant to Miss Janet Newhall. It was extremely humorous when one rather forward, but at the same time obnoxious, student stated to Jewett that it was very hard to talk to the librarian. Jewett said innocently, "I have not found her that way." After a bit more exchange, he confessed that she was his wife. The other student sputtered an apology and beat a confused retreat. He spent less time at the checking desk trying to shoot the breeze with the librarian after this episode. Mrs. Jewett became librarian in the Fuller Seminary library and her husband a theologian on Fuller's faculty.

There were some very fine fellows of all varieties of theological orientation whose scholarship pushed one to his limits in competition. Charles Speel, a United Presbyterian, and I regularly rode the train from Providence, R.I., together. Charles made a career in Monmouth College. Dewey Phillips went directly from the Divinity School to an assistantship in Washington, D.C., the largest parish in the Unitarian Association. Paul Karnes came back from the war after having suffered a minor wound, later served the Unitarian church in Memphis, Tenn., and then rose to be head of the Unitarian-Universalist fellowship before his death. Edwin Freed, who persevered with me through Nock's seminar in John, has done a career as a specialist in John at Gettysburg

Seminary. Albert Sundberg, interested in the canon of Scripture, went to Garrett Biblical Institute. The *Harvard Theological Review* published his dissertation on the canon as a monograph shortly before my article on Jamnia was published. The *Review* rejected my article; but at one of our last meetings, Sundberg said in a cordial way, "Your article on Jamnia has been a thorn in my side. People never stop to look at the date of my monograph." In the festschrift for Charles Speel, Sundberg tried to have a further word about Jamnia. Sundberg had had an embittering experience before coming to Harvard, but he no longer refers to "the stinking fundamentalists" in my presence as he did when he first came. Some of these, and others, I have annually looked forward to greeting at the Society of Biblical Literature meetings where scholars gather to hone the intellects of each other.

It was probably in the second year of my stay in Harvard that an older student, Samuel Schultz (later author of *The Old Testament Speaks*[6] and *The Prophets Speak*[7] and dean of Wheaton College Graduate School), engaged me in a conversation in the hallway of Andover Hall and asked how the Church of Christ boys were doing. He voiced concern and said he thought he could detect change in their attitude by the questions they were asking in discussion classes. With years of experience in high school and college debate, I knew how to take either side of any question. The problem with that procedure is that one can forget which side he is really on. The encounter with Schultz was to me sort of like the old cartoon where one view had the heading "This is a watchbird watching a watchbird" and the next view had "This is a watchbird watching you!" I knew that Schultz, though talking in the third person, was not concerned about someone down the hall. When Schultz passed his 65th birthday, I was especially honored to be invited to contribute an essay to his festschrift.

Can you look across our campus at the towering oaks and say, "Next year this one will be gone, but this one will be here for generations"? Whatever your choice may be, next spring when the rains and the winds come, there will be some of those enduring oaks on the ground, and only then will one know that they were hollow. Why does one man leave the church and another man with about the same background in about the same setting stay? I cannot tell you.

Perhaps one has had more experience than the other. Perhaps some element in his training helped. Is there an intellectual pride that draws one man to a teacher in a greater way than another man of less pride is drawn? Perhaps there is a native stubbornness in one. Richard Walker once said of a brother whom we both knew in Salt Lake City, "He is so stubborn that if he had anything to say, he would be too stubborn to say it." I personally know that emotion. Perhaps some did not react against their father in the way that Cecil Franklin (who came to Harvard from Abilene Christian via Phillips University) describes for himself in *Voices of Concern*.[8] On the contrary, perhaps the influence of parents who had sacrificed so much and whose heart would have been broken played a part in one's stability. Or was it a wife who made clear she was not in the slightest sympathetic to any liberal leaning? Or was it that one was turned off by Robert Pfeiffer's irreverent humor and by the stories in the "bull sessions" told by the Unitarian fellow students? Auer's Humanism certainly had no appeal! Could it have been that having to present a gospel lesson each week to the congregation kept one loyal to something positive? Is it that one area of study offers more problems than another? Is it possible that the lack of intellectual integrity (a charge made in the accusation of those whose positions are not accepted) is really there undetected? Is it possible that those positions have in reality been accepted and one is sailing under false colors as some brothers have always thought was true? For these two groups, one can only say, "Who are you to pass judgment on the servant of another? It is before his own master that he stands or falls. And he will be upheld, for the Master is able to make him stand" (Romans 14:4). Or is it none of the above things but that there is a power that shapes our destinies, rough hew them as we will?

J.W. Roberts, once writing about a brother whom he had heard had departed from us, said that he did not know where he had gone, but he for one hated to see him go. So it was for all of those who had come to Harvard from our Christian schools and then chose to cast their lots with other groups; I for one hated to see them go. I do not for one moment think that "Where can I park my car?" was the greatest problem they faced in Harvard Divinity School. Rather, I would say with John Bunyan, "There but for the grace of God go I."

During the summer following the completion of my first year in Harvard Divinity School, Lynell and I decided that for our work with the church we really needed to live in Providence; and so we gave up our apartment and moved. Living in Providence 20 minutes from the train station and an hour's ride on the train to South Station in Boston, a 10-minute subway ride, and a 15-minute walk to Andover Hall made school the second year something different. Despite these problems, I learned that when the snows came, one could make that trip when the professors would not show up for their classes though they lived much nearer. Because major classes met on three days a week, getting to them was not such a problem; but A.D. Nock's "History of Religions" and some of the practical courses met on Tuesday and Thursday. I could not see riding the train five days a week even though monthly passes made the expense of five days about the same as for three – $20 a month. I asked Nock's permission to study on my own instead of attending his class. He did not like the idea. I had to make a special visit to find him in his study in Widener. He fussed with me about taking up his time; but he did permit my taking the class, sure in his own mind that I could not succeed.

Nock was a world expert in his field and was respected by all in the academic world; but he was reputed to be the poorest lecturer on the staff. His British accent, his pacing back and forth with loud foot noises, and his tendency to make statements under his breath all added to the pain of trying to follow him. I attended the first two weeks just to get the feel of the class. I borrowed my brother's class notes which he had earlier made. He had gotten Nock's fancy and had developed into one of his paper graders. The notes were as hard to read as Nock's lectures would have been to listen to. When examination time came, my paper was not graded by my brother; but I made one of the few A's given. Nock could not believe it; he never forgave me. When I signed on for his seminar in the "Gospel of John," he saw to it that I had enough extra work to do to demonstrate that I was not a shirker. Only when I learned to be completely informed on any item I mentioned in a paper did he move on to pick on someone else.

The schedule I had worked out made me take the practical courses the third year rather than the second where they might otherwise have come. When I applied for admission to the doctoral program, the faculty commented that by my program it looked like I was heading for a career in the ministry. I had to explain that the transportation problem had made the course sequence; then I had no more problem over it. I would not recommend the procedure followed in the "History of Religions" course. Though I passed the course and though I made an acceptable mark later on the comprehensive examination for the S.T.B. degree, I never have known much about world religions.

Comprehensive examinations at Harvard were the major hurdle to a degree. They were to be taken at the end of the second year; and if passed, one could then begin work that was needed for the doctorate in his third year, though this did not reduce the two-year residence requirement for the doctorate. If he failed the examination, he had to do additional work to get ready for the exams at the end of the third year. Dean Sperry explained all of this plainly in his orientation sessions with first-year students. I spent every spare moment in my summer going over my class notes for the first year. Then there was an additional period of major cramming as the time for the examinations drew near. Joe Yowell, a former school acquaintance from Abilene who was in the Merchant Marines, periodically came into Providence and visited us. One of these stops came in examination week. I arranged with Louise and Kent May to come by to entertain him while I hibernated in the public library. The examinations covered Old Testament, New Testament, Early Church History, Reformation, History of Religions and Systematic Theology. They were held for three hours each day through six days. Following the written examinations, there was an oral examination the next week for one hour in which one could improve his grade if he had done poorly but could not lower it. No Harvard man will live long enough to forget comprehensive examination week.

In my oral examination, Dean Sperry asked me about the nature of my work in the Biltmore Hotel in Providence. He was willing to designate it "a home missions venture of your denomination." Professor Cadbury asked me about the education of preachers in the Churches of Christ. He also asked about instrumental music. He wanted to know if we put great stress on Greek, and he commented that he had had many letters inquiring

The P.G. Lewis Family
Front row: Loreta, P.G., Anna and Roy
Back row: Clyde, Jack and LeMoine

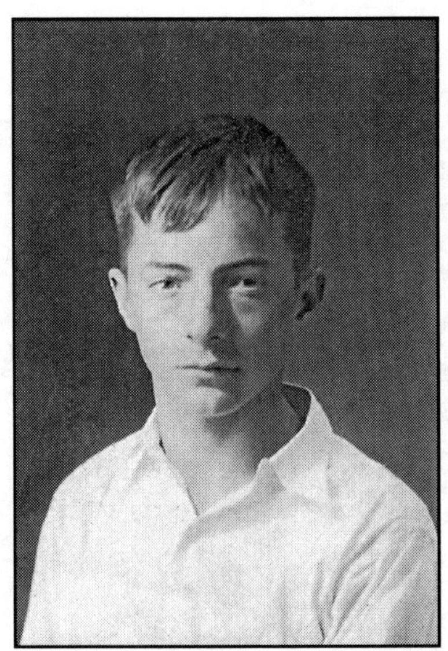

Jack Lewis, 6th grade, Midlothian, Texas (left) and a senior at Abilene Christian College (right).

Lynell and Jack Lewis
Huntsville, Texas, 1944

Annie May and Jack Lewis, Distinguished Service Award, April 6, 1979.
Photo by Harding University Public Relations Office.

Jack Lewis, studying in Harding Library, ca. 1975 (left).
Jack and brother LeMoine at Harding book sale, ca. 1980 (right).

Jack Lewis, lecturer: Haruna Bible Camp, Ochanomizu, Japan, 1992.

Jack Lewis, lecturer: Preachers Seminar, Cebu City, Philippines, 1995 (left). Nigeria Christian Bible College Lectureship, Africa, August 5, 1998 (right).

Harding Appreciation Dinner for Annie May and Jack Lewis with Dr. David Burks, 1989 (above). Lewis Tower, dedicated to Annie May, Jack and Clyde Lewis, at the Oliver and Norma Rogers Research Center, Harding School of Theology, Memphis, Tenn. (right).

Hebrew Union College, Cincinnati, Ohio, June 2, 1994. Alfred Gottschalk, President HUC; Jack Lewis, graduation speaker; and Alan Cooper, Bible HUC (left to right).

Jerry, Jack and John Lewis (left to right), 1999.

Annie May and Jack Lewis at ground breaking for addition to L.M. Graves Library, Harding School of Theology, March 31, 2005. Photo by Jeff Montgomery, Harding Public Relations Office.

Jack Lewis, tour guide in the Holy Land, 1996 (left).
In Israel, Dead Sea Scrolls Cave, May 23, 2007 (right).

In Egypt, Second Pyramid, May 17, 2007.

Jack Lewis, student for life: in his office at the Harding School of Theology (top) photo by Liz Copeland, June 26, 2012. In home study working (bottom left, photo by Cindy Putnam McMillion, June 19, 2012, bottom right, ca. 1995).

about the meaning of Greek words. Then he asked if I did not consider that I had done myself a disservice in coming to Harvard. I replied that I did not see that I was in a different position from those men who had gone to the University of Chicago. Nock roared back, "And that is worse, if possible?"

The oral examination was supposed to determine in part one's admission to the graduate program. Cadbury asked me my personal attitude toward things taught in the Divinity School. I replied that the courses had raised many new questions about which I had not thought adequately before, but that I was willing to investigate. Both then and now, I think investigation offers the only possible solution to intellectual problems.

One fellow student said to me that he had not crossed the professors. My reply was that if I could keep silent three years, I assumed that I would be silent the rest of my life. He did not reply. I did not feel then and do not feel now that it is the student's place to try to straighten out his teachers or to try to take over the class. It is his task to try to understand the teacher. The student is the guest of the school, in my opinion, not the operator of the school. If he is asked his position, he should forthrightly state it.

Finally, graduation came after three years in Harvard. Meanwhile, John, our first son, had come along on March 23. Lynell, worn down with taking care of a new baby, did not find it desirable to go. It was a gala occasion held out of doors in Harvard Yard adjacent to Memorial Church. All the old graduates of the university marched in the procession with honor given to the oldest class represented. A senior of the undergraduates gave a Latin oration. Honorary degrees were conferred on George C. Marshall, Omar Bradley, J. Robert Oppenheimer, Thornton Wilder and also upon some other literary figures. It was in his address on this occasion that Marshall announced his Marshall Plan. In a *faux pas*, the dean of the School of Public Health announced that he had so many candidates for "the following diseases." President Conant welcomed the doctoral candidates "to the company of educated men." The whole assembly then struck up "Fair Harvard" (to the tune of "Those Endearing Young Charms") which I had never heard before and have not heard since. Sixty winters have not dampened the tingle of the spine.

The Doctorate

Time has clouded my exact memory of the chronology of my experiences at Harvard. With Professor LaPiana's retirement, George H. Williams came to Harvard in Church History. I read with him on the canon of Scripture. He asked me one day why I had done it under him. I was completely frank, stating that knowing that he would be on the committee for my qualifying examinations, I thought it wise to take a seminar with him. His reply was, "There is nothing like honesty." The procedure with him was to read a book, write a review of it, and read the review for his criticism at the next interview. He introduced me to the index in the *Revue d'histoire ecclesiastique*, and I combed all the volumes and compiled a list, some of which I have not yet gotten around to reading.

John Knox came from Union Theological Seminary one semester and lectured on Christology. He was an interesting lecturer; but from my viewpoint, one vocal student who differed with Knox and who wanted to debate with the teacher consumed far too much time.

"Greek History" under Sterling Dow and "Roman History" under Mason Hammond met in the Yard and drew large groups of undergraduates. These topics were completely new areas for me but were important for New Testament backgrounds. For a paper in Greek History on the topic "Why the Athenians Killed Socrates," I entitled my paper, "The Gadfly – Swatted." The grader was not impressed with the actual historical documentation of my position and thought it more theoretical than factual. I drew a grade of "B" on each of these two courses.

I began planning the doctorate without having had either German or French. I persuaded Nock to let me audit German in the Yard. The opening session held in the Germanic Museum revealed that beginning German had an unlimited number of sections at Harvard. I drew a young instructor who was a German himself, probably a graduate student trying to make his way. I devoted many hours on the train to vocabulary; and in the next fall when the university offered the qualifying exam, I passed it, though I cannot say that I ever knew much German.

One of the summers, I resolved, "Come fall, I am going to pass French!" I bought the books at the Coop and bought the vocabulary cards. If there then were records, I did not know of it, and it was pre-tape recorder days. Regular hours devoted to French made progress in reading a language whose sound had never entered my ear. I got a pass on the first effort at the examination, much to the chagrin of LeMoine, who had taken French in a class in the Yard the preceding year and who did not get a pass on the same examination. He had to come up the next year a second time. What I have known about French also would be better left undiscussed.

Professor Nock insisted that I must have some "Classical Greek" to supplement the study I had done in *Koine* Greek. But again, the transportation problem was in the way. We could not reach an agreement on the question, but he found me wasting his time. He demanded that I come in the afternoon to his study in Widener Library. It was quite a chore finding him there, but he was no more sympathetic than he had been in the first discussion. Finally, I convinced him that I could take Classical Greek at Brown University in Providence without spending all that time on the train. The Greek courses at Harvard just did not come on the right day for my other program. A couple of winters in Brown found me in a Greek course there, struggling through Homer and some other Greek poets.

The end of my fifth year in Harvard brought completion of the class requirements for the Ph.D. and also brought qualifying examinations. Professor Pfeiffer came to the examination to ask questions in Old Testament. I had read E. Schürer's *History of the Jewish People*[9] and J. Juster's *Les Juifs*[10] in a private seminar with him. Though he asked other questions, he asked me if Julius Caesar died before Herod became king. I did not have the slightest idea. After supplying me the answer, he left before the examination was over. Professor Cadbury asked about the Corinthian correspondence I had read on Paul with him; but he soon found that my concentration had been on the teaching of the Corinthian letters rather than on literary criticism. He was sympathetic and asked if I had not misinterpreted the requirement. Then he suggested that I inform any other candidates I encountered. Sherman Johnson from Episcopal Theological School asked questions about the canon of Scripture on which I had prepared adequately; then George Williams asked about church history.

Oral examinations have always been humiliating experiences for me. When I knew something, the examiners hurried on; when I did not, they probed the ignorance thoroughly. After my cooling my heals for a time in the corridor, I was recalled to be informed that the committee had decided to pass me. W.B. West, Jr., dean of the Harding Graduate School during the first part of my career as a teacher, liked to talk about students passing with flying colors; but I responded that when the play is over, your nose may be in the mud, your teeth may be gone and your jersey may be torn off, but if the nose of the ball is one inch over the goal line, it is still a touchdown! In qualifying examinations, "Pass" is the magic word; never mind the rest.

In the fall of the year, a thesis topic had to be chosen. My classes and seminars had not made clear anything in which I saw a thesis topic. I went to Professor Nock, who advised graduate students, and told him that since I had spent five years in studying the critical approach, I would like to study and write on what the conservatives had to say on the same topic. I confessed that I had some emotional involvement in the question. Nock smiled at me and said, "That is reason enough why you should not do it."

For the next interview, I had made a list of a dozen topics I thought I might find interesting. One of these was "Messianic Ideas in Judaism." Nock seized the opportunity to send me to Professor Harry Wolfson to discuss it. I had earlier taken a course with Professor Wolfson in Judaism. I found Wolfson in his study in the Yard, but he was reluctant to see me. He wanted to know if I did not understand that he was on leave that year. However, he gave me a few minutes and talked about the difficulties of the topic and the fact that most of the material would be in difficult languages. It seemed obvious that if I wanted to make progress that year, it would not be on that topic.

On my next interview with Nock, he was impatient at my blundering efforts and with the amount of his time I was consuming. Out of the clear blue, he said, "Why don't you write on 'Christian Interpolations of Jewish Writings' and investigate *The Testaments of the Twelve Patriarchs*?" I had never previously heard of *The Testaments of the Twelve Patriarchs*; but I thought, "If that will get me out of this place, *The Testaments of the Twelve Patriarchs* it is!"

Uninformed people have talked about the scholars of the church avoiding crucial topics in selecting theses. They show a lack of understanding of the problems involved in selection. One cannot write on what has been used in the university before; if he does not make some new contribution to what has been said elsewhere, his thesis will be rejected. It must be worthy of publication. The directing professor has to be willing for the topic to be done, and the student's own interests and competence enter in, as do those of the director. The possible topics in theology are not likely to be clearly relevant to church life as it is seen by the man in the pew. Rather than avoiding crucial questions, before he gets a topic approved, the candidate is willing to take anything that offers a prospect of getting him a degree. Could he know in advance the tedium and boredom he is to experience while he is researching and writing, he might think a little longer.

Starting with no knowledge at all did not speed up the thesis in my case. I tell my students to take an area they already know and then to research it more thoroughly. Indices were not in 1949 what they are today. Though Elenchus was already being done, I did not learn of it until 20 or more years later. I did know of the *Revue d'histoirie ecclesiastique*. I combed it for bibliography. Professor Cadbury directed me along, and periodically I went to Cambridge to report on my progress and to get other materials. Somewhere along the way, my thrust became more an introduction to the *Testaments* and less a study of Christian interpolation of Jewish writings. I do not recall that there was ever any formal action taken on the shift. I had some preliminary copy and was nearing what I thought was the end of the writing stage when time to go to Cincinnati in the fall of 1950 came. There, I finished the thesis, typed it myself during the next summer and fall, and sent it back for approval.

The defense of the thesis took me back to Cambridge from Cincinnati in 1952. Professors Cadbury and Pfeiffer conducted the examination. For some reason I do not now remember, Professor Nock could not be present, though I had expected him. Before going for the examination, I had applied for a research grant for a program abroad and had given, with their permissions, the names of Pfeiffer and Cadbury as references. Pfeiffer had been quite generous in his recommendation and had sent me a copy of it. The foundation offering the grant, however, in returning my documents with their rejection slip had by mistake included the supposedly confidential references. I told Pfeiffer I would like to meet the fellow he was describing in the reference. He graciously affirmed that he meant every word of it. Cadbury, whose recommendation, though generous, had made suggestions about needed modifications in the project proposal, remarked, "I thought those were supposed to be confidential."

On the examination, Cadbury asked questions for which I had specifically prepared in careful study in F.C. Burkitt's *Jewish and Christian Apocalypses*.[11] Pfeiffer stumped me by asking me who was the last person in the Old Testament to have a pseudepigrapha written in his name. As I said earlier, oral examinations have always been humiliating experiences for me. Despite my blunders, they passed me – the first man of the church known to me in my generation to complete a Ph.D. from Harvard in the History and Philosophy of Religion. LeMoine would have been that person had he not gone to Abilene to teach for several years before he took a leave and returned to finish his degree.

The examination gave me another chance for a visit to Providence to see my friends there. Though few in number, they gave a party and rejoiced with me in the completing of my degree. Remembering the inspiration of the S.T.B. graduation, I dreamed of going to my Ph.D. graduation, and I thought that my mother ought to be present. My father had died six months earlier. However, I was not to go to graduation. Jerry was about six months old. My mother and my brother Roy were coming up from Abilene, and we were going together; however, just before they left home, it had to be called off. Graduation is like a friend's funeral; when it comes, it is once in a lifetime. If you miss it, you regret it the rest of your life. The diploma was mailed out to me eventually.

The Harvard I Remember

In the *Harvard Magazine*, a successful lawyer in New York, while acknowledging the unparalleled contribution her Harvard years made to her career, said that she had never been able to decide whether to love it or hate it. These men of Harvard were not men with whom one played golf in spare time. The fact is, there was no spare time. One caught from them the spirit that scholarship was the important thing.

The spirit of putting a premium on ignorance and of making jokes at the expense of scholars quickly eroded. During my first weeks at Harvard, at lunch a graduate student in another department of the university asked me what my professors had written. I had no notion. I had never heard of them outside of the Divinity School catalogue, nor had I heard of their works. I now tell my students, "Pick out the authority in the field you want to study, and go study under him." I did not do that. As the poet said, "There is a destiny which shapes our ends."[12] I had lucked out by falling unintentionally into the hands of the world's leading scholars in the biblical field.

I cannot say with certainty that this is how Harvard was 60 years ago. I can only say that this is how I remember it.

Chapter 6

CASTING BREAD ON THE WATER

I never knew who started the Sunday afternoon meetings in the Biltmore Hotel in downtown Providence. I assume it was some GIs who then appealed to the Brookline congregation in Boston for aid. Providence was not a port of embarkation; most of the people stationed there were returning from the war. Harold Thomas, preacher for Brookline, encouraged the effort before I came, as he did also for other groups meeting in the general Boston area.

At that time, there were no courses in ACC in mission work or church administration. I had a year in preaching as the first located preacher of Throckmorton, Texas. That was followed by three years at Huntsville, Texas. Huntsville had a 15-minute Sunday morning radio program. I was also in charge of whatever young people's work was done in that college town.

I went to Cambridge in the fall of 1944 at the age of 25 to attend Harvard University Divinity School. Before I went east to attend Harvard, it had been agreed that I would work with the church in Providence, R.I. Early in November, the first Sunday Lynell and I were in New England, we visited the Brookline congregation in the morning. LeMoine was preaching his first sermon as their newly selected preacher. Then Harold Thomas took Lynell and me by train to Providence for my introduction to the congregation at the afternoon service. We caught the train at the Back Bay Station. A large black man was the caller at the station, and he rattled off the stops down the line all the way to New York in an impressive manner. The State House, first seen through the train window, is unforgettable.

In Providence, perhaps 15 to 25 people were present for the service in Parlor A of the Biltmore Hotel. Not more than one or two of them were native New Englanders. The rest of them came from all over the country because of the war and were there for only a brief time; then more would come. There was Dorothy Ingham, a local school teacher, and Lea Reasoner from Jacksonville, Fla., whose husband Jeff was on temporary assignment as foreman for the repair shop of Union Tank Car Company. Jeff was not a member of the church. All the others present were GIs and their wives. The fellows mostly were returning from overseas duty in the Pacific.

One young lady had come up from Texas to visit her very bashful sailor boyfriend, and they wanted to get married the following week. Lea Reasoner offered her house for the wedding. Monday morning found me at the State House to get the papers needed in order to perform a wedding in Rhode Island. I then took a city bus to the Reasoners' apartment, and the wedding was done. Some years later at a service in Houston, I encountered the couple again who by that time had children.

I lived in Cambridge the first winter and went to Providence on Sunday and Wednesday afternoons. I arranged my school schedule so that I had two days without classes. The many hours on the train gave me time to study Hebrew vocabulary. Throughout the winter, on Sunday we usually went to Brookline in the morning and to Providence in the afternoon. Sometimes, we were back to Brookline at night. One Sunday, we went early and visited the service of the First Baptist Church whose building had been built in Revolutionary days between the battles of Lexington and of Bunker Hill. As I recall, the sermon that day was entitled, "Angels Are Singing: Listen Softly." It was my first time to encounter the fenced-in pews which were owned by individual families.

I went down to Providence one afternoon a week for visitation and to conduct a mid-week service at the hotel, again in the Biltmore but this time in Parlor D, which was much smaller as was the attendance and the rental price. With no car and only public buses to depend on for transportation, one or two calls an afternoon were all that could be done. One of the ladies asked me if I wanted a "tonic." Seeing my confusion, she explained that a tonic was a cold drink. Children from Maine called them "beer." Stores had signs offering "Cabinets to Take Out." I learned that meant an ice cream float. Children were asking permission to go to the basement. Somebody explained that in the schools, the facilities were in the basement. I heard people talking about what sounded to me like "the lore of Moses"; but eventually, I learned that they were talking about "law." I also heard of girls whose names were "Eller" and "Emmer." But perhaps that is not worse than my "warshing" the clothes. I took a preaching course in Harvard under Professor Packard, and it was gratifying to get a $25 prize in a preaching contest for having made progress in correcting my southern accent.

I was bold enough to attempt a call at housing on the Quanset Point base. The ground was covered with snow. The lady was cordial but never got around to attending another service. All seats were taken by sailors when I attempted to return to Providence. In Providence, many of the GI wives had only one room in a large house and shared the kitchen with all the other GI wives who also had rooms there. They were not in much position to have a caller. A plate of a frank and Boston baked beans at a street eatery was my regular supper.

There was no summer school at Harvard, so we students joined in aiding the small congregations with Vacation Bible Schools at Natick, Worcester and Mauldin. It proved the best way to open doors. At Natick, there were so many children that half had to be played with while the other half were in class, and then there was the reverse.

We exchanged gospel meetings with other workers in New England. Quite often, it was a series of services held in a different home each evening of the meeting. These took me to Bangor, Maine, and brought Harold Thomas to Providence. We had no place for him to sleep except on the divan in our living room. Thomas Page from Worcester also came to Providence, and I went to Worcester. At Worcester, my colleague and I were calling on a former Salvation Army captain who was at the time attending a Congregational church. Once the visit got under way and we talked about baptism, he made clear that he had no opposition to the idea of being baptized; but he had never thought it urgent. Then he wanted to talk about the millennium. I felt that such a discussion would merely remove focus from his major problem and confessed that I knew little about the millennium. He did not see the point in pursuing the question with an uninformed man. We parted with his promising to come hear Ellis McGaughey preach that night. Following discussions after the service, he wanted to be baptized; and the baptism took place, with police permission, in the lake in the city park at midnight. The next morning, the Worcester paper carried a picture and a story of his baptism on the front page. At the next service, he asked me how his being baptized would affect his membership in the Congregational church. It seems that he had not thought that question through, and I had never given a thought to the fact that it would be a problem. In time, he made a proper decision and worked with us. About two months later, the Worcester church had a lectureship, and I was asked to speak on the second coming of Christ. As he came past me after the lesson, he grinned and said, "I see that you have learned quite a lot in the last two months."

During the rationing of the war, many items were unobtainable in Boston. Among these were eggs. During the vacation school in Worcester, LeMoine and I were delighted to discover at the end of the week that the stores all had an abundance of eggs. We bought for all our friends back in Boston and, along with our other luggage, went home with shopping bags full of eggs. The overload made it necessary to set the bags down for rest from time to time; before long, the telltale moisture coming through the bags revealed what had happened to the bottom eggs. Once back in Cambridge, ready to distribute our bounty, we learned that Cambridge stores also had acquired an abundance of eggs that weekend and that everyone we knew had stocked up.

Though we had a satisfactory apartment in Cambridge well located for school, Lynell and I agreed that to accomplish anything in Providence, we must move to Providence. How to find an apartment in war-crowded Providence was another question. I hit upon the idea of going to the church hospitality center in downtown Providence. Though they were organized to be working with service families, they let me have an address on Broad Street. I went by the place and found that it was three rooms on the third floor just under the roof. One of the three rooms had vertical walls on all sides. I passed it up; but once back in Cambridge, Lynell and I decided it would do, and fortunately, it had not been taken. It was our home until our son John came along. The owner did not look with favor on having children in her apartment; we also needed to be on a lower level so that John could have some fresh air and could be taken out.

Multiple trips on the train moved most of what we had in Cambridge. At the Providence second-hand furniture stores, we acquired the furniture we had to have. We soon discovered that the ice man would not carry ice to the third floor. Many times, we took a stick between us, put a string around the ice, and carried the ice back strung between us with the string and the stick. It was a half-dozen or more blocks. The first post-war refrigerator that came on the market put an end to my purchasing of ice for good. The ice man has disappeared from society.

Lynell had given up her job at Raytheon to move. We did not have the foresight to know that the war was drawing to an end and that the job market would change drastically. Before the summer was out, the war was over, and there was no work for secretaries to be had in Providence. Lynell was never able to find work. Our timing put us through some lean times. Whether she had worked enough by combining the time before marriage and afterward to be due compensation, we were not sophisticated enough to find out.

Throughout the winter, I had combed Providence looking for a possible property for the church to get us out of the hotel. I turned up a monstrosity whose roof had fallen in, and the pigeons had taken over; and I also found a smaller place on a side street that had been a black church, but its roof was not much better. There seemed to be nothing desirable available. I finally found a dwelling house beside a lake on a good street that another religious group owned but had not been able to get a city permit to use as they wanted to. I did not know about this last problem; my experience had not informed me about building codes. It looked like one might live on the second floor and use the first and the basement for worship and classroom purposes. I had persuaded LeMoine to come down from Cambridge with me to have a look at it, and we were on the city bus when the news of the end of the war with Japan came over the radio. The driver said, "I am glad that I am not going back to town." Somehow, LeMoine made it back to the train station and on home. Later in the evening, two service couples came by our apartment. We took transportation as far toward the center as we could go, and then walked with the mobs. The center of the city had been closed to traffic. I have never seen so many people in the streets in my life. The whole city had turned out. The sailors and soldiers were grabbing every girl they met and kissing her. Gas rationing would be ending and people who had cars were out in them where the police would allow it. A car passed with a loud speaker system blaring, "Happy Days Are Here Again." One loop through the center was enough for us. We walked all the way back to our apartment.

Though I had never been through anything like it before, it was obvious that with a 99 percent service personnel congregation, the end of the war meant changes. In an earlier conversation, LeMoine had once commented, "I do not think there will be a congregation in Providence after the war." The thought had never really entered my head, and I was shocked at it. Now that question had to be faced a lot sooner than I had been able to foresee. Quite promptly, the people we had began going home. We finally got down to an attendance of Lynell, me, and four others. Then men began coming through on their way home from the war, and their wives came to meet them while they waited for their discharge. We were a place for them to worship. Now and then, there was a career family who stayed longer.

The end of the war with Japan gave a great turnover of attendants; but with the Korean War, a new group came. We had people stationed in Newport as well as at Quonset Point. Among them was the Gaines B. Turner couple who were very desirous to adopt a child. They finally found one to adopt. It was amusing to see how zealous Sister Turner was over who was making over her baby. Years later, I saw the child, married and a faculty member of Great Lakes Christian School. Earl and Willene Priest came from the Memphis area. After service duty, Earl became an elder at the White Station Church in Memphis. The Van Winkle family drove 80 miles from the air base on the Cape to attend worship. They later served as missionaries at Nazareth, Israel.

We tried to call on every person whose name we received who had any past connection with the church. Some had lost interest in the church completely.

Bob Houle grew up in a Catholic family in Pawtucket and married a California girl during the war. Being released by the church from the restriction of eating meat on Friday during the war did not make sense to him, and he was baptized. The Houles came back to Pawtucket to live when he was out of the service and shortly had a beautiful baby. Two months later, they were on my porch at 9 p.m. sobbing, "The baby died." We buried the baby the next day; the tragedy shook us all up. Without her baby, Sister Houle was not satisfied in Rhode Island, and they went back to California to be near her mother.

Kent and Louise May had a baby while Kent was still in service and were attended by a student doctor in the medical school. That is where we found help also when John was born.

The Frank Perrys came from the Fort Worth area. Sister Perry had a charming daughter, Patricia, from a previous marriage. They lived out in Pawtucket; Frank was a manager of a division of one of the large department stores in Providence. Sometimes, he came to church; sometimes, he did not. Ann Lake once told me, "If you would assure Frank that he could continue his highballs, you could baptize him next Sunday." I did not consider that "marked down" sales in Christianity would benefit the candidate. Alvis Bryan and I took Frank out for lunch and talked to him when Alvis came for his meeting. I was told that Frank appreciated our interest, but we got no action. Once we got into the new building, Frank was baptized. After we left Providence, the Perrys went back to Fort Worth for Frank to take over a responsible position in a department store.

Frank and Mary Maynard came up from the South. Frank was an attendant at the Veteran's Hospital. Upon his unannounced arrival in Providence, he called me to pick him up at the train station. He was not a member of the church, but his wife was. I took him out to the hospital where he was to work. When he learned that we had an auditorium not yet ready to use, he wanted to store their furniture in it until they found a flat. Mary, who was a school teacher, arrived with their two early teenaged children. They really were a nice family; Frank was just one of those who imposed on people. We picked up Mary and the children many times to go to church while Frank sat at home; but eventually, we baptized Frank. They were in the church in Providence until his retirement. Frank has gone on now. Mary has sent a card now and then. She has retired from teaching and has been in a congregation in Florida where Jackie Stearsman, one of our ex-students from the graduate school, preaches. I saw Mary at the Warren-Matson debate in Tampa, Fla., in 1978.

I met Mrs. Pierce, who lived in East Providence, through Miss Kent, who brought her to a few classes. She was a second wife, married late in life to her childhood sweetheart after his wife had died. Both were very old. He had a stroke; it did not occur to her that the police would help her. After many hours, she got him on the bed and got a doctor. His case was terminal, but he lingered. I called on them and found the house in pathetic condition; she was completely worn out trying to care for her patient. I went by Frank and Mary Maynard's to ask Mary if she would help me clean it. Frank, who was not a member, responded, "Are they members of the church?" Mary and I scrubbed the place from top to bottom. Mrs. Pierce commented that she had never dreamed she would see a preacher scrubbing her floors. She asked me to do the funeral. As I drove her back to her flat, she commented on how grateful she was that the Lord let her have 15 years "with that wonderful man." A relative held an auction the next week of everything she had and took her to Connecticut in order to be able to look after her.

I saw a notice one day in *United Evangelical Action* (which Miss Kent supplied me) that the chaplain's office in Washington had war-surplus New Testaments it would send to anyone who could use them. I sent a request and then arrived home one day to a surprising freight bill of $12 and a hallway stacked high with cartons containing thousands of pocket New Testaments. I offered them to all workers in New England to give as awards in our vacation school programs. We also offered them in advertising, hoping for new contacts. We had a free Testament for anyone who wanted one throughout the rest of our stay in Providence. In a bookstore one day, I chanced on a remnant sale of a printing of the ASV complete Bible and acquired a group for a dollar each which I then passed to anyone in the congregation who wanted one at that cost.

Mr. and Mrs. Arthur Lewis lived on relief in the direst poverty in a very depressed section of Providence. He was physically unable to hold a job. He told me that if he worked a day or two at any odd job that he would be put off of relief and that it would take him two weeks to get back on; he just could not afford to do anything. I learned one of the problems of our relief program which has not yet been solved: How does one help people without stifling any initiative they may have? How does one help people and avoid the problems of those who would abuse the relief program? The Lewises' marriage was a second marriage for both of them. Though I did not probe, I judged from passing remarks I picked up that their past had been sordid. She spoke of an infant daughter she had long ago put out for adoption and had never seen since. In a general conversation about outlook on life, he one day commented in her presence, "One loves a second wife, but it is not like the first one."

After Cecile Farrar was baptized, she devoted attention to the Lewis couple and at times got them out of their flat into car trips with her. Once, late at night, the Lewises called. Mrs. Lewis was seriously ill, and they wanted me to come pray with them. She thought she was going to die and said, "Pray that this is not the end of the story for me." We prayed, and I sat for hours with them until she felt better and finally said, "Brother, you can go now."

Mrs. Lewis was baptized in September 1949; but her husband's health was such that he feared he would not survive baptism. He wheezed at any exertion. His doctor told him that he would never get his breath again if he was baptized. That was a new problem for me. When one is young and healthy, death is not as real as it is when one is old. I could not make myself think that he would really die; but then it was not my life on the line. By the end of November at her and my urging, he had mustered his faith into a try. There were a couple of gasps as he came up from the water; but if he was adversely affected in any way, it did not show. Though they were only babes in faith and knowledge, we rejoiced with them in the Lord.

Bill and Doris Kildow came up from Fort Worth, Texas. Doris worked in the bank and was a natural to handle the funds of the congregation and to pay its bills. Bill had been in the South Pacific and had come back in one piece. He was a great guy, good natured, but with a slight speech impediment. He did a great deal of talking about his "Muvver." On one occasion, I helped him move their things from the room they had occupied to an apartment. Doris was sick and unable to lift. A taxi carried all they had. The war was over for Bill, and he was awaiting a discharge. We had another brother who had chosen the route of being a conscientious objector. He had been assigned work in a hospital for retarded children near Providence; but he had an evangelistic zeal on his heart for his war position. In an almost 100 percent GI congregation, he lost no opportunity in asking those he could what they were doing with a uniform on. Though my words are not exactly those used, Bill and others felt, "We built this congregation, and if he does not like it, he can go build one of his own." Doris insisted that the Seabees were no worse off than the conscientious objector. They had not killed anyone. Bill retorted, "Honey, now I would not say that!" I knew better than to inquire further. Returning servicemen did not care to talk about their experiences. The congregation survived with both opinions. Bill and Doris returned to Fort Worth. Doris taught school, and Bill made a career out of the post office. They served actively and faithfully in their congregation across the years. If I were in Fort Worth today and needed anything, I would call on Bill and Doris. One of the last times I saw him, at his suggestion he took off work and drove me out 30 miles to see my "Muvver."

It was a great day for the congregation the day Jim Black, a sailor from Tuscumbia, Ala., arrived. Jim was doing shoe repair in the post-exchange. After his discharge, he stayed on in that capacity as a civilian employee. Jim played a guitar but had little experience in song leading; however, he took over that task for the congregation as well as anything else that needed doing. Jim and I gouged each other a lot about the James P. (Plunk) Black and the Jack P. (Pearl) Lewis. Both of us had just as soon let it remain "P." Jim found himself a little fiery Irish Catholic girl, and it looked like he was headed for quite a life; however, he finally decided that she was unchangeable and that he was on a wrong road. After recovering from all the anguish that frustrated love brings, he found himself a very charming girl named Peggy Weir, who was secretary to one of the prominent Baptist churches. We had a very lovely wedding, reception and all for them in our new building. Later, Peggy was baptized. Jim and I worked on the building and at many other tasks together. He was my right hand. Years after I left Providence, Jim and Peg moved back to Tuscumbia. The last speaking engagement I had in that area, I enjoyed a talk on the telephone with them.

The couples who married during the war – one from the South and the other from the North – had the difficult problem of deciding whose family they were going to live near. Glen Monroe of Clyde, Texas, was persuaded by the little Catholic girl he married to come from Texas to Providence to be near her mother. Glen's parents were Christians back in Clyde. Glen was baptized and pitched right in to help in all sorts of ways; but he suffered a breakdown, became violent and was confined to the state hospital with a very unoptimistic prognosis. The doctor told his wife to be prepared to make a living for herself and her children. It was touching when I took his wife out to see him immediately after his confinement. He pushed aside her hair which she had arranged over the bruise he had made on her head, and he apologized for it. Glen dived off the state hospital water tower in a suicide attempt. Jim Black and I took his pregnant wife out to the hospital that night to see him all wired back together; it was pathetic. The nurse in charge told us that if he had a special nurse, it might save his life. His wife could only say that they had no money. I told the nurse that the church would pay for the nurse; we never received a bill. In the many months that followed, I took his wife and children to see him one afternoon each week. If her attitude toward the church ever mellowed, I never detected it. From first to last, she never attended a service. Finally, Glen's parents managed to get him transferred to a hospital in Texas, and his family went there with him. Jim Black did tell me that some years later on one occasion, the Monroes came back to see her folks and that they came to church together. I have long since lost contact with them and do not know their final outcome.

I learned in Providence that men can see opportunities where they are not living and be blind to those at hand. A young man from Woonsocket was converted somewhere while he was in the army. Then he went to Abilene to study preaching, and he married. He came back to visit his family, all of whom were Catholics. Woonsocket was almost solidly Catholic and was French-speaking. He had his eyes on preaching in California; the idea of "Go home to your friends, and tell them how much the Lord has done for you" (Mark 5:19) did not cross his mind. Even today, no effort has ever been made to establish a congregation in Woonsocket.

A lady in south Texas sent me an urgent, registered letter begging me to look up her son in Woonsocket who had ceased to answer her letters. She had only the name and address of his girlfriend for us to go to. One of the young sailor brothers and I went hunting on Sunday afternoon. The family, who was supposed to know him, spoke only French. They seemed unable to tell us how to locate him but made clear enough for me to get it that I should inquire at a local bar. There I learned that the name the mother had given was a man's name in French, not that of a girl. One bar referred me to the next. At each, as well as at the house, I left him a note asking him to call home. I also tried the police. They assured me that the French name was a man's name. We had to go home without finding him; my companion thought he had never been to stranger places with a preacher. I wired the boy's mother the sad news that we had failed to find him. Weeks later, he came once to service saying that he had called home in response to my notes the night after I had looked for him. His mother had insisted that he must come and report to me that he had called home. I never saw him again. Strange things happen to Christians when they are away from home.

The war years without transportation and perhaps also Jim Black's purchase of a car touched off urgency for me to acquire a car before cars had again become available. I had had one car before I went east. It was Jim's first car, and he was proud of it. I saw a possibility on a car lot and took it to a mechanic known to Jim. He advised against it and then offered me one he had on hand. The price, despite its age of about eight years, was more than it would have cost new before the war. I reasoned that a mechanic's car should have been kept in good condition. I failed to reckon with the fact that a mechanic rebuilt wrecks and that he knew how to get it running again if he were out in it and it died. We proudly went to the Lakes' that night to show them our "new car." Later, Ann told me that Fred had commented to her that I was going to have a lot of trouble with the car. A few days after we got it, as I was giving Lynell driving lessons, we must have overheated it in going backward and forward at slow speeds. It blew a gasket. The repair place at the Dodge dealer insisted that it must have rings also. When we were through, I had spent in the purchase and repair as much as a new car would have cost had one been available, and I still had an old car that knocked. The mechanic advised that it only be driven slowly; and in the years I kept it, I took his advice – top speed not over 35 and usually 25. Later, the gas tank developed a leak which I vainly tried to mend. Then the gas gauge went out. I never knew how much fuel I had. Once in heavy traffic at rush hour approaching a bridge over the river, I was in the middle of three lanes and ran out of gas. It was an interesting experience to get the side lane to make way and even more interesting to persuade anyone to help me push it out of the traffic so that I could go for gas. No one has been able to sell me a used car after I finally got rid of that one. I also learned something about advice. If one asks advice, he should be certain that he is asking someone who knows more than he does; and he should be sure to ask enough to find out what he needs to know.

Seeking Support

It must have been our second Christmas in New England that Joe and Lois Sellars, Lynell's sister and her husband, offered us a trip to Mississippi to spend Christmas with them. We were excited about the possibility. But when we tried to buy tickets on the Southern Railroad's all reserved seat "City of New Orleans" which went from New York through Meridian, we hit a wall. There were no seats available.

It was not until our fourth summer when John was about fifteen months that we got to make a trip home for the grandparents to see their first grandchild. Because of John, we took the first plane ride for any of us. It was a DC-3, making the milk run, stopping at what seemed every field en route to Atlanta. I think there were nine stops in all. John got into the spirit of it and bucked excitedly each time the engines were gunned. During the layover in Atlanta, I had him in a child's harness on a leash, and he showed me the airport. Now, people frown on the use of harnesses; but in my opinion, it was an excellent way to let a child have freedom without worrying his parents to death in keeping him from straying off.

Lynell spent her time in Meridian with Lois, but Joe had to work as a bus driver for the state transporting people to the hospital in the state compulsory venereal disease treatment program. I went with him on his pickup run. Most of the patients were black; and when Joe declared a rest stop, it was out in the bushes somewhere. People disappeared up the bank and behind a tree. Blacks in New England were treated differently.

Joe was an incurable enthusiast for car driving, which lasted until his death. On Sunday, he took me to Tuscaloosa, Ala., to a congregation from which we got help. A GI from there had persuaded his home congregation to send money; but before any came, they had to know the preacher's stand on pre-millennialism. I sent them a brief of my speech at the Worcester lectureship. They faithfully supported us for several years. This particular Sunday, they let me address the congregation 10 minutes about Providence, teach a Bible class on Jeremiah, and then deliver the Sunday night sermon. Much later, when they decided to discontinue their help, they wrote to that effect. I wrote them and thanked them for their help. I told them that mission works were like government agencies; once they got started, they were self-perpetuating and eternal in their wants. I stated that I did not see how we could do without their help; but perhaps it would be good for the congregation to see if it could not shoulder more of its own load.

A church in Montgomery, Ala., had helped some. I caught the bus from Meridian over there in time to speak on Wednesday night at one congregation. A couple from my home town, Midlothian, had moved there, and I was surprised to see them. They were living on the farm of Joe Greer, one of the members of the board of the new and struggling Alabama Christian College. At that point, Montgomery was plagued with extremists on women's hats in worship and other hobbies. The school was not free of these ideas. As the crowd gathered at the congregation, someone asked if anyone knew Jack Lewis; my fellow townsman did, vouched for me and made the introduction in a gracious way. I helped them with the hay on Brother Greer's farm for a couple of days. I got a view of black sharecropper conditions in the Deep South where one got money advanced on the coming crop but was always behind. Greer had built for the sharecroppers on his farm new cement-block houses, which were an improvement over the shacks one saw elsewhere. Brother Greer seemed favorable to my work, but nothing ever came of the visit.

I spoke on Sunday at two congregations, and then I took the bus back to Meridian; to my surprise, there was Joe Sellars waiting for me at the bus station at about three in the morning.

Joe loaded us into his car and drove us to Center, Texas, where Lynell's parents were living. I preached at a place or two around there, and the Carpenters got to see their first grandchild. It was Lynell's last visit with her parents before her father's death. Lynell and I made a hurried trip to Port Arthur, where she had been born, to visit a lady who had been kind to her in her first three years. I had also sold books there and in Orange in my college days. Lynell's father took me to New London to speak; a couple who had been in Providence was there. We went to Tyler. I got an appointment to come back to Marshall, which I did; but no help came from there.

At my parents' home, my father took me to Dallas to talk to people he knew there. We tried to call on Brother Achen, who was known to be wealthy, had helped Freed-Hardeman College and had a foundation to aid the church. One knew from the reports of others that getting an appointment was impossible. My aunt who lived in Dallas and who knew him had tried for someone and had been turned down. To our knock, Brother Achen answered the door, and we asked to talk with him and told him our subject. He did not invite us in. He told us it was time for his nap and excused himself. Despite the people my father knew and the preachers I had known from my childhood, I did not get a single speaking engagement in Dallas or a single dollar.

My father suggested that I might do better in Fort Worth on my own. One of our members had a brother whom she assured me would help me. I called on him and found him drunk; he in turn called a philanthropist who was supposed to help. I was granted an appointment. The philanthropist had known an uncle of mine in Fort Worth at an earlier time, and we spoke of him; he explained that since he had recently made a contribution to ACC, which they announced, he had been bothered a great deal by people with appeals; then he commented that my contact would be better off if he hit the bottle less. I could only say, "Yes, he was drinking when I was there."

Robert Jones, a prominent preacher in Fort Worth who had been in Providence, suggested that I call an elder of one of the congregations and ask for an appointment the next day, which was Sunday. The elder's reply was, "Why don't you preach for us?" That was just what I wanted. I even called a friend or two who had been in Providence and invited them to meet me at worship. My mother accompanied me, and I arrived on time and introduced myself. The elder got a couple of brothers into the office to talk to me, and they explained that they already had Fay Star to preach. I hardly got a word in about Providence. At the service, the presiding person in a warm auditorium opened with, "See how miserable you are this morning? If you will contribute to the building fund, we can be comfortable."

In the afternoon, I had made an appointment with another set of elders whom I had never met. Harold Thomas had understood them to promise to divert to Providence the money they had supplied him before a single large congregation in Fort Worth had taken over Harold's full support. But no money ever came. I had corresponded with the preacher but had not received more than stalling. They listened, gave no explanation for what had happened, and never sent any money.

I had a brief visit in Abilene with my sister, Loreta, who had married V.W. Kelley after I went to Providence. My brother Roy was then a student in ACC, and I saw him. V.W. took me back to Throckmorton, where I had done my first local preaching, for a visit. I made a stop at Stamford, where the brother-in-law of one of our members lived. The man had only gone through the fourth grade in school but had climbed the ladder to ownership of a prosperous Cadillac dealership. He, through the congregation in Stamford, was helping Providence. An ACC classmate of mine was preaching there. He gave me a glowing introduction that said more than I could say. One brother, a bulldozer operator, offered to give up his job and to come to Providence to work; however, we never got the details worked out for him to get work in Providence. Stamford helped us for a long time.

It had been suggested to me when I had visited Huntsville that Conroe, the next town south, might become interested. I made an appointment there after my West Texas visits. D.B. Rambo, an elder at Huntsville, took me down and introduced me, explaining that Huntsville sponsored my work. They responded favorably and continued to help Providence even after I left it. It was the most fruitful stop of my trip.

The Conroe appointment upset my fixed schedule. I was supposed to be in Batesville, Ark., the next night. The only way it could be done was to take the bus down to Houston, fly from Houston to Little Rock, catch the bus to Newport, and then catch another bus to Batesville. Billy and Marie Goodin were there and had been sending money through the congregation there since they had left Providence. Billy met the bus. Their first baby had just arrived. I addressed the mid-week group. Next morning, I caught the bus back to Newport. It crossed the river on a ferry but was late and got into Newport an hour after the bus I needed to St. Louis had gone. If I waited for the next bus, I would miss my connection all along the way. I took my suitcase, walked to the highway, stuck out my thumb in my last hitchhiking experience, and caught a ride. We passed the bus at its lunch stop. Finally, my benefactor turned off the highway. I waved the bus down and got on. Two days later, after an exhausting bus ride, I was at the airport in Providence to meet Lynell and John, who had stayed with my parents during my travels and then had flown home from Dallas.

I learned in trying to raise money that one has to be prepared to face many attitudes. Some preachers were willing to help one make contacts; others were not. Some seemed to feel that helping other programs would deter their own; others said, "Look, any money you can get out of these people just makes it easier for me to get them to give for our own programs."

There is always a basis for difference of opinion about how to fulfill the Lord's commission. My plans were wanting in the opinion of some. Burton Coffman once said to me when I first started making appeals to get to Providence, "Tom is going to publish a paper. You are going to school. Who is going to evangelize New England?" When I returned to Huntsville, my sponsoring congregation, D.B. Rambo, one of the elders, said of the preacher, "He is not one of your friends." Olan Hicks once pointed out to me that there were many works going on in the post-war age that were more exciting than Providence. I am sure that was true. The hope that carrying the gospel to the battle zones would end war once and for all caught the imagination of all of us. However, there were not any areas where the masses were more lost than they were in Providence. There were none where souls were more valuable. One did not have to learn a strange language to teach them. How grateful I am to God and to those who saw that at that time and made the work possible!

It seems to me that churches now are more systematic in their mission programs than they were then. It is quite possible that absorption in my own dreams brought some wishful thinking on my part and that I understood people to be making promises they never kept when they had not really made them. It may be that I mistook courtesy for promises. It may be that there were valid reasons why they changed their minds. May the Lord grant his mercy to all of them and to me when we stand before him!

Win Some, Lose Some

How does one build a congregation in a highly Catholic eastern metropolitan area? After years of schooling and 30 years of teaching, I am not sure that I have any more certain answer to that question than I did in 1944 as a 25-year-old beginner. One spends most of his time in complete frustration. He can dream that time on the radio might bring someone to teach; but unless he has been able to talk some supporters into footing the bill, that door is closed. Besides, radio stations are not much impressed with unheard of congregations meeting in hotel parlors in a city where there is a strong ministerial alliance.

The first hope in an American city is to find some members who have moved into the area from other places but who do not know that a congregation is in their new location. One sees to it that his work is listed in all the directories that circulate among the people of the nation's congregations. He sees that the church papers keep carrying reports of his work so that someone may see them and inform the people they know who are coming his way.

One opens his home to all comers. In an atmosphere where boys are away from home in the military and are on leave with time to kill, the preacher's home was home away from home. Youth and appetites seem to go together. I learned in short order who had to issue invitations for meals. It was the one who cooks the meals and knows the limitations, not the one who talks to the guests while the meal is being prepared. A WAC captain we had known in Brookline showed up for service.

In the open-door hospitality policy, I said, "Come home with us!" But on the way home, there had to be a grocery stop made to supply the barren cupboard with even the making of sandwiches. From then on, Lynell gave the meal invitations.

Furthermore, disproportionate sums (compared with the size of the budget) spent on advertising on the Saturday church page seemed a hope, particularly in an area and time line of 1944-1945 where service personnel were on the move each week. The advertising accomplished the purpose of letting those members looking know that a congregation was there; but it also attracted the curious and the religious misfits of the community who had moved from one new thing to another and who would listen for a while to this new thing also. It did make one feel like he had the possibility of accomplishing something; but if more than one or two stable persons who did not previously have a connection with the church where they came from were won by this means and stayed with us, I never identified those persons. The person who stayed the longest was Miss E. Winifred Kent. She kept company with a Mr. Dix, who was retired. His children (and maybe his own judgment) saw to it that they remained just friends. Miss Kent was very kind to us; but she was clearly emotionally unstable. We had many classes in her home and in the home of her friends over several years. When we met elsewhere, she brought her car full of elderly friends; but we never moved any of them.

We had a Mrs. Barney, a Swedish lady whose English was not always understandable. She was reputed to have earlier footed the bill for the founder of the Providence Bible Institute. She had the notion that the Lord was going to set up his kingdom in the Biltmore Hotel, and we seemed to her to be his forerunners. She was more faithful in attendance than a lot of the members – the Lord rest her soul! We did some better with Alice Goff, who came out of a Catholic background against her family's wish. She was the first native Rhode Islander to be baptized. None of her family were ever won. Later, we married her to William Nelson and also baptized him. After I left Providence, they moved to Colorado, and I am sorry to say that I lost track of them.

Correspondence lessons offered some hope, it seemed. Others in other areas reported favorable results in their areas. Our advertising of lessons resulted in only one telephone inquiry but in no students at all. Clipping family news items in the paper and mailing them along with a tract to every person whose name appeared in the paper can take a lot of time. It brought a few thank-you notes, but no one came to service from it.

How does one proceed? He grasps at straws! Missionaries abroad were reporting finding indigenous churches in their areas. Perhaps Rhode Island had such people who needed to be found. If a curious person came claiming to believe what one does, one probed the case thoroughly with great hope. Perhaps the person who believes the Scriptures on baptism but who is confused on instrumental music or on the millennium can be taught. An American Indian who preached for a small group claimed agreement and invited us to speak at a night service at his group. I took several with me and gave the best survey of the Restoration plea I could muster; people were kind, but neither he nor they moved. Mrs. Barney insisted that he was a scoundrel and would not speak to him or come near him when he came to service. With her problems with English, I never got straight whether his problem was women or money. The affair was hopeless.

A cordial person insisted that we agreed on baptism. He attended a small church on Rochambeau Avenue. They had the Lord's Supper every Sunday and did not use instrumental music. Four of us made it there the next Sunday morning, hopeful that we had found kindred spirits. It was a Plymouth Brethren group. Soon, they drew their circle for closed communion, leaving us in the rear. I found that the man thought that one should be baptized but thought it was not really necessary. He argued that because Ananias said, "Brother Saul" (Acts 9:17), and that "Brother" was capitalized, the passage shows that Saul was already a Christian. The employees of the place where he worked were on strike. I asked him if he was also striking, and he emphatically said, "No! The Bible said that one should be 'no striker'" (1 Timothy 3:3 KJV). He asked what we thought of the Rapture. I was about to go into a detailed exposition; but Harold Thomas, who was with us in a meeting, said, "Rapture? Is that a biblical term?" The guest answered, "Well, no, and I do not think that it is very important anyway." I asked permission to come to his home. I went through all the conversions in the book of

Acts with him and his family stressing baptism. It ran on to a very late hour. They were sure they were saved before being baptized and did not care to consider it otherwise. He did not come to service again, and we did not get another invitation to his place.

The gospel meeting was a proven tool in the areas in which I grew up; but how do you get people out where there is not already an audience to preach to? Though a preacher well known in the south was sent to preach, he was unheard of in Providence; and the 5000 door-to-door personal invitations turned up not one person that we did not already have coming. It is still very sad to me to remember the preacher who came up from the south. A black man came to the service, and the preacher suggested to the man that it would be best for him to sit in a certain area. The man left without staying for the service. He never came again.

How does one meet people in a metropolitan area where everyone goes his own way? It struck me that the Council of Churches service center where people did volunteer work might offer some possibilities. I helped them paint the interior of a vacant house that someone was furnishing rent-free for their charity center. Later, the group met on the lower-floor level of the near downtown church building of a Baptist congregation which was rapidly on its way to a permanent demise. The congregation was no longer large enough to use its auditorium for its services. I did meet some Providence preachers and church workers. The most productive of these acquaintances was with an elderly Baptist preacher of the congregation in whose building the work was done. He had been a machinist by trade. He told me that if he had his life to live over, he would read theology less and the Bible more. We talked many times, but I made no progress in changing his beliefs.

How does one make himself known? Perhaps it was not letting one's light shine but trying to shine it that took me to as many public lectures as possible where there were likely to be question periods. It then led me to ask questions, not because I particularly wanted information, but because I hoped people would say, "Who is that?" One visits all the religious services of as many groups as he can, hoping, usually in vain, that some conversation may supply a prospect.

One searches for unusual topics for lessons to announce which he hopes will touch off someone's curiosity. That perhaps did not accomplish its intended purpose when Eddie Couch was invited up from New York to speak on "You Should Be a Skeptic!" Couch arrived not very sure of the orthodoxy of the one inviting him. The curious of the community (the few who turned out) did not by the topic grasp the idea that you should be skeptical of tradition, of human religion and the other items that was intended in planning the program.

I never learned to play church politics. Perhaps I would have gotten farther along if I had. It struck me in Providence that having a campaign might advance us along. I had earlier participated in two campaigns in Salt Lake City. The only person I knew who might help bring it about was B.D. Morehead, and we began to lay plans in that direction. Meanwhile, Paul McNiel was making a trip through the south to stir up interest for work in New England. A.M. Burton in Nashville had up to that time made a generous contribution to each congregation which had acquired property. I asked Paul to present Providence's case to Brother Burton in hopes that he would do the same for Providence. Paul told me flatly that there was opposition to Brother Morehead in Nashville and that if Morehead was coming to Providence, he could not help Providence any more. I do not recall why the campaign never got off the ground; help for Providence from Nashville never did either.

How does one establish a church where he has no backlog of people from which to draw? Others may answer differently, but my answer would be that one does his best in teaching the husbands and wives of the few he has. His time spent on them is more productive than that spent knocking on doors. It is more effective than use of evangelistic gimmicks than any other procedure he can come up with. This is all the more true when he chiefly has contact with people who are away from home, out of their native setting.

There was Jeff Reasoner, whose wife Lea was with us from the beginning. Lea had been reared in the church in Arkansas and had come to Rhode Island via Jacksonville, Fla. Jeff, foreman for Union Tank Car Company, though in about his 40th year, was out of Christ. He, Bill Kittel and Alice Goff came to be baptized the same night during the Roy Lanier meeting. Hotel parlors do not furnish baptisteries, so we took them 50 miles to Brookline, Mass., and got back home in the wee hours of the morning.

Someone wrote of Nan Frasier, daughter of an army career man stationed at West Point, who was coming to school in Providence. She was the fiancée of Harry Walker, a West Point cadet from Memphis. She came to service and brought a Lutheran friend with her. We had them to our house. I visited the Lutheran Church hoping for additional contact with them, saw them there and chatted with them. It was not many Saturdays until Nan saw me in the public library working on my sermon for the next day, and she told me she wanted to be baptized. But where could we do it, I wondered? An idea hit me; just maybe the old First Baptist Church would let us use their baptistery. I called the preacher, and to my pleasant surprise, he said it would be permitted if I would tip the sextant $5.00 for his trouble. That put an end to our long trips to Brookline for baptisms. We used the Baptist Church until we got our own building. After a military career, Nan and Harry have worked with Pepperdine College and with Freed-Hardeman College.

People came and went with our paths crossing theirs sometimes like ships passing in the night. In other cases, we tarried a bit longer. Kent and Louise May came when Kent, a navy chief, came back from the Pacific. His ship had capsized in a typhoon, and he had spent several days in the sea before being rescued. Louise was from the congregation in Delight, Ark. After a few months, Kent remarked to Louise, "I believe you all are trying to convert me." She replied, "If the shoe fits, wear it." He did and shortly after was baptized. They were among our most faithful until he mustered out, and they went to Orlando, Fla.

Harold Thomas introduced me to the Howard family, whom he had met while he was coming to Providence before I arrived. Mrs. Howard's father had been in a congregation on the edge of Providence which had ceased to exist years before. Of the people that I had heard of before, only the name of a preacher, Randolph Wright, came out in the conversations with Mrs. Howard. They had had some contact with him. I do not know how long the congregation was there or how it got started. The dates of its existence were never clear to me; its people had all dispersed and were untraceable. Mr. Howard never showed an interest, but Mrs. Howard infrequently attended.

The Howards' son, Warren, came out of military service with a medical discharge. He was very interested and talked about his grandfather's faith; he wanted to preach. He was baptized. One Sunday, the contribution plate had a roll of bills, about $2000, in it. Though he never made it known, we knew it was an anonymous contribution from Warren. His pension had given him more money than he had ever had before, and he wanted to use it for the church. During the summer, he wanted me to hold a meeting at their summer cottage. He was able to get the use of a church building which no longer had a congregation. He would have bought it had I not discouraged him. We had no people in that area. Lynell and I were the Howards' guests for a week. Together, Warren and I canvassed the area; he was well known to the summer residents, and a few people came out for the evening services. One man asked me a question that surprised me very much. He said that Jesus and the disciples were walking one day and passed the carcass of a dog. The disciples said, "How that dead dog stinks!" But Jesus said, "Yes, but he has clean white teeth." The man wanted to know what Jesus meant by that. When I informed him that the episode was not in the Bible, he was completely surprised. Years later, I found the story in an Indian gospel. How he had known about it, I never could imagine.

In the fall, Warren went off to Abilene to prepare to preach; but on the way down, he suffered a nervous breakdown. His family wanted the money returned he had given the church, and it was. They felt that we had taken unfair advantage of him. Actually, nothing had ever been said to him about giving, and nothing had been asked of him. All that he had done had been at his own initiative with only the encouragement that one would give any willing new Christian. After a long hospitalization, Warren recovered and came back to church. He attended Brown University and got a degree in one of the sciences; he married an Episcopal girl, but he finally converted her. He has written several books. The pair of them ended up in the Los Angeles area where he was an elder in one of the congregations. When I saw him last, he was looking forward to retirement to devote his full time to eldering. He and his wife sent Christmas cards until she passed away.

Fred and Ann Lake came one Sunday. Ann had grown up in the church in Fort Worth, Texas, but she had gotten away from the church and had been through a couple of previous marriages. She had two married daughters, one in New England and one in Syracuse, N.Y.

Harold Thomas, at her mother's suggestion, had looked her up and had persuaded her to come back to the church. She and Fred had married – a third marriage for each of them. Fred was an Episcopalian and worked as a right-of-way engineer for the state. We were in their home many times, and they in ours. Fred was baptized in time, and they sort of became parents to us.

Fred and Ann helped us find a flat on the first floor; John was on his way, and we needed to move from the three rooms on the third floor which we occupied. When time came for Lynell to go to the hospital, Fred insisted on coming over to take us. It was early on a Sunday morning. After church, the Lakes sat with me at the hospital until John arrived. They took Lynell and John home with them for a week from the hospital. Meanwhile, I moved everything into our new flat and got things ready for the enlarged family. I had acquired a crib, a chest of drawers and a toy chest at a secondhand store and had scraped them down and painted them ivory and blue. I thought that it was as lovely a nursery as one could want.

I learned a lot from Fred Lake. On occasions, when he had a trip to make down state, he would drop by and invite me to go with him. Most of what I saw of Rhode Island outside of Providence was on these trips. He knew something of handyman work, and I learned a lot from him. He knew about property, and he and I looked at a lot of places hoping to find some way to get out of the hotel. He had his eye open for a house the state would condemn in taking a right-of-way that he could get for Lynell and me, but that never went through. We were so indebted to Ann and Fred! It was a great disappointment to me when their marriage finally broke up. Afterward, each of them was only spasmodic in church attendance.

Jimmy and his girl friend came down from Brookline to attend the Rhode Island School of Design. Jimmy had a singing voice as clear as a mocking bird. It was really a pleasure to relinquish leading the singing to him and to do only the preaching. The girl had been Miss Red Feather for the Community Chest of Boston. Jimmy was madly in love with her; her father was a prosperous real estate agent; but out of the blue, she married an heir to a large fortune. Jimmy was never the same again. He was studying architecture; he tried a few houses and went bankrupt.

Jimmy called me one day and said that the congregation wanted to have a business meeting without me present. I did not object. I thought the people needed to take more responsibility and that I should run things less. There was no organization. Most of the time, we had no one who was a remote candidate for being an elder. After the business meeting, I learned from others that Jimmy had attempted to persuade the people to fire me and to hire him. It did not go over. I guess it never occurred to him that I had raised what outside help we were getting and that it would continue or stop on my recommendation. Jimmy later decided that he could influence for good the people at Arthur Murray's dance studio if he would go and participate with them. His worth to the church became nil. At the last word I had, Jimmy never married. He went south, from where he had come, and was working for the state of Alabama.

I found what happened to some people when they were uprooted from their accustomed setting to be very strange. The idea of a church meeting in a hotel parlor turned some people off completely. A Navy commander and his wife, graduates of Harding College, came a few times. He confided to Ann Lake that he did not care for my sermons. Then he and his family started going to the Aquidneck Baptist Church, which was nearer to where they lived and was more the strata of society that benefited their status. He had been in the Philippines and was sending his contribution there to support some worker. After we got our building, they did some better in attendance. He and I painted the floor of the auditorium one Christmas Eve, getting it ready for use. Once out of the service, these people seem to have returned to their loyalty to the church. They sent their daughter to Harding, and she became student body president. Years later in Memphis, my wife invited a couple for lunch on Saturday who were studying in Mission 1000 preparing to do mission work somewhere. As we were eating, it dawned on me that the family name was the same as that of the commander in Providence. I asked my guest if he knew the commander. It was his father. He was the small boy I had known years before in Providence.

One Sunday morning, a very attractive young lady showed up at services. She had moved to Providence from Florida. She was positive about the fact that we should not try to visit her. We offered her a ride home after the service; but we got only to a neighborhood, not to a specific address. I later surmised that she had relatives coming to visit, and she likely wanted them to think she was going to church. She did continue to come for a time; then the story surfaced. She had married a Catholic boy on the agreement that she would leave the church and he would leave the Catholic church. He did not know that she was going to church. When he did find out and demanded that she keep her bargain, she asked the people of the church not to try to contact her. The two of them joined the Episcopal church.

One Wednesday night, a new lady came to service and asked to see me afterward. There were never more than a half-dozen to a dozen people present, so personal attention was always given to any visitor. She sat there and told me of a youth in Louisiana with a father who was an elder. All the great preachers had been in her home: Hardeman, Wallace, Nichols and others. But then during the war, she had married a Catholic boy, had taken instruction, and had gone to the Catholic church. Several children later, she was fed up with no birth control and with the pregnancy of which she had just learned. She wanted to know how to come back to the church. The last contact I had with her, she was attending with her children (without her husband) and was active in the programs of the congregation.

Larry Forrester from West Tennessee met an army nurse in North Africa and married her. The army sent her home when she became pregnant. Larry, when he was discharged, came to Providence where his wife's parents lived. His wife was a large, jolly Catholic girl, cordial enough when called on but not open to religious teaching. Larry came to worship just often enough to be teasing but not often enough to be depended on for anything. One day, they showed up together, and she wanted to be baptized. As we rode to Brookline to baptize her, she spoke freely and made explicit that she would put up with no demands that they forego birth control and there was to be no assigning them any specific financial obligation to the church. You have probably guessed already that she was pregnant again. Her choice of the church was a price I never had to pay in serving the Lord. When she told her mother, the mother said, "Don't ever mention religion again to me until you have returned to the faith of your fathers!"

Larry's sister married a Yankee, and they settled in Foxboro, Mass., to run a country filing station-store combination. It was nearer to Providence than to Brookline, but not near either. She came at infrequent intervals, particularly when her mother came to visit her. Carrying infants and small children on the bus was not easy. I stopped by their place one morning on my way to Cambridge, Mass. It was an inopportune time. With some embarrassment, he ushered me in to talk to his wife and mother-in-law while he went back to his friends. Years later, I was back in New England at Camp Ganderbrook in Maine for a men's retreat. There he was! Somewhere along the way, he had become a Christian and was trying to do right. He was apologetic for his earlier carelessness.

Tom Stevens, transferred by his company to Rhode Island, brought his family, including three children, up from Georgia. They lived a long way out of Providence, but not farther than the people who had been coming from Quonset all along. They talked about their activities in the church in Georgia. Tom could sing. Whether it was the hotel, the distance or something else, they never got into the life of the church in Providence. After much spasmodic attendance on their part, Jim Black and I decided that we would try to get Tom coming and into activity by asking him to teach a music class on Sunday nights. He agreed to do it; however, after two Sunday nights, he ceased coming without explanation. He just did not show. I got a new understanding of the Lord's statements, "He who is faithful in a very little is faithful also in much" (Luke 16:10) and "You have been faithful over a little, I will set you over much" (Matthew 25:23). Seek out faithful people and put them to the task; it just will not work to give people responsibility to motivate them. When I went back to the Ganderbrook men's retreat, Tom was there a different man. He was embarrassed about his earlier behavior. Perhaps it was losing his children to the church; perhaps it was that a congregation was established near him; or perhaps it was something else. But I was grateful that the Lord had been merciful to him and had opened his eyes.

Mrs. Martin, a life-long member of the First Baptist Church, was in her 80s. The burden on her heart was a 12-year-old son who had wanted to be baptized; but in New England, it was the custom to have baptisms for the year at Easter. Before that time came, he had died unbaptized. She came to worship more faithfully than some of the members did – perhaps because we met in the afternoon and that did not hinder her attendance at First Baptist also. Church going was her recreation. When I called on her, her husband, who had lost his hearing, made plain to me that he thought Providence had enough churches already. When he was out walking one day, a car knocked him down. The driver helped him to the sidewalk and, since he did not think Martin was hurt, left him without identifying himself. But the accident affected Mr. Martin's mind. Mrs. Martin could no longer deal with him, and she placed him in the state hospital. In a few months, he was dead. It was pathetic when she said, "If I had known it was for such a brief time, I would not have done it." They had been married over 50 years.

I picked Mrs. Martin up and took her to mid-week class each week after I got a car; and even after she moved to her son's house in Pawtucket, the next town that adjoined Providence, I still went for her. Her vocal insistence that baptism was not necessary was a greater hindrance to others I was trying to teach than the good I was able to do her; but if you have only a half-dozen in attendance, you cannot spare one. While there is life, there is still hope for a change; but we never made it with Mrs. Martin.

To Those Who Wait!

About my fourth year in Providence, my telephone rang. It was that elderly Baptist preacher whom I had met earlier while doing volunteer work. He was calling to tell me of a Swedish Lutheran church building in a depressed area of town that was for sale by its trustees. They had only one prospective buyer, but he lacked adequate money. The key to the building was available at a neighboring food store. I could inspect the building. To me, it offered the one opportunity for getting out of the hotel and building a permanent congregation. After examination, I called the trustee and told him that we had the money. We had been saving for a building since we first started. No price had been arrived at. The trustees decided to let us offer sealed bids and promised the building to the highest bidder. Fred Lake and I considered that the other buyer might offer $4000, so we offered $4004. The building was ours!

The Beacon Street property was frame and needed some repairs and painting both inside and out. It was seated with folding seats in rows. The pulpit was one sitting to one side at the front, and the preacher climbed up into it. There was a large mural across the front of the auditorium – no masterpiece, but not ugly either. There was a cross on the top of the building. As we saw it, a baptistery had to go in where the mural was, the building needed restrooms, and the pulpit had to go. Iconoclasts that we were and ignoring the pulpit's possible antique value, the lot of us turned it on its side, and Fred Lake dismantled it. I later wished that our idea of what an auditorium should be like had not been so rigid.

We had spent all we had in getting title to the property. Money had to be raised to put the place into shape for use. People from all the congregations in driving distance responded to our appeal for a work Saturday, and we did a fair job of painting the basement level in two Saturdays. One of our helpers was Alvon Richardson, who though willing was somewhat retarded. His mother evidently felt that if she taught him the Bible, he would not hurt anyone. Alvon knew much Scripture and was very opinionated. He and his wife were among the faithful at Brookline, Mass., and they had been in the Phillips Brooks House congregation in Cambridge which antedated Brookline. When noontime approached, someone was needed to go to my house to bring lunch. It seemed to me that we could spare Alvon better than any other. I explained the bus route to him carefully and then asked him, "Do you understand? Do you think you can find the place and then find your way back?" Alvon answered in his booming voice, "If I can't, I have a tongue in my head!" The hundreds of laughs I have had over the reply might suggest that I overestimated Alvon's retardation.

In the refurbishing, James Black and I made tables for the children's class in the basement. We also built coat racks for the main floor. Harold Thomas was invited to be the speaker at the opening of the building. His text was, "What have they seen in your house?" (Isaiah 39:4). With the building, we could have gospel meetings as we chose. We could have a morning and evening service as well as a mid-week service. I now could have a study apart from my apartment.

We had two weddings in our building. Alice and Bill Nelson were married. There was a shower along with the wedding. They later moved to Denver, and I lost track of them. Also married were James and Peggy Black. Once out of service, James became a respected school teacher. When their golden wedding celebration came, their daughter invited me, and I was honored to be able to go. James passed away in 2010, and again I was invited to his funeral.

There was some difference of opinion among us about the policy of using the building. We met in the basement auditorium some months until we were able to open the main auditorium. Some felt that we should have continued in the hotel until all was completed and we could make a more impressive entrance into the community. I felt that the rent paid the hotel could help pay the bill for repairs – money we badly needed.

Only after we got the building were my mother and father able to make their only visit to see us. With them, we took our one and only trip down the coast opposite Black Island. We took them around the 10-mile drive at Newport where the rich had their summer cottages which cost millions. Then we went to Boston and, with LeMoine and Shirley, visited Lexington, Concord, Bunker Hill and Salem. My car coughed on in a dreadful way. After making a very miserable day for us, the problem proved to be minor – a stopped-up fuel line – but it was disgusting. Another day, we all went to Benson Animal Farm in New Hampshire. John was two years old and was a considerable joy to his grandparents. On another day, LeMoine and his wife, Shirley, took my parents on a boat trip to Cape Cod. Lynell did not feel like more sightseeing than we had already done. We never got that trip in; LeMoine and Shirley did it several times.

Money to refurbish the church building did not come in from our mail and church paper appeals as we had hoped. It seemed that the only thing to do was to make a trip through the churches I knew to make a personal appeal. Almost before my parents left, I was on the bus for Nashville. My plan was to work the congregations from which we had service people in Providence. It was a defective plan in that it involved traveling too far and staying too briefly in each place. I went through Nashville, Memphis, and all the way to Texas; I returned from the trip with what I thought was adequate commitments to complete the repairs on the building.

When we left Providence, we were followed by Carl York Smith, who was also a Harvard student from Nashville via Yipselanti, Mich. His wife was teaching school to send him through university; but as his beliefs changed, she finally told him her conscience would no longer let her support his education. Carl later became a preacher for the Universal Church of Homosexuals in Denver, Colo.

The state put an expressway through Providence, wiping out the Beacon Street area. The money from the building went into the Appanoag building located in an area more convenient to the Quonset Air Station. Later C.M. Tuttleton, a very blunt man, came to Providence from Little Rock to start a congregation over again in Providence. He did not waste time on people over long periods of time as I had done. He gave them a few lessons and then demanded that they commit themselves one way or another. One either got on or got off. Brother and Sister Tuttleton lived on a pittance but raised money to build a new building in East Providence on land that once had been the Kent farm. It was a stone's throw from where E. Winifred Kent had lived when I knew her.

The East Providence people had me up to speak at the opening of their new building. Though the membership had turned over and only a few of the people I knew were still there, it was gratifying to see the Blacks and a few others that were still there. The Appanoag and East Providence congregations are still at work; and besides, there is a congregation in Middletown that was developed by service people in Newport. The congregations now have a larger percentage of civilians and fewer military personnel than we had in earlier days.

Considerable progress has been made for the church in these 66 years. There are now seven congregations meeting in Rhode Island. May the Lord bless all those who have labored.

Chapter 7

I'D DO IT AGAIN!

Who in his wildest dreams could have envisioned that a boy from the cotton rows of a white rock farm of east Texas, growing up in the Great Depression, whose mother had only a high school education and whose father had only one year of college, would have opened to him the opportunities offered in three years on Interfaith Fellowships at the Hebrew Union College leading to a doctorate? I had first thought of learning Hebrew in college where I and a blind student were the only ones in the class. As the blind student's reader, I drew the Hebrew letters in his hand so that he could envision what they were like.

The Interfaith Fellowships at Hebrew Union College first came to my attention by an announcement on the bulletin board at Harvard Divinity School. I knew of Hebrew Union College only from a set of the *Hebrew Union College Annual* occupying a prominent position on the bookshelf in Professor Robert Pfeiffer's study. I was taking a seminar under him on the book of Psalms.

The announcement of the Interfaith Fellowship Program was not specific on what the class requirements would be. Perhaps it was the *yeṣer haraʿ* that suggested to me that the Torah could be used as a spade to dig with, though I did not at that time know R. Zadok's saying (*Aboth* 4:5). I confess that it seemed to me (busy at the time with serving a church as well as trying to go to school) that a fellowship might offer a chance to complete a dissertation that was already underway. What a delusion that proved to be!

The fellowship offered furnished the recipient $2,400 and was one of the largest I knew of available to a student at that time. When the news came that I had received it, I really hated to leave Providence. The task there was not completed. At a lectureship at Manhattan, I called Harold Thomas aside and said, "I have a problem." Without hesitation, Harold replied, "I know which side of it I am on." Men were hard to come by in New England at that time.

To HUC

We sold what furniture and toys we could and shipped the rest, which we wanted to keep, into storage in Cincinnati. We loaded the car until there was room only for the three of us in the front seat. On the way, I took Lynell on a run down through Manhattan and Times Square, which she had never seen. I expect that I was more interested in it than she. There were plenty of stares at the loaded car. With the car in the shape it was, it took three nights to make it to Cincinnati; it had to be driven slowly. Near midnight the last night, we turned off the highway at a motel sign in Ohio onto a back road. In a couple of miles, a police cruiser whistled us down; I wondered if I had failed to see a stop sign. I crawled out more asleep than awake and fished for my owner's registration and my license. The patrolman took a look at the stuff in the car, at Lynell, and at sleeping John and said, "We did not see that you had your family with you. What are you doing on this back street?" I said, "There was a sign back there that said that there was a motel up here."

Upon arrival in Cincinnati, we were fortunate to find a "for rent" in the afternoon paper and acquired a one-room apartment with bath and kitchenette near the University of Cincinnati and also within walking distance of Hebrew Union College. After our two-bedroom flat in Providence, the apartment was crowded for three; but it was available for only one month because a daughter of the owner was getting married and would occupy it. However, that would give us time to find what we needed, and nothing else was advertised. At the end of the month, we found another, even smaller; we took it and started moving in. Then we were told by the previous landlady that the daughter's wedding had been postponed; the move would not have been necessary. In our second place, the neighbors fought all night; however, because we already knew we were moving to Garrard Street in Covington, Ky., we made it through that month.

Hebrew Union College opened at the end of Succoth (the feast of Tabernacles). On opening day, Professor Sheldon Blank took me on a quick tour of the facilities. There was opening chapel and then a reception in the Succah (booth) as a part of the holiday season. The Christian fellows greeted me cordially as a curiosity from Harvard who knew Robert Pfeiffer. They wanted to know what he was like. They all used his book.

The interfaith program at Hebrew Union College was fairly new, as was also their doctoral program, and no Christian fellow had yet graduated. The honor of being the first went to Ron Hals, who was then on hand but still lacked a couple of years. Ron made a career at Capitol Seminary in Columbus, Ohio. Entering fellows the first year I was in Hebrew Union included James Sanders and Francis Williams. Williams (a brilliant linguist) and I had suffered together through Edwin Broome's Beginning Hebrew at Harvard. Sanders and Williams took to Hebrew just like a duck takes to water. Gaston Cogdell, as a preacher in the Cincinnati area interested in preparing to work among Jews in Israel, was taking classes and accumulating credits, but he never completed a degree program. Gaston worked very diligently with rabbinic students and formed some fast friends; as far as I know, he never succeeded in getting one to convert. A Jew who converts pays a great personal price.

Both Matitiahu Tsevat and Jakob Petuchowski, who later became professors, were then doctoral candidates in the Hebrew Union program. Tsevat was a brilliant linguist from Israel who had the misfortune of defective sight; Petuchowski came out of an English orthodox background and knew more Judaism and Hebrew than most of the students did. He became the teacher when Dr. Epstein became ill the second semester.

I will not mention other rabbinical students with whom I had classes, but we shared a great experience together. My former students have returned from HUC asking me if I knew Dr. So-And-So. I have reflected, "Why, I went to the college with him."

The program for all entering students was an 18-hour-a-week first semester Hebrew program. I went through elementary Hebrew for the third time. The course included classical grammar, modern Hebrew, biblical Hebrew and Mishnaic Hebrew. It was taught by Sheldon Blank, Elias Epstein, Eugene Mihaly and Robert Katz. During my graduate program at Harvard, I had let my Hebrew stagnate. Ask any Interfaith Fellow how sick he felt after listening to Jewish students read Hebrew orally the first day. They could articulate Hebrew with sickening ease; Sanders and Williams were linguistic geniuses who made better marks than the rabbinic students did. I was struggling to survive whether in pronunciation, grammar or translation. I knew what it was to look at a section of Hebrew on an examination and not recognize that I had seen it before. I later jokingly told Dr. Elias Epstein that I understood that mothers no longer threatened their mischievous children with hell; they merely told them if they were not good, they would send them to HUC to take elementary Hebrew! James Sanders recently described his statement to his beginning Hebrew students as, "If you do not curse me now, you will not bless me later." The elementary course and the following courses did lay the foundation for a career of 35 years teaching biblical Hebrew at the seminary level.

Students and teachers smoked freely in class; rabbinic students were cordial to the fellows. The student body was a tightly knit organization equal to any labor union. At the first announcement of a student body meeting, I turned up only to see a complete silence come over the group. Someone informed the chairman that a person was present who was not a member. When I said, "I am a fellow," he said, "The meeting is not for you." I made an embarrassed exit. Later, another student came to me and explained, "The fellows are not a part of the organization because we deal with appointments and other matters that would not concern them."

A student came back once from his bi-monthly appointment in a synagogue telling of being involved in a minor mishap in which a pedestrian had walked into the side of his car at an intersection and had been shaken up in a minor way. A man came running up shaking his finger in his face and saying, "I want you to know that Presbyterians have the right of way in this town!"

The library at Hebrew Union had open stacks but had the checking desk in the reading room. On one occasion when the conversation of a person was loud and long, I just started reading from my desk out loud until he took the hint and left. Furthermore, the reading room served as the meeting place for the board of governors and, on some occasions, for certain women's gatherings. On those times, the student vacated for whatever place he could find. On one occasion, ladies filled the hall with loud chattering. The student sitting next to me found concentration impossible, looked up at me, and said with all disgust, "*Nashim*!" ("Women!"). I have never had trouble remembering that Hebrew word since then. I had hoped before coming that Cincinnati would have study carrels, but they did not. When the campus planner later proposed that we have the checking desk in the reading room of our library in Memphis, I promptly protested with all the vigor I could.

Hebrew Union College had a nice gymnasium. My usual day included classes and then library until closing time at five, after which there was a swim in the pool. Chapel was held each day. The Scripture was read in Hebrew, and the liturgy was sung in Hebrew in melodies that still ring in my ears. Chapel served the rabbinic students a place to practice for their careers as leaders in worship. It enabled the fellows to accustom their ears and eyes to Hebrew. For the first time, I was with people who prayed standing with their eyes open, fixed straight ahead of them. I have never thought that Scripture bound people to one posture for prayer. The liturgy for the day included a prayer for the memory of all those connected with the college who had died on that day in times past. One can pick that which he participates in when he is in a group.

America was facing great change in the early 50s, and we fellows were impressed with HUC's lead in employing secretaries from racial minorities. We shared in the fellowship program with Murray Branch, an African-American. It was a good start (particularly for those of us who came from areas of great prejudice) toward the leadership we all needed to exercise.

Our world broadened as we learned of a culture to which we had previously not been exposed. Good natured humor was shared between the Christian fellows and the rabbinical students. At the Purim play, the theme was that of the rabbinic student who had flunked out, had converted to Christianity, and had returned as a Christian fellow. An item I remember best was when Scott Carpenter took his rocket ride, one said, "Another carpenter in space."

There were giants in the land in those days. The perceived stature of the particular giant depends on the individual interest of the student. Despite our theological and cultural differences, the Interfaith Fellows were treated with the greatest of courtesy. We learned to differ without being unkind.

A student who went through Dr. Julian Morgenstern's class on Amos might not have been convinced of the rearranging of lines in Amos, but he could not avoid the stimulus of Amos's message – a stimulus that will not die no matter how many times one teaches Amos. Laughter about Morgenstern's umpiring at the softball games with his "*kadurs*" and "*makahs*" did not dampen lessons in Amos.

Receptions in the home of Dr. and Mrs. Sheldon Blank were a part of the pleasure of each year. Going through Isaiah, Jeremiah and Ezekiel with Dr. Blank glued one's pants to the seat of a chair for long hours as he made his preparation. But it also made him love these prophets. I heard Dr. Blank read a paper at the meeting of the Society of Biblical Literature. Someone took exception to certain points he had made. The chairperson asked Dr. Blank if he wished to reply. He quietly declined with, "I do not believe so." I learned that one need not belligerently defend himself. His case can stand on its own merits.

Time came for thesis selection. If you have not personally been through the thesis selection process, it would be futile for me to try to describe the trauma it is. In the preceding summer, I had read Willoughby's *The Study of the Bible Today and Tomorrow*[1] in which it was suggested that there was a need for a commentary on the book of Zechariah. In my prospective thesis interview with Dr. Blank, I mentioned the possibility of attempting one. He kindly but quietly replied, "I think that might be more suitable at the end of your career than at its beginning." Much additional study of Zechariah leaves in my mind no doubt concerning the wisdom of his statement about the beginning of a career, but it does raise questions about the ending point. Now that

I am working on a commentary on the twelve prophets, I am not sure that a creditable commentary on Zechariah can be done even at the end.

Who among the fellows did not benefit from the academic demands and the charity of Dr. Julius Levy? We always remember his pleasure (though not necessarily ours) in his cigars. Students joked by calling his course in Hosea "Moon River." Levy raised a question about a Latin phrase, and a student said, "Dr. Levy, it has been a long time since I studied Latin." Levy replied with a smile, "But it has been much longer since I studied Latin." Levy insisted that he had never studied anything for which he did not later find a use. I have been amazed at how much I could see no use for at the time but which has served a need later at an unforeseen time. It has left me regretful that I was so eclectic in my sampling in the curriculum when a student. A student being chided for his errors in class returned, "But Dr. Levy, you are a genius!" Levy responded in his German accent, "But I was not born a genius. I became that way by hard work."

Semitic languages were not my forte. Aramaic I could crib through if enough time was put to it. I was having trouble enough with Hebrew, and Ugaritic was learned in transliteration from transliterated Hebrew. Only two of us were in the class. Despite the time I put to it, Ugaritic and I just did not connect. Years later, I apologized to Dr. Levy for my poor performance in class. His generous, smiling response was, "I do not remember it that way!"

A gentle soul was Dr. Alexander Guttmann with his own sense of humor. How I enjoyed his rabbinic tales and Jewish jokes as our classes read selections from the Mishna, the Midrash and the Talmud! How these sections have served me in writing and teaching! At times when I cited some wise saying of the rabbis, my wife joked me that I had more regard for the rabbis than for the Scripture.

During my years, Dr. Samuel Sandmel returned to the college to teach. From him I learned Philo and matters concerning New Testament backgrounds. He guided and endured my efforts at writing a thesis on Noah, a topic suggested by him because of his work on Abraham. I agree totally with the person who said of him, "He cared about students."

I sat in Dr. Nelson Glueck's archaeology classes in Cincinnati the few times his obligations as president allowed him to attend. When the New York school and the Cincinnati schools combined, rabbinical students were very concerned, tension was high, and the students drew up a series of inquiries for the president to answer. Out of curiosity, we all attended the meeting. Question: "Is the president aware that the incoming group of students from New York will create added competition for pulpits?" Answer: "He is." Other questions were dealt with like precision. Dr. Glueck gave the final answer: "No one forces you to come to school here!"

Dr. Sandmel reminded me on one occasion, after I was teaching, that the Chautauqua Society furnished speakers for schools and afterward made a gift of books to the school library. With my trying to build a Judaic collection for my school, I lost no time in getting an invitation issued. The speakers proved to be former HUC classmates. The time came for me to appear at a fundraiser in Memphis to express gratitude for the many books given by the Society over several years. I introduced myself as a parasite living off Jewish charities. Three years on Interfaith Fellowships in Cincinnati, my book begging, and two summers at the Nelson Glueck School in Jerusalem made the characterization apt.

Finishing the Thesis

After three years of residence in Cincinnati, I accepted a teaching position with Harding College. Hindsight is always 20-20. It is a delusion to suppose one can write a thesis that probably could have been done in a few semesters had he stayed at the library. A student makes a serious mistake when he supposes he can complete his class work and then write his dissertation in absentia. Preparing class lectures, giving them, grading papers, and preaching on weekends do not contribute to progress in research and writing. Though the dissertation for Hebrew Union College could likely have been completed in six to nine additional months of solid work, my dissertation stretched out almost eight years.

About the third year, Harding gave me a summer off to work on my dissertation. I also obtained a grant to attend a two-week seminar at Brandeis University at which Cyrus Gordon and S. Yeivin were the lecturers. The seminar was designed to launch Gordon on his career at Brandeis and was attended by, among others, a number of Evangelicals whom I am still glad to greet at Society of Biblical Literature meetings.

Following the seminar, I spent two weeks with my brother LeMoine, who had taken a two-year leave from Abilene to write his dissertation. We spent our full time in the Harvard libraries in diligent work on the theses. When the Divinity School library closed at five, we moved over to Widener, which remained open until ten. The first evening, I was slow in making my way out of the stacks where the study carrels were and barely escaped being locked in. It was rumored that if one got locked in, he had to wait an hour or so until the night watchman came around to free him.

On my way home from Cambridge, a stop at the Yale Divinity library turned up nothing new on the thesis; but then a stop at Union Theological and at Jewish Theological Seminary libraries gave some help on things I had no other access to. The trip also enabled me to spend a week at Garrard Street in Covington, Ky., and to have an interview with Professors Samuel Sandmel and Alexander Guttmann at Hebrew Union College. Professor Sandmel reminded me of the need to complete the dissertation by saying, "This is not your life's work!" Xerox copiers were not available in the late 50s. Beginning libraries had limited resources. While at the Brandeis seminar, I first heard from Dr. Beatrice Goff, a seminar member, of a portable copier for scholars that had been invented by someone around Yale. It was awkward and expensive; however, Harding was kind enough to purchase one, and it did help some. My files still have copies made that way.

Nevertheless, several more years were to drag by before the thesis was ready for typing – this time by a skilled typist. Though I had thought a second dissertation would be less strain than the first, I had stretched my nerves to the limit between preaching, teaching, research and home obligations. Intense chest pains took me to the doctor and the hospital for an examination. The cardiologist, after reporting that the cardiogram was normal, sat down by my bed to talk about burning the candle at both ends. I replied, "Burning at both ends never bothered me; it is when the middle is added to the ends that it bothers." Shortly, the pains disappeared, and I have not been bothered again.

At the end of the summer, the dissertation was shipped to Dr. Sandmel; but months dragged on with no word about its fate. During the winter, I crammed for the oral. Hebrew Union had in the intervening years more clearly defined its requirements in the various area of majors and minors. The field of Tannaitic Literature which I had chosen for one minor had a list of Hebrew materials I had not previously covered. I hired a local rabbi to read it with me; and, thanks to his tutoring, I made adequate progress. In the late spring, Dr. Nelson Glueck, president of the college, came to Memphis to lecture at Temple Israel and at Southwestern of Memphis. I asked his permission to take him to the airport. I wanted to talk to him about the possibility of a year in Israel. He led off with the question, "Why did you never finish your degree at Hebrew Union College?" I told him that I had sent my dissertation in the Fall and had heard nothing but that I expected to graduate at the next graduation. Within two weeks, I had a notice of the acceptance of the dissertation. It seems that the thesis had gotten put on some reader's desk and had been forgotten.

I planned to fly up to Cincinnati for the oral examination in the Tripacer that our flying group had. On the morning to go, the airport in Cincinnati was closed due to fog. I took off expecting to land at Louisville and then to go on from there as best I could; but by arrival at Cincinnati, the fog had lifted in time for me to make the afternoon examination. It was the longest flight I had piloted. When the gas was all out of one tank, I forgot to shift over to the other until the engine sputtered; but once shifted, it caught back immediately and ran without a problem.

When I had seen Professor Sandmel in Memphis the previous week and had suggested some anxiety about the examination, he said, "If you do not intend to pass, do not come!" His questions went off easily; then he excused himself and left. Professor Blank asked about flood material in the book of Isaiah which I knew well. And Professor Levy wanted to probe my knowledge of Near Eastern flood material. The area was outside that included in the dissertation; Levy felt that it should have been included. It was the area he knew. As I have said before, oral examinations have always been humiliating experiences for me. At the end, the Hebrew Union faculty passed me.

The people at Garrard Street in Covington, Ky., wanted me to speak at their mid-week service, and, never being one to know his limitations (was not an oral examination enough for one day?), I agreed to it. It was a pleasure to visit those good people again. I had lunch with Gaston Cogdell the next day, and he took me to the airport. He offered me a coke, which I refused. He asked why, and I replied, "It is a long way to the bathroom when one is flying." Down across Kentucky after I had passed Louisville, the thunder storms with reported hail blocked the way. I turned westward toward Evansville and Paducah thinking that the rivers would keep me from getting lost. At Paducah, there looked like a corridor between the two storms leading right down the Kentucky Lake; sure enough, it proved to be. After a fuel stop at Paris, Tenn., I was home for supper.

Having missed the Harvard graduation, I was certain not to miss the Hebrew Union College one. John, Jerry and I were weekend guests of Gaston and Janelle Cogdell. Festivities at the college began with a reception on Friday night, called an *oneg Shabbat* ("enjoyment of Sabbath"), at the home of Dr. Nelson Glueck. Dr. Jacob R. Marcus asked me if I had really learned to read Hebrew. I replied, "It depends on who is asking."

Dr. F.C. Grant was receiving an honorary degree for his service to the Jewish people; we had a cordial visit that evening. The news had just announced the execution of Adolf Eichmann by the Israelis. Glueck's comment to a judge who was receiving an honorary degree was, "They should not have done it." A rabbi who was also receiving a degree and who was eating at the table I sat at the next day was of quite a contrary opinion. When the conversation drifted around to Eichmann and I had commented that if commandos could enter a country and kidnap a person, then none of us were safe, he found me very narrow-minded in my feeling that the law should have its due process with even such a criminal as Eichmann.

The graduation exercises were held at the Rockdale Temple in Evendale, a section of Cincinnati. When I had been taking classes in Cincinnati, Evendale was one of the exclusive areas, almost solidly Jewish; but in the intervening years, it had gone almost entirely black. Following the awarding of the degrees, the college had the graduates as their guests at dinner. The day after that was a very pleasant visit for me with the Garrard Street church. The long road in school for me was finally ended!

Learning from All Men

The years have flown by so swiftly! As a teacher, the compliment I treasure most came from a student who had done very poorly on his examination but appended to his paper was the note, "I know more about the subject than I did when I started." The teacher is rewarded when the occasional student comes along who proves able to do what the teacher would liked to have done but either could not do or did not have the opportunity to do.

One of the greatest pleasures of teaching has been the occasional student who has reacted to my feeble efforts by wanting to follow the path I followed and who has felt that the Interfaith Program at HUC would help him to attain his goals. I am particularly grateful to the college for admitting those students I have recommended. I am humiliated by those very few whom I recommended who disappointed both the college and me.

The apostle Paul said he was debtor to all people (Romans 1:14). A scholar is debtor to his parents, to the schools he attended, to the teachers who guided him, and to the society in which he lives. It is a debt he can pay only by efforts to open doors of like opportunity to those who come after him. My life and whatever contribution I have been able to make would have been different had it not been for the Interfaith Program of Hebrew Union College.

I am today mindful of a literature that would be as foreign to me as any foreign language had it not been for my experiences at HUC but which through them has been a great stimulus. Ben Zoma said: "Who is wise? He that learns from all men, as it is written, 'From all my teachers have I got understanding' " (*Aboth* 4:1). "He who learns in order to teach, to him is given the power to learn and to teach" (*Aboth* 4:5).

Mr. Abraham Waldauer (*zikaron livracha* – "may his memory be a blessing") delighted in claiming that he was the only surviving buck private from World War I in Memphis. In the intervening years, all of the others had become majors, colonels or generals. Likewise, I make no claim to having been among the shining stars of the Interfaith Program of over 50 years ago. I am glad that I entered the program when it was new and competition was not so keen. Graduation requirements also were not as exacting as they have now become.

My interest has been in biblical studies. While I make no pretense of having become a world-class scholar in biblical Hebrew, the Interfaith Program at HUC gave me a facility in the Bible in its original language that I would never have attained without the program. I could not have worked in English Bible translation or in the preparation of *The English Bible from KJV to NIV*[2] without the training at HUC.

My other work which has attracted notice beyond my own fellowship challenged an accepted dogma about the canon of Scripture. The article, "What Do We Mean by Jabneh?"[3] published shortly after graduation, pointed to the lack of evidence supporting the concept of a Council of Jamnia. Without the training of Dr. Guttmann and Dr. Sandmel, I would not have been able to deal creditably with the required rabbinic and Hellenistic materials. Reviewers of my commentary on the Gospel of Matthew[4] have favorably noted its illustrations from rabbinic materials.

Unlike those schools where one has to sign the creed each semester in order to stay in school and to graduate, one's marks and progress in the HUC Interfaith Program were not dependent on acceptance of a prescribed viewpoint. Dr. Sandmel loved to say that there should not be Jewish scholarship and Christian scholarship. There should just be scholarship.

Life had gone full circle for me when the rabbi of one of the Memphis synagogues and when Mr. Naowitz, a teacher in the Memphis Hebrew Academy, enrolled in my Advanced Introduction to the Old Testament and in my Advanced Introduction to the New Testament courses. The tests and required papers were graded on academic performance, as I had been taught. Students have been welcome without regard to sex, race, religious background or present commitment.

To move beyond the atmosphere of one's background, culture and presuppositions and to subject oneself to a diverse culture even in the most cordial atmosphere is not the most comfortable thing one can do. Often, such a person is caught in no-man's land with suspicion from both sides. But it opens to him vistas he previously did not know existed. With apologies to Thomas Wolfe, "You can't go home again." You can only go forward.

A late mayor of Boston entitled his autobiography, which detailed his long political career, *I'd Do It Again!*[5] To those who made possible the fellowships, to the teachers who shared their time so generously, and to the students who were so tolerant, I would like to express my gratitude in the borrowed words, "I'd do it again!"

Chapter 8

TO STUDY, TO DO, TO TEACH

When Dr. George Benson and Dr. W.B. West began a graduate program in Bible in Searcy, Ark., and were gracious enough to invite some others to join them, the dream among other goals was to build a school where students would attain the highest academic degree. The educational world is like a pyramid. Those who aspire for education are far more numerous than those whose ability, opportunity and persistence allow them to climb up to where the crowd thins out. I have no exact statistics; but I suspect that out of 1000 people completing a B.A. degree, not more than 100 enter graduate school. Of that 100, probably fewer than 10 would finally complete a doctor's degree. Even these figures may be too high. Not every one needs a doctor's degree. I did a study some years ago which showed that though there might be a backlog of candidates awaiting a doctoral program at the Graduate School, the year-to-year graduates in all our schools combined were not enough to keep a program going.

In my student days, the Christian colleges did not think of themselves as preacher-training institutions. The schools of preaching were a generation or more in the future. The junior colleges felt their training of two years adequate for preaching. The student needed to get out and preach. It was assumed he could study on his own.

Charles Roberson was explicit that the schools were to give young people a Christian education. If one wanted to preach, they were glad to have him. The Bible Department covered speech, Greek and Bible. There was no training in missions, youth work, congregational leadership, performing weddings or conducting funerals. Psychology was taught, but counseling was not featured.

The few preachers who had higher training in religious studies had gone to denominational schools or secular universities. The casualty rate to the church (what some might call the brain drain) in the educational process was alarmingly high. It is sad to recall that of the about 10 brilliant young men who entered Harvard Divinity School in the seven years I was there, not more than about three remained with us. A 66 percent casualty list is frightening indeed. In crude humor, some preachers punned about the "theological cemeteries" where they buried the gospel. A few young men had gone to the seminaries and had left the church. It was assumed that would be the likely fate of any who followed.

As persons who had lived through the World War II years, we of the early days of the school were not blind to the fact that intellectual warfare has its casualties as other warfare does. I freely confess that I had considerable misgiving about what attitude the church would take and what attitude its preachers would take toward our efforts should we have a casualty. I am extremely grateful for the understanding and the charity extended us.

A.R. Holton and E.W. McMillan of the preachers I knew had schooling in religion beyond the B.A. degree. Academically inclined people majored in English, history, education or one of the sciences even when they intended to teach Bible. The Ph.D.'s were absorbed in school administration. It is only fair to recognize that self-trained preachers often knew by rote the English text of the Bible in a way that shames more highly schooled people. It is not my intent to cast any aspersion on those sacrificing servants of the Lord.

Before the war, W.B. West, Jr., went to the University of Chicago and then to Southern California for a degree. J.W. Roberts went to Butler for a B.D. before completing a degree in Greek at Texas University. During the war, J.D. Thomas went to the University of Chicago. My brother LeMoine went to Harvard Divinity. Carl Spain went to Southern Methodist in Dallas, and Homer Hailey also did an M.A. at Southern Methodist. Harvard would not get one a draft deferment; but if he had one, it could admit him while the deferment continued. Paul Southern did a degree at Southern Baptist, as I recall, but it was after Harding started its graduate program. A few others went to New Orleans Baptist and to Southwestern Baptist in Fort Worth.

West began an M.A. program at Pepperdine, a first for our people. West, with the support of George Benson, then moved to Harding.

There really was no great competition for teaching positions in our schools for people with a degree in religion. The state universities had not yet developed departments of religion. Ecumenism had not developed to the condition where teaching positions in denominational seminaries were open to our people. Nor would a position have been accepted if offered.

When Dr. and Mrs. West stopped by to see me in Cincinnati, on their way to the annual SBL meeting in New York, to talk to me about teaching at Harding in "God Knows Where," Ark., I had little concept of what I was being invited to. I had never visited Harding, and Texas people had reservations about the school. I had previously heard George Benson at lectureship on missions at Abilene when I was a freshman. I had met J.D. Bales in one of the Salt Lake City campaigns. I had met S.F. Timmerman, who had been a student at Harding. If I had received a bid from Abilene, I have no doubt that I would have taken it. Abilene was my *alma mater*. "Near the foothills of the Ozarks" did not move me very much and still does not. It was written for Morrilton and not for Searcy, anyway. The school moved, but the song stayed the same.

Dr. West talked about the fact that when you went to town in Searcy, you could find a place to park. Mrs. West smiled and said, "But you cannot buy anything." When later, after I moved to Searcy, in a chapel talk, I sarcastically commented on the advertisement "Conveniently located to all parts of the United States by rail, air and automobile transportation" that it took all of them to get there, I got a rousing cheer from the students.

West asked me what I wanted to teach, and I answered that it was Greek. He replied that Greek was already taken. Leslie Burke and Mrs. West filled that post. Decades later, when we had a program in the Memphis Harding Academy auditorium that involved some Greek terms, I commented that the school had never trusted me to teach Greek and "now they turn me loose on you." As I recall, in 30 years of teaching, I taught elementary Greek to a handful of students one semester.

Then and Now

In 1952, there was no ground swell from the churches for such a program as West was beginning. A preacher in Memphis is reported to have said that all one needed to preach were a few scriptures and the gift of gab. Much preaching was a rote recitation of relevant verses. People commented on and evaluated a preacher by how much he knew.

West, however, was a persuasive salesman for graduate education and persuaded many young men to participate. He, Paul Rotenberry, Mrs. West, J.D. Bales and F.W. Maddox were the teachers. Later, Don Sime in religious education and W.B. Barton in theology joined.

All aspects and details of the program had to be worked out by trial and error. This included graduate teaching load and level of graduate classes. Also, there was the matter of salary. Most of us had a combination of graduate and undergraduate courses to teach. I found myself teaching six two-hour courses. Added to that was Bible for the Academy, and there was an occasional radio sermon. Each semester, there were new courses. I also was preaching in Arkansas churches each Sunday. I found myself going back to my office in the evenings and working until 10 o'clock. West called me in one day, handed me a book on the history of the English Bible, and said, "The students are in the classroom. Go teach them." I had taken one semester as an undergraduate in Abilene in that area. However, that was the beginning of a love affair with that class which lasted until far after retirement.

My fellow students at Hebrew Union College were graduating to their permanent pulpits for $9,000 a year. Harding's scale at that time was $5,000. With two Ph.D. degrees and 30 years' teaching experience, before retirement my salary moved up to about $40,000. Before I moved to Searcy, someone rumored that Harding teachers preaching on Sunday received $75. When the churches open to me talked about $25 or less, I could see that rumors had gone astray. The policy also was that if one got an invitation from a church like Sixth and Izard in Little Rock for a gospel meeting, he could miss class and hold it. A person in my status could have gone to the moon (which then no one had done) easier than he could receive such an invitation. Hardly two weeks had gone by before General Campbell of the development office came to my office to find out what I would be contributing to the current financial drive.

The racial integration winds were beginning to blow at this time. Harding had not yet integrated. For an extension class I was conducting at Little Rock, I was instructed to inquire if the class would object to the admission of one African-American preacher. This was before the riot in Little Rock. I got a mixed response. One student, a controller at the airport, was indignant that such a question should have to be asked. Another student dropped the class because it was asked. He later was a participant in the riot. When we moved to Memphis, this question was never an issue from the very beginning. We had Robert Bond and Nokomis Yeldell as students. Dr. West liked to compare our program to a person flying over the city to get a general view. He next landed and went down the individual street to get a more detailed view. Finally, he went into a specific house to see close detail. After several meetings of class, Brother Bond said to me, "Brother Lewis, when are you going to land?"

At a scholarly meeting on the west coast, a speaker from Chicago who worked in the inner city in a joke asked if we knew that Simon of Cyrene was a black man. He replied, "He was the father of Alexander and Rufus. How many white men do you know with the name of Rufus?" He added, "That may not be much exegesis, but it goes a long way on the block."

After a beginning of about seven years in Searcy, about 35 young persons were in the program leading to the M.A. Dr. West and Dr. Benson were ready to enlarge the program to a three-year program. As a part of Harding, the plans had to be approved by the entire Searcy faculty. Many emotions came into play, and every imaginable basis for opposition was suggested. West, Rotenberry, Barton, Sime and I were imports and not alumni of Harding. As I see it, Harding faculty were predominantly Harding graduates. Some seemed to lack confidence in West. One person ordered a copy of West's thesis to examine. Others had no grasp of graduate Bible study. Some talked of the lack of resources to write theses. The library was not adequate for such a degree, and traveling around the country to do research would be too expensive for the students. I had written no thesis for the three-year program at Harvard. Some expressed fears that that much training would kill the mission spirit which had characterized Harding in the past. Such a program would take away from Bible teaching for the undergraduate students. John Lee Dykes, former mathematics teacher but then popular bookstore manager, said to me, "If you are going to do it, I hope you will not do it here." A popular mathematics professor, as we drove out together on a Sunday morning to our preaching places, said to me, "Dr. Benson has gotten away with so many things, we are determined that he is not going to get away with this one." The faculty vote was negative.

The proposed program also faced opposition in the board, with some resignations when it was approved. I have been told that Dr. Benson used leverage to get a favorable vote, threatening to resign from the presidency if the three-year program was not approved. People fear what they do not understand. The opposition proved to be one of the greatest blessings to come to the Graduate School in its early days.

I saw in the *Reader's Digest* once where a father who made his living by digging ditches gave advice to his six daughters: "If the door doesn't open, climb through a window. If the window is closed, try to get in through the cellar. If that is locked, go up on the roof and see if you can get in through the chimney. There is always a way if you keep trying!" Dr. Benson was that sort of a person. Blocked in the center, he made an end run. Dr. Benson not only operated a grade and high school but also transferred the graduate program to Memphis where he did not have to have permission from the Searcy faculty to operate. The Memphis Christian School could not raise funds, and the property came to Harding to run the school. The Graduate School became at that time the only free-standing graduate school of the church. I have lived long enough to see some of the board who were vigorously opposed become our enthusiastic supporters, and for that I am grateful. When Jeremiah asked, "Can a leopard change his spots?" (Jeremiah 13:23), he was not giving a universal.

Before the move was proposed, I had preliminary plans for a career in Searcy. I acquired a building site in a new development the college was opening. My site was about where Harding House is. In fact, a tree and a bush or two on that lot are ones I set out at that time. The first rumor I got that I might be moving was from other faculty members who wanted to acquire my lot. Every one seemed to know it before I did. After a mid-week service, Dr. Benson came by where I was sitting and informed me that he wanted me to move; but he assured me that if I was unhappy in Memphis, I could come back to Searcy. I earlier had been granted permanent employment.

I am no longer sure of the chronological sequence of some events. Dr. Benson proposed to Abilene one cooperative graduate school that would not necessarily be in Searcy; Abilene rejected the offer. Back then, we could not see the junior colleges all moving up to senior colleges and each starting its own graduate program. We could not see the rise of the preachers' school movement. I believe in training in all honorable forms at all levels.

In preparation for our advanced program, Dr. West invited an advisory curriculum committee made up of Paul Southern of Abilene; Reuel Lemmons, editor of the *Firm Foundation*; B.C. Goodpasture, editor of the *Gospel Advocate*; and Batsell Baxter of David Lipscomb. At the day of the committee meeting in Searcy, Lemmons was unable to attend. It seemed to me that Southern was primarily interested in learning what we were planning in order to know what Abilene should do. From the beginning, we have been one step ahead of Abilene in every move. Baxter cautioned us to go slow and to be sure before we went ahead because we could not back up. Through the day, when Goodpasture was asked if he had comments, his reply was, "I believe not." At the end of the day, he informed us that he thought we should include study of the Septuagint in our program. We never got around to undertaking that. He did assure Dr. West that the columns of the *Gospel Advocate* would not be open to attacks on the program, and he kept that promise. With both the *Gospel Advocate* and the *Firm Foundation* in our camp, that is one battle we did not have to fight. I came out of the committee meeting feeling that the day had been a complete waste of time and of money. The committee never met again.

In the summer of 1957, I was assigned an extension class in Memphis which met in the administration building. Earlier extension classes had met in the Union Avenue church building. The east room upstairs of the mansion which now is divided into faculty offices was the class room. The Academy still had offices on the main floor. Student housing was on the second floor. The faculty did not have telephones; the public address system was for Miss Sisco, who filled multiple roles, to step out into the hall and loudly call anyone who was wanted. The library was where the dean's secretary now has her office. We had two rows of shelving less in expanse than a row in my present study in the library.

Park Avenue was yet a two-lane suburban road but was being widened, paved and curbed. On opening day, the school was completely unapproachable from the north. Dr. L.M. Graves, board chairman, in his opening address assured us that the problem was only temporary and that we should be patient. That year a flash flood brought water temporarily over the bridge near the front gate – water that covered cars on Dee Road between my house and school. These conditions have never been repeated in the years since.

The school property was surrounded by a wire fence left over from the time it was privately owned property. The gate on the Cherry Road side was kept locked except during school hours. Charlie, the aged caretaker who earlier had served N.B.Hardeman, had one room on the basement floor which is now a storage room. The back entrance on Dee Road was a lover's lane.

On opening day in the fall, the Academy was still using what later was my office as its school office. The Academy building was still under construction. What we know as the bookstore had been furbished as a library. An Academy class met where the exercise room now is until the fire code inspector became aware that the furnace is under that room. It had to be cleared out immediately. At about this time also, the Academy class that met in the basement, where Mrs. Huffard's office now is, also moved to the Academy building. The Academy offices earlier had moved out.

By fall, the library furniture for what is now the bookstore area had arrived. During the years the Graduate School was in Searcy, some purchases had been made for the graduate program; but no one had dreamed of moving the school. What was to come to Memphis was a heated question. The librarian was determined that the Searcy library would not be impoverished. Dr. Benson said that the graduate teachers should select what they needed. Dr. West, Don Sime and I were coming to Memphis. I headed to the catalogue to make up a list. Miss Alston, the librarian, asked me what I was doing and said, "Why don't you go back to your office?" I did. After considerable conflict over the matter, Dr. Benson ruled that all the books we wanted out of the Searcy library that had not been checked out in a past specified time should come to Memphis.

On the opening day of school, not one book was on the shelves – all were in boxes on the floor. A Miss Anna Maye Johnson had been employed to divide time between the Academy and the Graduate School as librarian. After my class on that day, I went over to the "library" to help and found her wringing her hands over the unpacked boxes of books and saying sadly, "I thought it would be ready for me to run." I offered to put the books on the shelves if she would arrange them. So the next day, the library, furnished with light-colored maple furniture, was open for business. It next migrated to the basement of the administration building, where in flooding times the furniture got water marks. You can see the marks on the shelves in the library workroom.

Another year, the dean's student assistant also had library duty for a time. Money was hard to come by, and the dean, who had spent a fortune on his private library, felt that if a faculty member needed a book, he could buy it. The library could not buy books that the dean already had in his uncataloged collection. You can see something of the outcome on the walls of my office.

There have been many humorous and many very frustrating episodes across the years. Under the original arrangement, the Academy administration had responsibility of maintenance of the Graduate School building. The furnace was always unreliable. The maintenance man would allegedly light the furnace in the morning, and then it would go out. I would relight it and complain, and then there was the jawing over whether I was telling the truth about being cold and having lighted the furnace or the maintenance man was about his lighting it. I learned that it is easy to be complacent when your office is not where it is cold.

The first year in Memphis after school started, Dr. West became ill and had to have surgery. He had extension classes going in Florence, Ala., as well as classes on campus. I ended up with my own classes plus most of his in both places. If you want to know how I became teacher of Introduction to the New Testament, that is how it was. He was teaching that course in both locations, and he never took it back. I was stuck with it. Believe it or not, I think I also taught the book of Revelation. In addition to that, Dr. West was scheduled to speak at Michigan Christian College lectureship on "The Christian College as Seen by the Teacher." You can guess who got to work up and make that speech. The lectureship was published; you can read the speech if you wish. Finally, graduation came. You can see the picture of the graduates on the wall outside the dean's office. You will notice that no faculty pictures are there. The policy was that one had to pay for his own picture, and the faculty did not see fit to do it.

The bookstore had its beginning when Maurice Hall, a former missionary in France, enrolled as a student and opened the store in the west end of the building where the development office is today. It later moved into the carriage house space.

School then was different. There were no faculty secretaries. For classes, I had the book of Isaiah, History of the Reformation, Church History, Hebrew Readings in Amos, Beginning Hebrew and the Gospel of Matthew. The Gospel of Matthew met at night, and the students included 19 auditors, 12 undergraduate students and 13 graduates. To enlarge the pool of candidates for graduate classes, we had to offer undergraduate credit for those needing it. The dean had persuaded Memphis people to turn out for the classes. A class might have undergraduates taking the course for credit and working on a degree, miscellaneous auditors and a few graduate students. I must confess that I thought if a class was a graduate class, it ought to be conducted on the graduate level. The auditors and undergraduates could catch what they could, if anything, as it went by. Needless to say, the attendance was less at the end than at the beginning. I never had such a mixed crew again. A student had to do six or more term papers if he took a full load; and a full load was then counted as a minimum of twelve hours rather than the nine it now is. At the beginning, with some teachers, if one read an extra book, he got graduate credit for a course that otherwise was undergraduate.

Don Sime flew over one day a week from Searcy the first year. Dr. West was in New Testament, and E.H. Ijams, for whom our administration building is named, became a valuable adjunct faculty member. His being a part of us meant much in gaining status among the church people. W.B. Barton, Jr., came in the area of Philosophy of Religion but later became full time in the Department of Religion of the University of Memphis and left us. In time, Richard Batey became a professor of New Testament and James Zink a professor of Old Testament. George Gurganus came in missions. Near the beginning, Earl West started coming from Indianapolis to teach Restoration History.

Early on, Dr. Benson secured professional planners to plan our campus. Dormitories, classrooms and a lovely New-England-style chapel were included in the plan. Our progress has compromised that plan; but in my file, I still have a copy. I counted it a sad day when it was decided to sell off the Park Avenue end of the property, leaving us squeezed in the middle of a block.

Dr. West persuaded friends of S.P. Pittman to furnish the chapel in his honor. Pittman was a long-time beloved teacher at Lipscomb. Former Lipscomb students have legends about him. Dr. West and I brought him down for the chapel's dedication. All along the way, he was pointing to one house and another where his former students lived.

We reasoned that we needed single-student housing, and we enjoyed watching the building go up. At first, married students found apartments farther south on Cherry. Time took the single students' building, but you can now see the pavement where it once stood. Then came married-student apartments. The wife putting her husband through school became a part of our community. FedEx's development also made school possible for some students. A student could work at night and sleep in class.

We had our round with the neighbors. They were not happy about the Academy and Graduate School operating on this property. When it came time to get city permission to build student housing, the neighbors turned out in force to oppose giving the permit. Some insisted that they had been told that the school had no plans for developing the land. Apparently, they thought it should be maintained as a private park for them to view. Others were afraid that the student wives would create an unsightly scene by hanging laundry. Others felt that the fine homes on Fair Meadow in time might become fraternity houses. If you ever wonder why the unsightly hedge is on the eastern boundary of the Graduate School and Academy properties, it is to pacify the neighbors who wanted to be separate.

It was exciting when the first stage of the library went up. Annie May Alston insisted that she could do without an office, but she had to have a book lift. You will find the lift used to this day.

Along the way, the former students of West presented a Festschrift, *The Last Things*,[1] to him on his 65th birthday. It was a first in our fellowship. Festschrifts have now become quite common among us.

Then came the classroom building now named after Dr. West. As the walls went up, we left them standing in the evening only to return in the morning to find them fallen flat. Dr. Hazelip jokingly asked if we had seen any marching around during the night.

Looking backward, one of the humorous times was when the dean decided that we needed to teach biblical Aramaic. There was no Xeroxing at that time. The war had not left Aramaic grammar books available. I had taken Aramaic at Hebrew Union College with Julius Levy, a transplant from Germany, and he had used a hand-drawn syllabus. Gullibility persuaded me that the school's future rested in Aramaic, and I made 100 copies of that syllabus. Aramaic lasted one semester. Somewhere, packed away in my study, you could find about 90 copies of the syllabus.

It was a very shocking time when in the before-daylight hours, Jane Tomlinson called me to tell me that the building was on fire. Dr. West, from the beginning, had feared that, lest he lose his books. With his retirement, they had been moved to his house. Annie May and I pulled our clothes over our night gear and hurried to campus. Seeing the flames and thinking of books, notes and papers, I lamented, "My life's work is in that building." Annie May corrected me, "Your life's work is in the students, not in the building." It was heart wrenching when the cupola on the top of the building came tumbling down to the ground. After the flames were put out, Annie May said, "I must go home and write about it," and that is what she did.

It was encouraging when later in the morning, Dr. Burks arrived with information that the building was covered by insurance and could be rebuilt. The books were to be freeze dried, but the contractor was unable to find a refrigerated truck. The books went three days, instead of a few hours, before they were frozen. The glue in the books is still coming apart.

My books that were on the shelves did not get wet. My papers in the files were protected by the files. Those on the desk and on the floor did get wet. Boxes appeared out of heaven, the window was broken out, and a crew of friends passed the books out the window separating the wet ones from the dry ones. The rumor spread that I had lost my library in the fire. Hebrew Union College Library offered to replace from their duplicates what they had that I had lost. I was able to thank them profusely and to decline their generosity.

Others like Allen Black lost more than I did, and Evertt Huffard lost also. Their offices were on the second floor. Our neighbors across Cherry to the west furnished lunch for the rescue crew that day. Rick Oster and I found study space for the next year at the back of the classroom auditorium. Other faculty crowded into what is now the hospitality room.

The rebuilt building is more suitable for a graduate school than the lost one was. We are no longer dependent on the undependable furnace in the basement for warmth. The building has thermostats and air conditioning.

The school in its early days did not seek financial support from the congregations. It was a great day when the elders at White Station decided for the congregation to give regular financial support to the Graduate School. Other congregations like the Highland congregation have since followed.

Christian schools from an early day have aided teachers financially to take time to complete their degrees. A teacher who already had his degree when employed created a new problem. Sabbaticals are standard in schools like ours. A teacher needs renewal. Such problems were: Does the teacher forgo a raise if he is not on campus at the time of year raises are given? Can he take a sabbatical in the spring, or must it be done in the fall? Granting regular sabbaticals is another first for our schools.

One of the great days of the school was when the decision was made to keep the school in Memphis and not move it back to Searcy, over which problem we had worried many months and years.

Commencements I Remember

Life for me has been full of ironies, perhaps none greater than that I would spend a life annually attending commencements! The first time I wore a cap and gown was on a day in June in Texas in the pre-air-conditioning age. There were small black crawling insects which we called "oat mites" but which my uncle said should be called "church mites" because they were particularly bad at church. In their annual appearance, they made life miserable for all. I vowed I would never again wear a cap and gown. I have also made a lot of other vows that I have broken; but this one explains why I have a mental block that makes memories of all graduations of the past 25 years vague.

During the years the Graduate School was in Searcy (1953-1957), the commencement of the Graduate School was not separate from that of the college. The graduates marched in the regular graduation line and received their degrees as a part of the graduation exercises. The first graduation in Memphis in August 1959 marked a banner day in Dr. W.B. West's mind (but was less momentous for the teaching faculty); he marked it by having a picture made of graduates, along with pictures of Dr. George Benson and Dr. West, as the first graduating class.

Through 1963, graduation was held in August rather than in May and was in the White Station Church building. After the friends of S.P. Pittman had furnished the Pittman Chapel, it served for graduation from 1962 to 1967. Then the O.O. Emmons Auditorium of the Harding Academy was used until 1977. Finally, the classroom building was constructed on our campus with an auditorium adequate for our graduating classes, and there we now hold commencement.

A recent issue of the *Reader's Digest* carried the quotation: "Almost nobody listens to a commencement address except, perhaps, a few parents engaged in one last effort to get something for their money." If that has been true of our graduations, it was not because there were not good speakers. It was appropriate that the first speaker in Memphis was Dr. George Benson, under whose administration the Graduate School developed. We have had other Christian college presidents, and faithful and infectious gospel preachers have served us well. Dr. W.B. West, Jr., spoke after his retirement from the office of dean.

Not all speakers register for an equal time in one's memory. Reuel Lemmons made an outstanding address in which one point stressed how much is yet to be learned. His illustration was of an untrained healer who had considerable success with mudpacks but who was thought by the medical profession to be a "quack." After medicine had made adequate progress, her source of mud was analyzed and found to contain almost pure penicillin. She could not have known why it healed, but it did. We have not learned all there is to know!

At our 1981 graduation, the speaker was Batsell Barrett Baxter. In his accustomed masterful way, he challenged the graduates. It was his last visit to our campus. How we miss his gentle ways and noble personality!

In the early days, L.M. Graves, for whom our library building is now named, regularly brought a message from the Board of Trustees. Later, others took over this task; in 1974, Jack Goode assumed this function. Earlier, music was furnished by the "Words of Life" television chorus and then later by the Harding Academy chorus; in recent years, we have had congregational singing. Something of the history of Memphis churches could be reconstructed from the list of preachers who have graciously interrupted their schedules to lead prayers for us.

Something of the life of the Graduate School itself can be reconstructed from the degrees conferred. At first, there were the Master of Arts and Master of Religious Education degrees; but in 1960, a new degree, Bachelor of Sacred Literature, appeared for only one year with Vernon Boyd and Neale Pryor as recipients. By the next year, the name had been changed to Master of Theology. The Master of Religious Education was phased out after 1967. After 1977, the popularity of the Master of Arts gave way to the Master of Arts in Religion that required no thesis. As the number of recipients of the M.A. decreased, the number for the

M.Th. increased. In 1983, there were three M.A.'s and 28 M.Th.'s. By 1984, there were two M.A.'s and 35 M.Th.'s.

Graduates prepared themselves for preaching, for work in the mission field and for teaching. It would be unfair to those whose sacrificial service is known best to God to list some above others. Look about you. You will see them teaching in the colleges, Christian schools, pulpits and the mission fields. However, some categories do demand notice. Shirley Thompson, Nancy Codner and Miriam Mieher in 1960 were the first women to finish M.A. degrees with us. That same year, Yung Jin Lee of Korea graduated also. We trust that the Lord will find us making some contribution to the demise of racial and gender prejudice.

It has been a special pleasure to see older men graduating, who with Ulysses realized, "'Tis not too late to seek a newer world." Among them were J. Marvin Powell, Cecil N. Wright, O.P. Baird and James Anders. We sincerely hope that other older men will prepare themselves for better use of their last years.

Commencements also have their humorous sides. The year Dr. West was in Japan, I, as a faculty member, was left to do in the August graduation what I had never given any thought to. Miss Nona Sisco, West's secretary, managed the details. Once we were on the platform at the White Station Church, I announced the first item on the program; Dr. Benson whispered to me that he would preside. I should not have had to be told! At the time of the recessional, the graduates at the first bar of music began marching out, leaving the platform party to follow them. Dr. Benson said, "That is not right. Who is responsible for this?" I could have gone through the floor. We had not thought of instructing the graduates about the recessional.

Early graduates were to a large extent commuters. At graduation, it was announced how many miles a fellow had commuted to get his degree. Finally, someone in jest asked if we transported a donkey a certain number of miles, would we confer a degree on him? That ended the mileage count!

One year, the newspaper carried a cartoon just shortly before graduation time showing a father congratulating his graduating son with the words, "Well, son, despite the emphasis on finances, I made it; and despite the emphasis on academics, you made it!" I showed the cartoon to graduating Raleigh Wood (of blessed memory, who was not a bad student) on graduation day; he got quite a chuckle out of it.

The Retreating Dream

When one considers where we were when we started and where we are now, it seems to me that we have a great deal to be rightly proud of and thankful for. The congregations no longer fear graduate education. From the beginning, a large part of our graduates have gone into the pulpits or served in other capacities in the local congregations. Think of an Oliver Rogers, a Jim Howard, a Jimmy Moffett, a Harold Redd or a Rodney Plunkett. There has been a steady stream of people like Leslie Williams and Ron Burnett going to the various mission fields around the world. The Graduate School has not killed the mission spirit!

I see no reason to be ashamed of a goal of training scholars. Furman Kearley became the editor of the *Gospel Advocate* before the Lord took him from us. The current owner of the *Gospel Advocate,* Neil W. Anderson, is one of our students. Oxford University Press has published a new translation into English of the Septuagint; George Howard translated the Minor Prophets. At one time, we had 10 men on the Bible faculty of Freed-Hardeman. The recently appointed president of Ohio Valley is our graduate, and we have had other representatives there. Cecil May is chairman of the Bible Department at Faulkner. Charles Coil was the founder of International Bible College (now Heritage Christian University). We have people at Oklahoma Christian and at Pepperdine. Look at the Bible faculty in Searcy. One could think of Jimmy Allen, John Fortner, Tom Alexander and others. Why should we be ashamed for the part we have had in the lives of Eddie Randolph, Allen Black and his brother Mark?

Professor Arthur Nock of Harvard once said that if a calamity destroyed all the buildings on Harvard's campus, but Widener Library was left standing, it still would be a university. We have a theological library unmatched between Nashville and Dallas and between New Orleans and St. Louis – a library to grow as long as the Mississippi flows past Memphis, useful to students and also to researchers. "Those who are wise will shine like the brightness of the heavens, and those who lead many to righteousness, like the stars for ever and ever" (Daniel 12:3 NIV).

It is with great sadness that we have seen some brilliant young men start to climb the pyramid of education and then make shipwreck of the faith. J.W. McGarvey said at the end of his career that he had never destroyed the faith of any boy who had been entrusted to him. I feel certain that no teacher connected with Harding Graduate School has ever consciously or purposefully destroyed the faith of any student who has come our way. It is our regret that our skills have not been such that we were able to save all and to see that not one lost his way.

Along the way, there also have been those students for whom the training offered in this school has been a stepping stone in their climb up the educational ladder. It is my opinion that they went better prepared for the problems to be faced than we did 60 years ago. They have attained the highest degree but have attained it elsewhere than in one of our schools. They serve in various capacities in the Christian colleges and in the churches. The number, the names and the positions they fill are impressive.

People fear that which they do not know and do not understand. Each step upward in the educational pyramid for the Harding Graduate School has been difficult to take. But the Harding program has been the pioneer in all ways. Harding's three-year program was the first one. She was the first to have a specialized library aimed solely at religious study with two professional librarians. Harding's library is the only one which for a generation has had an adequate budget for book purchases and is the only one which has a beginning endowment. Harding is the first school to attain accreditation for its program and was the first to get accreditation by the American Association of Theological Schools.

Harding pioneered in sending its professors to the national meetings of the learned societies. While in Searcy, before we came to Memphis, Dr. West, who himself had attended national meetings, urged me to write papers for the programs. The college bore a large part of the expenses. Back then, none of our colleges sent their teachers. Only Frank Pack and I attended the first year I went. In recent years, there were more than 50 people who came to the morning worship in Annie May's and my hotel room on Sunday, and there were other members of the church at the meetings. Many presented papers.

Harding pioneered in giving its teachers sabbaticals for additional study after they completed their doctorates. Other schools have aided teachers to finish degrees but did not grant sabbaticals after degrees were obtained. Harding allowed me to spend two different winters in Jerusalem in research at the American Schools of Oriental Research which had become the Albright Institute by the time of my second stay.

Our dream of a school where students could be trained at the highest level, though an admirable dream, proved unattainable in our lifetime. The school has turned to other goals as men have seen needs differently. I am no longer certain that part of that dream has any priority in the planning. Across the years, some have repeatedly asked when the next stage is to go on the pyramid. At times, it seemed to be within the talking stage. As I see it, some of the steps taken in the meantime which were alleged to be preparation have proved to be permanent hindrances. With retrenchment, the dream seems to have retreated beyond any imaginable horizon.

I was among the minority of Graduate School faculty who stood in opposition to the shift to the Doctor of Ministry degree. The D.Min. was developed by schools whose dropping enrollment left them desperate for student recruits. Though approved as a bona fide program by the AATS, of which Krister Stendahl was a member, it might be noted that Stendahl's own school (Harvard Divinity School) never went to the program.

Although the D.Min. was promoted as a step toward the Ph.D., I saw it then, as it has proved to be, the death knell of any movement in that direction. I saw the D.Min., with its focus on technique rather than upon biblical knowledge, as further progress along the road which has left our people high on enthusiasm but short on conviction. Though marketed in the beginning as not being a teaching degree, it has been accepted in certain cases as qualification for teaching and even as qualification for being head of a religion department.

I have never been opposed to training at any level at which people are willing to acquire it: the congregational Bible classes, the preachers' schools, the junior colleges, the senior colleges and the graduate schools. I do believe that each level should recognize what it is and not pretend to be what it is not.

I had a capable student once who had taken four years at an

unaccredited college which then decided to cut back to two. He was then admitted to a seminary program which became defunct, and he lost more years. At the time I met him, he was (after these tragedies) enrolled in a senior college trying to get a degree which would admit him to a graduate program. We in education owe it to the student to operate with integrity.

As I see conditions, the continuation of having all our college and university teachers trained at the highest levels in denominational seminaries and secular universities dooms us to a continued high casualty list. The brain drain of the church will go on until the Lord raises up men who not only dream, but who labor, sacrifice and persuade people that the accomplishment of the dream must be a top priority!

There is not a one of us who would be willing to entrust the care of his physical body to a doctor who has no better training than the person has to whom he is willing to entrust the welfare of his soul. The one is temporal, but the other is eternal.

J.W. McGarvey in 1865 said,

> That one who is to preach the gospel, and teach the disciples the whole will of God, should be educated for his work is a maxim of common sense. In every other department of human labor, whether physical or intellectual, a man is expected to undergo some preparatory course of instruction; then why not in this? If to teach the arts and sciences which pertain to earth alone a man must be appropriately educated, how much more to teach that master-science which pertains both to earth and heaven![2]

Today, as I have done many times in the past, I would like to point out that expertise in the speech arts, in how to win friends and influence people, and in like techniques may equip a man to entertain the people. They can help him communicate what he knows, but they do not equip him to deal with eternal questions. They do not equip him to answer ultimate spiritual questions.

Some people are more gifted than other people are. There will always be the geniuses who by self-training accomplish unbelievable things. One by training could not make me into a Jimmy Allen, a Neale Pryor, a Harold Hazelip, a Max Lucado or a Billy Graham. One can learn in school in a relatively short time what it would take him a lifetime to learn by experience. Whether gifted or ungifted, he can be aided to accomplish more than he would accomplish on his own.

Every person has to decide where he should spend his short day the Lord gives him. N. Rudenstein said, "Significant new knowledge depends on the rigorous work and imagination of prepared minds."[3] Alexander Fleming, the discoverer of penicillin, said, "The unprepared mind cannot see the outstretched hand of opportunity."[4]

I never had my IQ tested so that I would know whether it is 30, 40, or 60; but I want to take Ezra as my model. Ezra set his heart to study the law of the Lord, to do it and to teach his ordinances in Israel (Ezra 7:10). I want to spend my energy in further study of the word the Lord gave us, in trying to apply it to life, and in teaching people that word. No longer despising study as I did when a freshman, I am quite satisfied to be a student until the Lord shall see fit to call me home.

Chapter 9

DREAMS OF TRAVEL

My dream of traveling in the Middle East goes back to grade-school chapel when a speaker sang "The Holy City" while he drew a stylized picture of Jerusalem in pastel colors on his easel. I did not get the picture as I wished. The only one was for the whole chapel.

A distant cousin, who with her husband operated a boys' school, gave us her collection of back issues of the *National Geographic Magazine*. I spent hours looking and reading about distant lands.

When I married, I discovered that my father-in-law had earlier been on a trip to the Holy Land with a friend, and he liked to talk about it. In his day, ships were the only transportation to the Middle East. It took longer to get there than a tour now lasts.

In Harvard Divinity School, Dr. Robert Pfeiffer whetted my interest further with tales of his experiences as an excavator. At Hebrew Union College, tales by Dr. Nelson Glueck, who had spent 18 years in exploration, only sharpened interest in what seemed to be the impossible for me with a young family.

My day of dreams awakened into reality when New York University offered a summer seminar in 1963 in Israel directed by Professor

Abraham Katsch and funded by the government. A lawyer friend gave me a supplement from the Kress Foundation, and a student friend gave $200 for incidental expenses.

The seminar covered Israel in a wonderful way. I could extend my time by crossing one way into Jordan through the Mandelbaum Gate. I was then on my own. During the first night at the YMCA in East Jerusalem, bombardment of the Jordan area revenged an afternoon incident. My room was on the border just above the Gate. I lay on the bed as flat as possible for safety. When the bombardment ceased, the dogs stopped barking, and the roosters began to crow.

A trip through Hezekiah's Tunnel was a necessity, so I gathered others to go with me, including 14-year-old Evertt Huffard who, with his missionary father, was new in Jerusalem. A rental car took me to Hebron; to the site of ancient Tekoa, home of Amos; to sites north of Jerusalem, the location of which Evertt had learned; and to ancient Jericho. The ancient stone tower there, the oldest in the world, had been uncovered by Kathleen Kenyon, and I had to try its interior circular stairway, permitted then but later forbidden.

East of the River Jordan was Mount Nebo before its church had been restored. The road was unpaved, but Madeba with its ancient map had to be seen, though an extended funeral greatly delayed its viewing. A few minutes at the site of Dibon, where the Moabite Stone had been found in 1868, gathered an annoying escort of idle children, all of whom wanted "baksheesh" (a gift). From there, I set out alone over unpaved roads to reach Petra. I had little concept of the time involved to cover the distance, and the gas gauge lowered as did the sun. Once Petra was reached, no eating places were visible. A bunk at the police post was the night accommodation. It was already occupied by bedbugs. A high-school-aged boy named Mohammed was available as a guide. His English was too sparse to learn much, but he could climb even to the upper sites not seen by tourist groups. Late in the day, I set out the 15 miles to reach the new highway with its gas station and to get back to Amman in the darkness.

A brief flight from East Jerusalem took me to Beirut, center for northern investigation. Here, I tried local transportation – service taxis that picked up a load and then took off when full to Tyre, Sidon and

Baalbeck. I had to see the cedars of Lebanon. From the last village to the cedars had to be by private taxi, and a taxi from Beirut was also necessary to reach Damascus to see the Damascus museum, the street Straight and the gate alleged to be the one Paul was let down out of. A trip to Palmyra out in the desert required first a service taxi to a town on the north-south road and then a crowded bus ride of several hours. No one had told me that one was assigned a seat with the ticket; foreigners took what they could find at the rear. At a rest stop, I never found the facilities. The ancient ruins at Palmyra were most impressive. A return by bus and a further service taxi ride brought me to Aleppo. Noise at a cheap hotel at the transportation center limited sleep. Food could be had in a shop just by pointing. The museum and castle there were quite rewarding.

An early morning taxi ride to the airport somehow ended at the seaport, and I had to persuade the driver to continue on to the correct destination. After a plane flight of several hours, we landed at Baghdad. The summer temperature was quite oppressive. The customs looked at my book on history and archaeology until it looked like I might not be admitted. A taxi, rather than losing a fare, agreed to take me to the YMCA at a price I was willing to pay. In the late afternoon, I inquired at a tourist office without encouragement about getting to the ruins of Babylon. A taxi driver volunteered to take me. First, a permit had to be acquired at a government office to travel in a police state. Much time was required. The Ishtar Gate and the procession street at Babylon had been reconstructed. Once outside the main ruins, once again I picked up an escort of children each claiming he had something to show. I had to ask my driver to show me the remaining foundation of the destroyed ziggurat.

The local train station was on the Baghdad to Bosra line. I got a second-class ticket to Ur Junction. The driver was to meet me the second morning when I returned to Baghdad. The train put me off at the junction about 4:00 a.m. Nothing was to be seen except a bench. As I sat down to wait for daylight, a guard said, "You cannot stay here." He took me to a shed which had a lock on the inside of the door. There was no furniture, only a cement floor. With a camera case for a pillow, I awaited the day. Once it came, at about two miles across the desert was what I had come to see. There was only one way to get there, and the heat was oppressive. The Iraqis had encased the remains with modern bricks. Only the first stage of the ziggurat remained. I climbed to the top and sat down to read the book I had brought. Shortly, the police arrived wanting to know what I was reading. Having satisfied themselves that I was not dangerous, they left me to deal with the two locals who thought they knew what I needed to see. We shared no common language. Of course, the treasures of any archeological site are not to be seen at the site itself. They are in the museum.

With my curiosity satisfied, there were the two miles to negotiate back to the station. At the time of my arrival, there was a train leaving for Nasyria. I got a view of the Euphrates at Nasyria and then bought a ticket back to Baghdad. This time, with some fatigue, I thought I could afford first class. The journey involved changing trains at Ur Junction, which itself was an experience.

The taxi driver met the train at Baghdad as agreed. My morning schedule included a visit to the museum to see its antiquities. There were stamps, tablets, art objects and other treasures found by those who had excavated in Iraq. The most showy, perhaps, was the ram caught in the bushes from Ur. When the museum was later looted at the overthrow of Saddam Hussein, I was thankful for the memory.

There then was the task of getting a permit to travel to Mosul. After rejection, I could only ask who the next higher official was. I finally was instructed to get the local scribe to make out a permit. It had to be signed and accompanied by a photograph. A photographer was on hand for the purpose. Because the permit was in Arabic, I could only hope it was not permission to be shot at sunrise! The YMCA clerk seemed relieved when I turned up for my suitcase after I had not occupied the room for two nights. There was no charge for them.

The taxi driver delivered me to the train station with instructions of how to get from there to the airport when I returned from Mosul. The second-class compartment had four bunks; I chose an upper one expecting a night of rest. But I had the fortune of having as a compartment fellow a student who had just been granted a fellowship to go to England. He was overjoyed to find a person on whom he could practice his English. He would not take a refusal of an invitation to go to his home for breakfast. I was uneasy about food, so it was a good omen when he was met by a car.

His home was obviously above middle class. Breakfast was served in the living room. A bowl of yogurt was placed on the coffee table. There was pita bread and the inevitable small glass of very hot tea with far more sugar than a westerner was accustomed to. There were no knives, forks or spoons. One tore off a piece of bread, dipped it in the bowl of yogurt and ate it. No women were to be seen, though a young girl had brought the food in. Only Arabic was spoken, and I knew very little.

With breakfast done, there was the task of going to the local police station. I learned that I had a permit for one hour in Mosul. There was no train back to Baghdad until night. A new permit left me freedom to cross the Tigris River and to see the remains of Nineveh. At Nineveh can be seen the ancient mud brick wall enclosing two mounds named Quyundjiq and Nebi Yunus. A modern road cuts across the ancient site as also does the small Khoser River. Alas, the museum there was closed, so a trip around on foot seemed the best choice. A local man who was watering down the dust let me fill my canteen from his hose. A local wagon offered me a ride; but I saw that I would fall by a sudden stop, so I decided that walking was safer. With the high temperature, I decided that halfway around was more realistic. I caught a city bus back to the train station for late lunch, and then set out to see the ruins on the Mosul side of the Tigris River. It was not long until, like the Pied Piper, I was accompanied by a band of children beating on pans and shouting, "Englisi, Englisi." I could only thank the adult who restrained them.

Upon arrival in Baghdad, I crossed the street from the station to the airport and acquired a ticket for the next flight to Cairo. The room to which I was assigned in the hotel in Cairo had bedbugs, and I quickly was given another with assurance that its furnishings were new. The next morning, I caught a city bus to Tahrir Square and the archaeological museum. One could with profit spend days there. Then came an afternoon at the pyramids. Climbing the big pyramid was still permitted, and I had to try that. About halfway up, I decided that my camera stand was not necessary to carry; I could pick it up on the way down. From the top, the view was most impressive. Coming down, my terror came on – where had I left the camera stand? Considering it lost,

I descended more and finally found it right where I had left it. No one else was on the pyramid. At the foot, there were still the second and third pyramids to see from the ground level.

I had come to Egypt to see also a portion of Upper Egypt. The way was by the overnight train which arrived at Luxor in the early morning. It seemed that only one hotel was open. And again there was the problem of the guide. I had not intended to use one, but I finally agreed to a guide to see Karnak and the Luxor temple with an American lady. The following day, there was the west side of the river, including the Valley of the Kings. We were given the privilege to climb over the mountain to get to the impressive view of the Deir el-Bahari of Hatshepsut from above. The guide had not seen fit to include the Ramesseum, so I insisted that we take it in. The size of the statues there, even though fallen, was most impressive.

There was far more than one could see in the time allotted. In the afternoon, I rented a bicycle and covered more of the western side of the Nile River before taking the night train back to Cairo. When checking me out from the hotel for a flight to Athens, the hotel clerk did not return my passport. That required a roundtrip taxi ride from the in-town check-in point for the flight to Athens.

When I arrived in Athens, the Middle East fever caught up with me, and I lost my cookies on the street before reaching my hotel. After a few hours in bed, I registered that the time was too precious to waste on rest. The Acropolis and Mars' Hill had to be seen. And then there was Corinth for the next morning. This also for me was a magical world, a continuing of the dream.

A second summer in Israel was in a summer seminar of Hebrew Union College. For a week, I was an apartment guest of Nelson Glueck. I went out in a morning of August and found the sky was dripping just a little. I rushed back in to tell him that it was raining. He insisted that it did not rain in August. When I finally got him on the terrace, he walked up and down saying, "My, isn't the dew heavy this morning!" He insisted that in eighteen years in the Middle East, he had never seen the equal and that we should make a record in our diaries.

Since these early beginnings, I have been to Jerusalem more than 30 times. Those included one winter as Thayer Fellow, accompanied by my youngest son, at the American School of Oriental Research and a second one as a Senior Fellow of the Albright Institute. I got a taste of dirt archaeology in a week at Arad on the low tell when we started with rows of cultivation of the recent season and came down in a few inches upon on a broken clay jar. It showed that a few inches under the surface were the remains of the ancient period. The whole area later was excavated. A second initiation was two weeks at a site near Jericho looking for the site of ancient Gilgal.

I have traveled widely, oftentimes in areas where our national political relations were reputedly poor. I have found the common man to be extremely cordial. He is not beyond "turning a fast buck," but I have never been robbed or molested in any way except by people trying to help. Now, transportation is but a few hours in a comfortable jet plane. Housing is in first-class hotels. Clean food and water are available all over the country.

All of these travels have allowed me to fulfill that dream begun in childhood of exploring in the Middle East. The Lord has blessed me with the privilege of traveling widely in the Middle East and of seeing with my own eyes most of the places of importance except Susa that are significant in the biblical story as those places remain today. I have been high up on Mount Ararat as a guest of the chaplain at the U.S. airbase at Adana, Turkey. I have been a week with a rental car in Turkey. I have been at all the sites of the journeys of Paul except those nearest Rome.

I traveled not only for my personal satisfaction but that I might have the knowledge that would allow me to be a better teacher. Biblical archaeology has as its goal the illustrating of various features of God's revelation. One can demonstrate from archaeological finds, or in some few cases from parallel historical records, that certain biblical people once lived. The interpretation the Bible gives to those events is the essential thing of faith; archaeology can neither prove nor disprove the veracity of that interpretation. But the first step in using archaeology is the finding and the collection of objects. There is no question in my mind that material of this sort is faith-strengthening to the person who will study it.

Chapter 10

IRON SHARPENS IRON

It was probably about 1954 that I went to the Society of Biblical Literature national meeting for the first time. At that time, the national meeting was a relatively small gathering with a New Testament section and an Old Testament section meeting after Christmas three years in a row at Union Theological Seminary in New York and one year at some other location around the country. E.W. McMillan and W.B. West, Jr., had attended some meetings, but not every year.

On another part of the week, there was also a meeting of the National Association of Biblical Instructors. That later became the American Academy of Religion. The archaeologists held a noon meeting, and the professors of Hebrew held one gathering. One had to forego a block of his Christmas vacation to attend.

It was unusual that Harding would send me. West was responsible for that. The condition was that I would write and read a paper. My dissertation had been on "The Testaments of the Twelve Patriarchs," and my paper was on the sort of literature known as "Testament." You can imagine where my ego went when, instead of the dead silence one feared, Theodor Gaster arose, was kind to the paper, and mentioned that he had his father's ethical will in his pocket.

Except for the two years I spent on sabbatical in Jerusalem and the three years for Annie May's terminal illness, if my memory does not fail me, I attended every year until 2008.

An item humorous to me occurred the year that my dean became ill after school and classes had started. I was the one to carry on his classes, including an extension class some distance away, for the whole semester. My reward for the extra load was that I could go to the SBL meeting if I would prepare and read a paper at the meeting.

Then as our staff grew, for economic reasons our administrator determined that we could go to sectional meetings rather than to the national meeting. Sectional meetings have their place; but in my values, they are no substitute for the national meeting. My president accepted the suggestion that we could pay for ourselves the difference between the sum allowed and the actual cost of attending.

In the past 20 years of retirement, there has been no school aid to make possible attending the SBL meetings. Why have I kept attending? The first reason is social. I have continued acquaintance with some of the fellows I met in my graduate classes. As the number from our schools has drastically increased, the worship on Sunday morning and the *Restoration Quarterly* breakfast have become a high point of my year. My path and theirs do not cross very often at other times.

But the real reason for attending is, I think, stated by a proverb: "Iron sharpens iron, and one man sharpens another" (Proverbs 27:17). The ancient rabbis have many legends about their scholars. One is about the very learned scholar who left the academy and then forgot all that he had learned. We have our isolated tasks in our various positions. One has only his own ideas to modify the prejudices which he has accumulated. Most of our teaching loads are heavy, and publication is a luxury, not a demand. For some, the thesis is the last scholarly article they produce. Richard Batey shared a story about the soldiers guarding the cross at Jesus' crucifixion. One said to the other of Jesus, "He sure was a fine fellow." The other replied, "Yes, but he did not publish anything."

Scholarship is not stagnant; it is moving. One can be awakened by others to the shortcomings of his own arguments. I grant that an SBL meeting never turned the world over; but the book displays, the new material coming to light that one can hear about, the forming acquaintance with those who are writing the papers and publishing the books is a rewarding and challenging experience. It is true that with some of the papers it seems that only the reader knows what he is talking about. Some seem so far out that they are close in on the other side. Robert Pfeiffer was once quoted in the newspaper about an SBL meeting he had attended as having confessed that he did not know what was going on. But the occasional paper one finds can say to him, "If you want to make any contribution to learning, you have to get off your easy chair and get on your bicycle and ride! Don't just come to SBL. Write a paper and read it!"

As I recall, the *Restoration Quarterly* meeting at SBL got under way in Houston through the stimulation of Abilene people and the generosity of Ray McGlothlin and his wife, Kay, who picked up the refreshment tab. The meeting has not always been a breakfast and for a long time was not actually listed on the official program. But it is the only time of the year when some of us see each other.

Progress of Scholarship

As I see it, the past 70 years have been years of exciting progress in *a cappella* congregations and schools. As a biblical student, I make no claims of being a historian or to being a theologian. At the beginning of this period, only Abilene and Harding offered four-year programs. Pepperdine began about 1942 and offered a master's degree. Freed-Hardeman and Lipscomb were junior colleges. Others we now know had not had their beginning. Oklahoma Christian began in 1950 and moved to Oklahoma City in 1959. Ohio Valley began in 1959.

The programs were designed for the rank-and-file young person. The colleges did not think of themselves primarily as preacher-training institutions. If a person was interested in preaching or teaching, he just took more Bible, Greek and speech courses. Schools of preaching were still decades, if not half a century, in the future.

The Bible tent was far more restricted than it has now become. Counseling, missions, youth work, congregational administration and other "how to" courses were only dreams of the future. A person graduated and went out on his own with no personal training in these areas.

During the war and after, young men were challenged to undertake advanced studies in religion. And following the admonition made by the men of the Great Synagogue to "Raise up many disciples," they have brought us to where we are. With Joshua, we can say, "There remains yet very much land to be possessed" (Joshua 13:1).

Don't Be Cowed by a Consensus

You likely have heard of the philosophy department that had on its door, "All work done on premises." Our trade proceeds on hypotheses. Absolute truth, which we are searching for, is hard to come by. Some scholar summarizes the evidence supporting a proposition and draws a conclusion as it had not been stated before. Others examine the evidence in the light of the proposed solution and agree or disagree with it. If a majority agrees, it becomes a consensus. If someone comes up with a new summary that gains popularity, then it becomes a new consensus. A consensus is not infallible. Of human documents, only a papal decree is claimed to be infallible.

In trying to teach students how to write papers and to avoid clogging their footnotes, I have told them if one takes any proposition and goes far enough back in history, he will find a scholar who stated the conclusion that became popular. He is the one who did it to us. The rest of the names are just of those who are saying, "Me too." That is, "I agree with what he said." The "Me Tooers" are inconsequential. Do not list them.

We can well keep in mind Oliver Wendell Holmes's "The Deacon's Masterpiece."

Have you heard of the wonderful one-hoss shay,
That was built in such a logical way
It ran a hundred years to a day, …
How it went to pieces all at once,—
All at once, and nothing first,—
Just as bubbles do when they burst.[1]

New evidence can change a question completely. That happened to Old Testament scholarship with the find of the Dead Sea Scrolls. For the New Testament, there was the discovery of the earlier Greek manuscripts.

I did not start out to challenge a consensus when I wrote my paper on

"What Do We Mean by Jabneh?" I was curious about the close of the Old Testament canon. I was asking for help where the evidence seemed to me to be lacking. I read my paper at the SBL meeting in New York and got that embarrassing silence when nobody raised question one. Henry Cadbury told me that I probably should have read it in the Old Testament section instead of the New Testament section, and he was right. I submitted the paper to *The Harvard Theological Review* and got a rejection. *The Journal of Bible and Religion* printed it.[2] Krister Stendahl later told me that at Harvard they were making copies of it and were reading it.

Opportunities in scholarship open on whom you know and even more on who knows you. The Jamnia article resulted in an invitation to be on a lower editorial committee for the making of the NIV Bible. The books on Bible translation resulted in an invitation to submit articles on Bible translation for the *Anchor Bible Dictionary*. All of that resulted in an invitation to spend a whole year on "The Textual History of the King James Version" that appeared from the American Bible Society in *Translation That Openeth the Window*.[3]

Martin Luther reports that his conscience during the struggle of his reform raised the question, "Are you the only one who is smart?" One does not have to be egotistical to probe well a hole in a consensus which others have not seen.

I Am Debtor

I would like to remind us all that others have labored and we have entered into their labors. Like many, I am a product of schools built by the sacrificial people who went before. There were teachers who never enjoyed the privileges I have had. Harvard was made possible for me by a program called "Compensated Church Work." I never knew what fund put up that money. Next came the Hopkins shares. Edward Hopkins was a British bachelor of the Revolutionary War period who left his estate for the education of preachers in the colonies. His charity is the oldest existing charity in America.

During my last year at Harvard, I saw that Hebrew Union College in Cincinnati was starting an interfaith program with attractive fellowships. Mrs. Workum was the only one of my benefactors I ever met. Her real interest was in Jewish students having openings in the fraternities and sororities of universities. I did not fit that pattern, but the school had persuaded her to finance a fellowship. The Horowitz and Rabinowitz money completed the three-year residence requirement. My first-hand experience in Palestinian archaeology also came by way of grants. I was aided by congregations which let me, as a student, preach for them.

My recitation is not at all motivated by pride of being a leech on charity, but only to remind myself of what a debt I owe. I would like to challenge others, as well as myself, over time to replace what we have received in order to make available funds for those younger scholars who follow in our footsteps. Our profession is not one of the high-paying professions of American culture. The grants I got look like chicken feed when compared to the costs of education today, and today's costs will look that way to the coming generation's costs. But by a bit this year and more next year, over the course of our lives we can replace the sums we have consumed. I challenge you to try it. Do not leave charity to the philanthropists.

The Church

Scholarship is the servant of the church and not the church the servant of scholarship. To strive to produce one article in the *Journal of Biblical Literature*, or one of the other scholarly journals, in one's career challenges all of us. At the most, a few hundred people will read it.

We still have the gap to bridge between the scholar and the person in the pew. Rabbinic tales have Akiba, who had become the renowned Jewish scholar of his day, say of his past, "When I was an *ʿam haʾarets,* if I had encountered one of the scholars I would have bitten him like a donkey." An associate corrected him, "You mean like a dog." Said Akiba, "No! A dog only breaks the skin. A donkey breaks the bones."

As scholars, we need to learn to work with the congregations where we are. We need to teach classes and be active in the various programs, active in the social life, and active in the services the congregation is rendering. A generation back, the Berkeley, Calif., congregation had two elders. One worked in maintenance at the university; the other was a Latin professor of world renown, still known for his translation of Augustine in the Loeb Classical Library series. They worked in harmony together.

I was honored to serve on the editorial board of *Restoration Quarterly* when Pat Harrell and Abe Malherbe began the journal. I have not done much editing, but from time to time I have submitted a paper which I am grateful the editors saw fit to print. The *Restoration Quarterly* is always seeking a wider readership. Scholars should keep sending in papers. We made a giant step forward when the magazine was put on the Web.

When I look at the popular level journals circulating among our people as well as the literature being used in our Sunday Bible classes, I do not find there materials written by our scholars. The Rabbis said that the Torah was not a crown with which to adorn oneself, nor was it a spade to dig with. The whole operation of scholarship is about people and for people. One must not forget about the people who have not had the opportunities he has enjoyed. He should make himself available and hone his skills of answering the questions people are asking.

It makes an old man's heart glad to be given the opportunity to reminisce. I would conclude with three items: The first comes from Satchel Paige, the legendary baseball pitcher. "How old would you be if you did not know how old you was?" The second comes from a baseball catcher Yogi Berra, which I apply to scholarly pursuit: "It ain't over till it's over." The third I borrow from the Jewish Passover observance, but take the liberty to change the place and occasion: "Next year in Atlanta!"

Chapter 11

EIGHTY YEARS OF MINISTRY

I deserve no special credit for the interest I have had and continue to have in the ministry of God's word. I was born the third child to a dedicated couple in Midlothian, Texas. My maternal grandfather gave the land on which the church building was built. A few years ago, there were three faculty members at the Harding University Graduate School of Religion who had come out of the Midlothian congregation, though we were not there at the same time. At the centennial of the Midlothian congregation a few years ago, it was pointed out that in the 100 years of its existence there had never been a Sunday in which the congregation had not met to observe the Lord's Supper.

I have no remembrance of there being any discussion in my childhood home of whether or not we would go to worship. I assume there must have been times when only those well could go. We did not know of allowances, but each child received a nickel for the collection plate.

My father grew up in a religiously divided family. He failed in various efforts to get religion at the mourner's bench. That led him into Bible study resulting in his being baptized.

Like many small town or rural congregations, Midlothian did not have a located preacher. Preachers from nearby cities like Dallas or Waxahachie filled appointments. Services were less formal then than those we have become accustomed to. Any brother who felt the urge might arise and give an admonition.

The summer revival meeting was the highlight of the congregation's year. A favorite evangelist was brought in to do the preaching. In our area, Horace Busby was a favorite. People from various congregations would drive miles to hear him. But the Wallaces and the Dunns also had a following as did Athens Clay Pullius of David Lipscomb College. The word of an evangelist was highly regarded.

It was the time when women began cutting their hair, and the act was highly debated. One lady said of her hair that she had rather have it and not need it than to need it and not have it. A lady in our congregation had dared to cut her hair. But it was her day to have the evangelist into her home. She spent the morning trying in vain to pin her locks back on. Finally, in tears, she telephoned the evangelist to confess what she had done. He agreed to come to her house for lunch as scheduled but admonished her not again to cut her hair. But of course, once the dam had cracked, there was no way to hold back the flood.

Childhood Impressions

In thinking about lasting influences on life, I recall that we walked to school in suitable weather. There was one vacant lot along the route, and one day a man in a covered wagon had parked it there and was giving out paperbound books of the Bible to the children as they passed by. The book I received was the book of Proverbs, and he marked Proverbs 28:1 in it: "The wicked flee when no one pursues; but the righteous are as bold as a lion." I never had the slightest insight into what religious group he represented; but I have never forgotten his Scripture.

In the pre-television age, a program on the radio from Dallas offered a New Testament to any person who would read the entire New Testament. I never knew what group was making the offer. They mailed out the Gospel of Matthew; and when it was read and returned, they mailed out Mark. Postage then was only two cents. I received the Gospel of Mark and finished it in a day or maybe two. My parents had to be convinced I had read it by a recitation of its content. I finally received and read the book of Revelation. I received my New Testament. The pictures of the book of Revelation impressed themselves in my childish consciousness. That is something I have to see! I have been blessed by the privilege of traveling widely. I have seen a lot of what the world has to offer; but as I approach the end of my pilgrimage, I am still registering, "The city with the street of gold and gates of pearl is something that I have to see." Do not underestimate the influence small things can have on the life of a child.

Education

My mother and father were not highly educated people. My mother probably finished the equivalent of high school. My father had to drop out of college after one year to operate the farm of his widowed mother and to provide for four siblings younger than he.

My parents were trapped by the Great Depression. When bills consumed an inherited farm, my mother's advice to her children was, "Get an education. No one can take that from you." All her children graduated from college. Three became college teachers.

At a family gathering in Abilene, Texas, of children and grandchildren, someone on the telephone asked to speak to "Dr. Lewis." The person answering the phone said, "Which one? There are five of them here." The latest count of doctorates in the family is 13.

Spiritual interest was somehow kindled. All the children went to Abilene Christian. Three of the sons served churches as elders. The fourth was invited but declined, though a Bible teacher and serving in other ways. He was asked to teach lessons on church history and agreed to do it if adequate time was allotted. The Wednesday evening class ran eleven and one-half years. The Harding Graduate School has the recordings of these lessons.

Over the years, various winds blew through the congregations of Texas. One was of the dividing of the congregation into various classes for Bible study. Midlothian had solved that question before I appeared on the scene by dividing the auditorium for various classes. It was only after I went off to college that the congregation was able to construct an education building.

In the early days, the common drinking cup was standard in rural areas. The gourd dipper was seen at the well for all to use without concern for spreading germs. The field had the common jug for all workmen to use. In small congregations, the building had a central aisle with seating on either side. In Depression days, one might see two snuff glasses on the Lord's Table, one for either side of the auditorium.

Again, Midlothian had worked through this problem before my day. I am told that they had a common glass in the center of the communion tray for those who wanted that and individual cups on the outside of the tray for those who preferred that. The next generation had no trouble over this topic. The children did not accept the feelings of their parents.

I saw a variation of this topic in the Ohio Valley the summer as a college student I sold Bibles in that area. Their compromise was to have individual cups, but the prayer had to be said over grape juice in a pitcher before the cups were filled. Someone had invented a device that when filled would fill half a tray. The tray could be rotated and the process repeated and the other half filled. This was done while the people waited until the number of needed trays were filled. People, despite differences of opinions, can worship in peace if they love the Lord and each other.

The Premillennial question was heated in the 30s. My father attended the Norris-Wallace debate in Fort Worth. He reported finding the assigned entrance doors locked and his having to climb in a window to get entrance. We all learned that "pre" means "before," "millennium" means "a thousand years," and "ism" means that it is not so. The joke was that when a church person in anger wanted to call one a bad name, he said, "You Premillennialist!"

I went through my baptism of fire teaching junior-high boys in the summer in Evansville, Ind. I was laboring away presenting the material for the day when a boy's hand went up, and I thought I had successfully made a point. I called on him, and he said, "There is a bug going up the wall over there."

I was not one of those boys who knew from early years what he wanted to give his life to. In my freshman year in college, an older preacher told a group of student preachers that if one intended to preach, he must plan to be a student all his life. I was convinced that was the last thing I wanted to do. Four years later, I saw the question differently. A floating joke around school was that Lewis was going to spend his money on books rather than on a girl; one could shut a book up when he got tired.

When graduating from college, I agreed to divide time between congregations in Throckmorton and Woodson, Texas, which were about 15 miles apart. The remuneration was $20 a week. I had a room and meals with a family in Throckmorton. After a month or so, the Throckmorton congregation decided they wanted me full time.

To get acquainted in the town, I decided to call on every house. I knocked on a door and introduced myself. I was cordially invited in. I no sooner was seated when my host led off with, "No one for whom God Almighty died will be lost." He was a rigid Calvinist, believed in a limited atonement as well as the perseverance of the saints, and that is what he wanted to talk about. I had studied the Bible but had not encountered Calvinism before. I did not make any gains in that conversation.

The Throckmorton congregation had been in debt 10 years during the Depression, paying the interest but not reducing the debt a penny. I preached about finances Sunday after Sunday, and we paid off the debt.

In the pre-war years, we had radio and the movies but no television. In a small country town, the revivals proved to be the best entertainment available. The Methodist evangelist in a friendly banter said in his sermon of his people, "We Methodists not only believe in falling from grace, we practice it!" That has stayed with me through the years. There are also some of the rest of us who practice falling from grace.

The Baptist evangelist was a showman called "Cowboy Crim." He dressed like a cowboy, often threw his saddle over the pulpit, and used sound effects to entertain and communicate with rural people. He had a sermon entitled "Climbing Fool's Hill" in which he depicted the sinful life people were living. It was as though one were trying to drive uphill on the mud road in a Model T. Country people knew that problem and its noise. Next day, the sun comes out and dries the road, but coming back down one has to cross the ruts he made going up. Maybe you have never heard "Whatever a person sows, that he will also reap" (Galatians 6:7) exegeted exactly that way; but it is rather pointed.

Country singings were a part of the community entertainment. The military camps had been built, and the draft had been registered for;

but I was at a country singing at Elbert when it was announced that Pearl Harbor had been attacked.

My second location was at Huntsville, Texas, which was the location of Sam Houston State Teacher's College as well as the Texas State Penitentiary with units for men and for women.

In small churches, the preacher was the total church staff. There was no secretarial help. The preacher taught a class and preached twice on Sunday. He also taught a weekday class for women and presented a Wednesday evening lesson. If there was a youth program, he likely directed that.

There was also a 15-minute radio program on Sunday morning. A listener from the distant rural area came to my study one day with the grocery list his wife had given him for the day. Along with bread, beans and potatoes was "Get baptized." In response to the radio program, I got a letter that in vocabulary and style could have been from the Apostle Paul. It was from a man in the prison who had been baptized by one of my predecessors. Now he wanted communion brought to him. He claimed to have taught himself to read and write from his Bible.

The congregation, though interested in evangelism, did not consider serving the prison was part of the work of its preacher. Not having been told that, I got one of the men in the congregation who was a guard at the prison to take me to see this fellow. We found him in isolation in a six-by-nine-foot room. I later learned that he spent nine years there and that he had worn a trench in the floor pacing back and forth. All sorts of stories were circulating about his deeds of the past. In my mid-twenties, I was soon persuaded that I could not handle that situation. Years later, the preacher who had baptized him asked me, "Do you remember Clyde Thompson?" I said, "Who could forget him?" He said, "He came to see me." A crippled lady had arranged a pardon for him and had married him. I was preparing to speak on an Abilene Lectureship when Clyde Thompson walked up and gave me two books. The one was a biography entitled *The Meanest Man in Texas*,[1] and the other was his autobiography written for prisoners entitled *The Best Way Out Is Up*.[2] They tell an entirely different story from that in the rumors circulating in Huntsville. He spent his last years evangelizing men coming out of prison. He is said to have baptized about 1700 people. I think this experience taught me what Paul had already said, that no one who is still alive is beyond hope. The Lord can save the chief of sinners (1 Timothy 1:15).

The mail in Huntsville brought a request of a prisoner on one of the farms who wanted to be baptized. The warden was cooperative and took me out into the field where the man was working. A nearby pool with its cattails served as a baptistery. Bare skin dries quickly in the sun. The prison had no provision for people to be immersed. The only possibility was the bathtub in death row. It is quite a trick to immerse a full-grown person in a bathtub.

A late-night call of a sister and mother at my place of residence wanted me to take a meal to the son and brother who was tired of prison food. The money they left bought a plate at a restaurant, and the prison accepted it.

There was a letter from a sister who wanted her brother saved whom she insisted was not really a bad person. The warden informed me that he had just been recaptured from a three-day break in which he had shot at the Texas Rangers. But the warden was still willing for me to talk to him. They put the two of us in the bull pen with armed guards looking on. He was very cagy even when I showed him his sister's letter. Weeks later, I was at the prison again and saw him in the visitors' room with a lady I assumed was his sister. He was all bleached out, and I assumed he had been in isolation.

In the depth of night, I was awakened in my second-floor bedroom by the sound of bloodhounds and guards on their horses ordering the escaped prisoner to put up his hands. In the morning, a discarded weapon was found in the shrubbery.

I have long believed that the gospel has hope for all. A few years ago, the *Christian Chronicle* had a story of a congregation which was located adjacent to a prison farm which had revitalized itself with the program it had for work with prisoners. This sort of work requires special training and is not a program for every congregation. One learns quickly that religion is considered a legitimate way to freedom for many prisoners.

New England

Before World War II, we had only about three congregations in the five New England states: one in Connecticut; one which met at the

Philips Brooks House on Harvard's campus in Cambridge, Mass.; and one in Portland, Maine. The shifting of population brought men and their families, as well as GI's, seeking conveniently located places for worship where there had not been such before.

At the same time, four of us, all from Abilene, entered Harvard Divinity School in the fall of 1944. Through the school's "Compensated Church Work" program, which aided in paying tuition, I picked Providence, R.I., as my congregation to work with. We had no congregation in Rhode Island before the war. Rhode Island is the smallest of the states but is the densest in population. There were many military bases around Narragansett Bay on which Providence is located. Men were continuously going to war or returning from it there.

Among the community projects I got involved in was one the churches had of packing clothing to ship to Europe to aid the needy of the war zone. The shoe factories around Providence supplied all their unmated shoes and unsalable shoes to be put into useable pairs. The pile seemed inexhaustible. One had to put together a left and right shoe that were approximately the same size and looked somewhat alike. It was a time-consuming affair. But a local religious section of the paper ran a story on the project, and I got the publicity of a picture as one mating shoes. I discovered that the participants in the project were the more zealous members of their congregations and not very ready prospects for the message I was offering.

I did meet a retired Baptist preacher who was a colorful figure about town with his beautiful collie dog. One day my telephone rang. It was this preacher who called to inform me that a small Swedish Lutheran church building in a depressed area of the city but only three blocks off a prominent bus route was up for sale. We put up the winning bid, and the building was ours. By obtaining this building, we now could have Vacation Bible School and could try to attract families through their children. We could have weddings and programs of whatever sorts we chose. If I had not mated the shoes (which at the time did not seem the most urgent way for a pressed graduate student to spend his limited time), I would not have learned that the church building was for sale.

I terminated my work in Providence, not because the task was completed but because I received an Interfaith Fellowship at Hebrew Union

College in Cincinnati. We had always tried to contact any person of whom we learned who came into the area. In the last month of my stay in Providence, I learned about a lady in Groton, Conn., about 50 miles away. We had GI's who were driving that far to worship on Sunday. We had tried not to let any person go unvisited who had any past connection with the church. I found a GI bride that had come with a husband who was not a Christian to her husband's home area. They had a new baby. It did not seem to me likely under the conditions that she could come to Providence with any regularity for worship. I suggested to her that because Groton was a submarine base that likely some members of the church were in the area if they could be found. If she would get a meeting place and put an advertisement in the paper, I would come on Sunday afternoon, and we would see if we could find people to worship with her. She secured the Grange Hall for an hour, but no one had called or showed up. So we repeated for the second Sunday with the same outcome. The third Sunday was my farewell at Providence, and she and her husband came to that. That was the only time I ever saw him. I went on to Cincinnati, became involved in church affairs there, especially with the Garrard Street congregation in Covington, Ky., across the river from Cincinnati, and then on to my teaching career.

Some 30 to 40 years later, a thank-you letter arrived here in Memphis from this lady telling of her getting help from another preacher, Wilmer Hebbard, who came down from Hartford. A congregation had been begun. Her husband had been baptized, and her four children had been baptized. Her husband was being considered for an elder of the congregation where they were worshiping. More recently, the congregation in Groton has celebrated its 50th year. Who can estimate the power in an idea planted in receptive soil?

The children of a couple married in Providence invited me a few years back to the 50th anniversary of their wedding. They live in Muscle Shoals, Ala. I get a card from them at Christmas time. A GI wrote me years after his baptism thanking me for baptizing him in Providence.

White Station

I came to Memphis when the Harding Graduate School opened here in 1957. We were introducing a level of education not previously known to our people. The first 15 to 20 years, in addition to teaching, I was preaching on Sunday in places like Brinkley, Ark.; 61 South in Memphis; Ripley; and Henning, Tenn. I told the elders at White Station that I knew they had Sunday morning members, and I was going to be a Wednesday night member.

Over the subsequent years, the congregation has let me teach in the Wednesday night program and also in the Sunday morning program. Some of my publications grew out of material put together for these classes. In recent years, my assignment has been the Sunday morning auditorium class. Though not primarily intended for seniors, it has attracted some seniors in their last years.

The congregation has granted me the privilege of serving about 25 years on the Missions Committee. In addition to many pleasant hours in planning meetings, we went for supervision and encouragement to the congregation's project in Campo Grande in Brazil. We went to Paris, Rome and Kenya also for supervision and encouragement of workers there.

About 26 years ago, I was invited to become one of the elders. I recognize that because of age there are many things I cannot do, but I prefer to do something rather than doing nothing.

I am appreciative of the schools which have over the years invited me to teach on their lectureships year after year, especially Harding, Freed-Hardeman and Faulkner. Some of the material prepared for these lessons is printed in Lectureship books; other of it is available on audio disks.

About 20 years ago, the Japanese churches became aware that they had only five preachers under the age of 50. They needed a preacher-training program on a financial level they could support. They did not plan a campus but would use the church buildings for classes and the existing preachers as the teachers. The first year, they had one student. The second year, they doubled the enrollment. I had two qualifications the Orient values: the first is age, and the second is education. So I serve as honorary dean of the Japan School of Evangelism. My obligation is for my name to be on the stationary. I have made a few trips over to teach and encourage the preachers.

New Opportunities

Across my years, one of the significant questions has been that of Bible translations. I started out with the KJV; but in college I shifted over to the ASV, and then in Graduate School over to the RSV. When I cite a passage, no one knows which influence will be reflected. This has resulted in two publications: *The English Bible from KJV to NIV*[3] and *Questions You've Asked about Bible Translations*.[4] Most recently, the Bible Society has included "The King James Bible Editions: Their Character and Revision History" in their volume *Translation That Openeth the Window*.[5] People ask me, "Which is the best of the translations?" I reply, "The one you will read and live by is the best of them for you."

Modern technology has opened a new door of service – that of answering Bible questions. I get an occasional question over the telephone from someone in the congregation; but e-mail brings questions from people I have never met and never expect to see both from this country and from abroad. One question I can likely answer; a dozen may go unnoticed.

As one looks over the losses and gains of 80 years of ministry, he may be reminded of the story of the person planting corn by hand in his garden. He was saying of the grains, "One for the buzzard, one for the crow, one to rot, and one to grow." Jesus did the same with the seed that fell by the wayside, that fell on stony ground, and that fell among the thorns. It is not likely that many seeds we plant will produce 100 fold. But may the Lord grant you at least that one seed will produce 30 fold.

I would not like you to see these things as items of boasting but rather as reminders of a passage of Scripture: "Cast your bread upon the waters, for you will find it after many days" (Ecclesiastes 11:1). A Christian life is composed of the insignificant things one does as opportunity comes.[6]

Endnotes

Chapter 1

1 Vernon J. Charlesworth, "A Shelter in the Time of Storm," in *Songs of Faith and Praise* (comp. and ed. Alton H. Howard; West Monroe, La.: Howard Publishing, 1973).

2 *The People's New Testament: The Common and Revised Versions* (notes by Barton W. Johnson; 2 vols.; St. Louis, Mo.: Christian Publishing Co., 1889, 1891).

3 Charlotte G. Homer, "All Things Are Ready" in *Great Songs of the Church* (comp. E.L. Jorgenson; Abilene, Texas: ACU Press, 1974).

Chapter 2

1 Bob Miller, "Seven Cent Cotton and Forty Cent Meat" (1932).

2 *The People's New Testament: The Common and Revised Versions* (notes by Barton W. Johnson; 2 vols.; St. Louis, Mo.: Christian Publishing Co., 1889, 1891).

3 Tillet S. Teddlie, "Earth Hold No Treasures," in *Great Songs of the Church* (comp. E.L. Jorgenson; Abilene, Texas: ACU Press, 1974).

4 Stephen D. Eckstein, *From Sinai to Calvary: An Autobiography* (Winona, Miss.: J.C. Choate, 1990).

Chapter 3

1 Charles H. Roberson, *What Jesus Taught* (Austin, Texas: *Firm Foundation*, 1930).

Chapter 5

1 Wilbur M. Smith, *Therefore, Stand: A Plea for a Vigorous Apologetic in the Present Crisis of Evangelical Christianty* (Boston: W.A. Wilde, 1945).

2 Robert H. Pfeiffer, *Introduction to the Old Testament* (New York: Harper, 1948).

3 Elton Trueblood, *The Logic of Belief: An Introduction to the Philosophy of Religion* (2d ed.; New York: Harper, 1942).

4 J.A.C. Fagginger Auer, *Humanism States It Case* (Boston: Beacon, 1933).

5 J.H. Newman, "Lead, Kindly Light," in *Great Songs of the Church* (comp. E.L. Jorgenson; Abilene, Texas: ACU Press, 1974).

6 Samuel J. Schultz, *The Old Testament Speaks* (New York: Harper, 1960).

7 Ibid., *The Prophets Speak: Law of Love, the Essence of Israel's Religion* (New York: Harper, 1968).

8 *Voices of Concern: Critical Studies in Church Criticism* (ed. Robert R. Meyers; Saint Louis: Mission Messenger, 1966).

9 Emil Schürer, *A History of the Jewish People in the Time of Jesus Christ* (5 vols.; New York: Scribner, 1897-1898).

10 Jean Juster, *Les Juifs dans l'Empire romain; leur condition juridique, économique et sociale* (2 vols.; New York: B. Franklin, 1914).

11 F. Crawford Burkitt, *Jewish and Christian Apocalypses* (London: British Academy, 1914).

12 William Shakespeare, *Hamlet*, Act 5, Scene 2.

Chapter 7

1 Harold R. Willoughby, ed., *The Study of the Bible Today and Tomorrow* (Chicago: University of Chicago Press, 1947).

2 Jack P. Lewis, *The English Bible from KJV to NIV* (Grand Rapids: Baker, 1991).

3 Ibid., "What Do We Mean by Jabneh?" *JBR* 32, no. 2 (April 1964): 125-32.

4 Ibid., *The Gospel According to Matthew* (2 vols.; The Living Word Commentary; Austin, Texas: Sweet, 1976).

5 James Michael Curley, *I'd Do It Again: A Record of My Uproarious Years* (Upper Saddle River, N.J.: Prentice-Hall, 1957).

Chapter 8

1 *The Last Things: Essays Presented by His Students to Dr. W.B. West, Jr., upon the Occasion of His Sixty-Fifth Birthday* (ed. Jack P. Lewis; Austin, Texas: Sweet, 1972).

2 J.W. McGarvey, "Ministerial Education," *Lard's Quarterly* 2 (April 1865): 239.

3 Neil Rudenstein, "The Fruits of Science and Serendipity," Harvard University Commencement Day Address, June 8, 1995, 134, http://www.neilrudenstine.harvard.edu/pdfs/fruits.pdf (accessed April 19, 2012).

4 Cited in Neil Rudenstein, "The Fruits of Science and Serendipity," Harvard University Commencement Day Address, June 8, 1995, 133, http://www.neilrudenstine.harvard.edu/pdfs/fruits.pdf (accessed April 19, 2012).

Chapter 10

1 Oliver Wendell Holmes, "The Deacon's Masterpiece or the Wonderful One-Hoss Shay," in *The One Hoss Shay* (Boston: Houghton, Mifflin & Co., 1982), http://www.ibiblio.org/eldritch/owh/shay.html (accessed April 11, 2011).

2 Jack P. Lewis, "What Do We Mean by Jabneh?" *JBR* 32, no. 2 (April 1964): 125-32.

3 Ibid., "The King James Bible Editions: Their Character and Revision History," in *Translation That Openeth the Window: Reflections on the History and Legacy of the King James Bible* (ed. David G. Burke; Atlanta: Society of Biblical Literature, 2009), 97-117.

Chapter 11

1 Don Umphrey, *The Meanest Man in Texas: A True Story Based on the Life of Clyde Thompson* (Nashville: T. Nelson, 1984); *The Meanest Man in Texas* (3d ed.; Dallas: Quarry Press, 2008).

2 Clyde Thompson, *The Best Way Out Is Up* (Fort Worth, Texas: Star Bible & Tract Corp., 1977).

3 Jack P. Lewis, *The English Bible from KJV to NIV* (Grand Rapids: Baker, 1991).

4 Ibid., *Questions You've Asked About Bible Translations* (Searcy, Ark.: Resource Publications, 1991).

5 Ibid., "The King James Bible Editions: Their Character and Revision History," in *Translation That Openeth the Window: Reflections on the History and Legacy of the King James Bible* (ed. David G. Burke; Atlanta: Society of Biblical Literature, 2009), 97-117.

6 Selections from a Business Lunch, White Station Church of Christ, Memphis, Tenn., January 2010.

Bibliography

Auer, J.A.C. Fagginger. *Humanism States It Case*. Boston: Beacon, 1933.

Burkitt, F. Crawford. *Jewish and Christian Apocalypses*. London: British Academy, 1914.

Curley, James Michael. *I'd Do It Again: A Record of My Uproarious Years*. Upper Saddle River, N.J.: Prentice-Hall, 1957.

Eckstein, Stephen D. *From Sinai to Calvary: An Autobiography*. Winona, Miss.: J.C. Choate, 1990.

Great Songs of the Church. Compiled by E.L. Jorgenson. Abilene, Texas: ACU Press, 1974.

Holmes, Oliver Wendell. "The Deacon's Masterpiece or the Wonderful One-Hoss Shay." In *The One Hoss Shay*. Boston: Houghton, Mifflin & Co., 1982.

The Holy Bible: King James Version. Nashville: Crusade, 1972.

The Holy Bible: New International Version. Grand Rapids, Mich.: Zondervan Bible Publishers, 1973, 1978.

The Holy Bible: Revised Standard Version. New York: World Publishing Co., 1962.

Juster, Jean. *Les Juifs dans l'Empire romain; leur condition juridique, économique et sociale*. 2 vols. New York: B. Franklin, 1914.

The Last Things: Essays Presented by His Students to Dr. W.B. West, Jr., upon the Occasion of His Sixty-Fifth Birthday. Edited by Jack P. Lewis. Austin, Texas: Sweet, 1972.

Lewis, Jack P. *The English Bible from KJV to NIV*. Grand Rapids: Baker, 1991.

_____. *The Gospel According to Matthew*. 2 vols. The Living Word Commentary. Austin, Texas: Sweet, 1976.

_____. "The King James Bible Editions: Their Character and Revision History." In *Translation That Openeth the Window: Reflections on the History and Legacy of the King James Bible*, 97-117. Edited by David G. Burke. Atlanta: Society of Biblical Literature, 2009.

_____. *Questions You've Asked about Bible Translations*. Searcy, Ark.: Resource Publications, 1991.

_____. "What Do We Mean by Jabneh?" *Journal of Bible and Religion* 32, no. 2 (April 1964): 125-32.

McGarvey, J.W. "Ministerial Education." *Lard's Quarterly* 2 (April 1865): 239-50.

The Mishnah. Translated by Herbert Danby. London: Oxford University Press, 1933.

The People's New Testament: The Common and Revised Versions. Notes by Barton W. Johnson. 2 vols. Saint Louis, Mo.: Christian Publishing Co., 1889, 1891.

Pfeiffer, Robert H. *Introduction to the Old Testament.* New York: Harper, 1948.

Roberson, Charles H. *What Jesus Taught.* Austin, Texas: Firm Foundation, 1930.

Rudenstein, Neil. "The Fruits of Science and Serendipity." Harvard University Commencement Day Address, June 8, 1995. http://www.neilrudenstine.harvard.edu/pdfs/fruits.pdf (accessed April 19, 2012).

Schultz, Samuel J. *The Old Testament Speaks.* New York: Harper, 1960.

_____. *The Prophets Speak: Law of Love, the Essence of Israel's Religion.* New York: Harper, 1968.

Schürer, Emil. *A History of the Jewish People in the Time of Jesus Christ.* 5 vols. Peabody, Mass.: Hendrickson, 1994.

Smith, Wilbur M. *Therefore, Stand: A Plea for a Vigorous Apologetic in the Present Crisis of Evangelical Christianty.* Boston: W.A. Wilde, 1945.

Songs of Faith and Praise. Compiled and edited by Alton H. Howard. West Monroe, La.: Howard Publishing, 1973.

Thompson, Clyde. *The Best Way Out Is Up.* Fort Worth, Texas: Star Bible & Tract Corp., 1977.

Trueblood, Elton. *The Logic of Belief: An Introduction to the Philosophy of Religion.* 2d ed. New York: Harper, 1942.

Umphrey, Don. *The Meanest Man in Texas: A True Story Based on the Life of Clyde Thompson.* Nashville: T. Nelson, 1984; *The Meanest Man in Texas.* 3d ed. Dallas: Quarry Press, 2008.

Voices of Concern: Critical Studies in Church Criticism. Edited by Robert R. Meyers; Saint Louis: Mission Messenger, 1966.

Willoughby, Harold R., ed. *The Study of the Bible Today and Tomorrow.* Chicago: University of Chicago Press, 1947.

Published Works

1941

"The American Way." *Proceedings of the 20th Annual Meeting of the Council of Alpha Chi* (March 28-29, 1941): 24-26.

1942

"Australia and New Zealand." Jointly with Brooks Terry. In *The Harvest Field*, 47-48. Edited by Howard Schug and D.H. Morris. Abilene, Texas: Abilene Christian College Press, 1942.

1944

"Why I Am Not a Denominationalist." *Gospel Broadcast* 4 (Nov. 30, 1944): 744-45.

"A Study of the Effectiveness of Poetry in Sermon Technique." M.A. thesis, Sam Houston State Teachers College, 1944.

1945

"Better Than Denominationalism." *Gospel Broadcast* 5 (Jan. 18, 1945): 42-43, 47.

"Gambling." *Gospel Broadcast* 5 (March 8, 1945): 150-51.

"The Church as a Building." *Gospel Broadcast* 5 (April 5, 1945): 214, 219.

"The Church—Body of Christ." *Gospel Broadcast* 5 (April 12, 1945): 234, 238.

"The Church—Family of God." *Gospel Broadcast* 5 (April 19, 1945): 252.

"Too Little and Too Late." *Gospel Broadcast* 5 (April 26, 1945): 266; *World Vision* 11 (May-June, 1945): 9.

"The Church—A Mighty Army." *Gospel Broadcast* 5 (May 10, 1945): 296-97.

"The Church—Vineyard of the Lord." *Gospel Broadcast* 5 (June 14, 1945): 362-63.

"Reviewing 'The Friends' Church." *Gospel Broadcast* 5 (July 19, 1945): 406-7, 415.

"The Church—'A Called Out' Body." *Gospel Broadcast* 5 (Aug. 2, 1945): 438, 447.

1946

"And Why Not You?" *World Vision* 12 (March-April 1946): 16-17.

1949

"First Building in the State of Rhode Island." *Gospel Advocate* 91 (March 24, 1949): 189-90.

"First Building in Rhode Island Opened." *Firm Foundation* 66 (August 16, 1949): 15.

1952

"The Northeast." In *Harding College Lectures*, 228-32. Austin, Texas: Firm Foundation, 1952.

1953

"An Introduction to the Testaments of the Twelve Patriarchs." Ph.D. dissertation, Harvard University, 1953.

"Priest and Prophet, False and True Prophet." In *Harding College Lectures*, 156-68. Austin, Texas: Firm Foundation, 1953.

1954

"Overcoming Modernism." In *Abilene Christian College Bible Lectures*, 82-113. Austin, Texas: Firm Foundation, 1954.

1958

"If I Had One Sermon to Preach: Our Greatest Need." *Minister's Monthly* 3 (May 1958): 13-16.

"Where Are the Dead Now?" *20th Century Christian* 20 (April 1958): 15.

"The Jewish Background of the Church." *Restoration Quarterly* 2 (4th Quarter, 1958): 154-63.

1960

"Why Study the Old Testament?" *Teenage Christian* 1 (April 1960): 20-21, 31.

"Ability," "Communion of Saints," and "Transcendentalism." In *Baker's Dictionary of Theology*, 16, 131-32, 528. Edited by E.F. Harrison. Grand Rapids: Baker, 1960.

"The Christian School as the Educator Sees It." In *North Central Christian College Lectures: Christian Education*, 76-90. Austin, Texas: Firm Foundation, 1960.

"Study to Show Thyself Approved to God." *Christian Bible Teacher* 3 (Nov. 1959): 4-5; (Dec. 1959): 4, 13, 17; (Jan. 1960): 5; (Feb. 1960): 4-5.

"The Synagogue." *Restoration Quarterly* 4 (4th Quarter, 1960): 199-204.

1961

"Ezekiel." In *Fort Worth Christian College Lectures*, 333-46. Fort Worth, Texas: Fort Worth Christian College, 1961.

"The Jewish Background of the New Testament." *Restoration Quarterly* 5 (4th Quarter, 1961): 209-15.

1962

"The Transmission of the Text of the Bible." In *Harding College Bible Lectures*, 46-52. Austin, Texas: Firm Foundation, 1962.

1964

"Bible Lesson for Jan. 12, 1964: Isaiah's Call." *Gospel Advocate* 106 (Jan. 2, 1964): 3, 7.

"What Do We Mean by Jabneh?" *Journal of Bible and Religion* 32 (April 1964): 125-32. In *The Canon and Masorah of the Hebrew Bible*, 254-61. Edited by Sid Z. Leiman. New York: KTAV, 1974.

A Self Study Report of the Harding College Graduate School of Religion. Memphis, Tenn.: Harding College Press, 1964.

1965

"The Suffering Servant." *20th Century Christian* 27 (July 1965): 15-16.

"Demythologizing the New Testament." In *Harding College Bible Lectures*, 163-75. Nashville, Tenn.: Christian Family Books, 1965.

1966

"The Schools of the Prophets." *Restoration Quarterly* 9 (1st Quarter, 1966): 1-10.

Review of *Luke and the Gnostics*, by Charles H. Talbert. *Restoration Quarterly* 9 (1st Quarter, 1966): 53-55.

"The Books of Kings." *Minister's Monthly* 12 (Sept. 1966): 22-25.

The Minor Prophets. Grand Rapids: Baker, 1966.

Reviser of sections V-Z. *Smith's Bible Dictionary*. Edited by R. Lemmons. Garden City, N.Y.: Doubleday, 1966.

Review of *The Bible in Modern Scholarship*, edited by J.P. Hyatt. *Restoration Quarterly* 9 (2nd Quarter, 1966): 118-20.

"An Exegesis of Romans 13:1-7." In *Harding College Bible Lectures*, 100-112. Austin, Texas: Firm Foundation, 1966.

"Old Testament Studies in the Past Fifty Years." *Restoration Quarterly* 9 (4th Quarter, 1966): 201-15.

1967

"Liberality in the Early Church." *Gospel Advocate* 109 (March 30, 1967): 195, 200-201.

"Shall I Speak Falsely for God." *The Mission Studies Quarterly* 1 (July 1967): 25-34; *Mission Strategy Bulletin* 5 (Nov.-Dec. 1977): 1-4. In *Abilene Christian University Annual Bible Lectures*, 117-35. Abilene, Texas: Abilene Christian University Bookstore, 1981.

1968

"You." *Firm Foundation* 84 (May 2, 1967): 275; *20th Century Christian* 31 (Dec. 1968): 29-31.

A Study of the Interpretation of Noah and the Flood in Jewish and Christian Literature. Leiden: Brill, 1968.

"Real Estate in Palestine." *Firm Foundation* 85 (May 14, 1968): 308; (May 21, 1968): 327; (May 28, 1968): 343, 346.

"Loaves and Fishes." *Firm Foundation* 85 (July 30, 1968): 484, 491.

"Tell Us the Dream." *Firm Foundation* 85 (Oct. 8, 1968): 643, 645.

"Eastern Turkey and the Bible." *Firm Foundation* 85 (Nov. 12, 1968): 726.

"The Effect of Affluence on the Church." *Contact* 15 (Fall 1968): 10-13.

"In Search of Gilgal." *Restoration Quarterly* 11 (3rd Quarter, 1968): 137-43.

"Translation Problems." In *Pepperdine College Lectures*, 44-47. Los Angeles, Calif.: Pepperdine College, 1968.

1969

"The Teacher in the Christian College." *Minister's Monthly* 15 (Oct. 1969): 56-58.

"Bring the Books and the Parchments." *Firm Foundation* 86 (Feb. 11, 1969): 89.

"Meeting Modernism." In *Abilene Christian College Annual Bible Lectures*, 238-52. Abilene, Texas: Abilene Christian College Bookstore, 1969.

1970

"The Bible and Archaeology." *The Spiritual Sword* 1 (January 1970): 26-27.

"The Ministry of Study." *Harding Graduate School of Religion Bulletin* 8 (April 1970): 2-3; *The Campus Journal* 13 (Spring 1971): 6-8; *Christian Bible Teacher* 15 (Nov. 1971): 368-69, 371.

"The New English Bible." *Firm Foundation* 87 (May 19, 1970): 312-13, 315; (May 26, 1970): 326, 332.

"Why New Bibles?" *Firm Foundation* 87 (Oct. 13, 1970): 647, 651; (Oct. 20, 1970): 663; (Oct. 27, 1970): 679, 685.

1971

Review of *The Prophets Speak*, by Samuel J. Schultz. *Journal of the Evangelical Theological Society* 13 (1970): 132.

Historical Backgrounds of Bible History. Grand Rapids: Baker, 1971.

"Doctrinal Problems and the King James Version." *Restoration Quarterly* 14 (3rd & 4th Quarters, 1971): 142-54.

"Modern Speech Translations." *Firm Foundation* 88 (April 13, 1971): 231, 236; (April 20, 1971): 247, 252-53.

"The Soul." *Bible Beacon* 9 (May 1971): 34, 39.

Review of *Protestant Biblical Interpretation*, 3d ed., by Bernard Ramm. *Christian Bible Teacher* 15 (Oct. 2, 1971): 349.

"The Mosaic Authorship of the Pentateuch." In *Harding College Bible Lectures*, 73-108. Austin, Texas: Firm Foundation, 1971.

"The New American Standard Bible." In *Harding Graduate School Bible Lectures*, 90-105. Nashville, Tenn.: Gospel Advocate, 1971.

"I Was in the Isle Called Patmos." *Firm Foundation* 88 (Dec. 14, 1971): 789, 795.

1972

"You Shall Love the Lord Your God With All Your Mind." *20th Century Christian* 34 (July 1972): 17-18, 27; *Christian Bible Teacher* 16 (Jan. 1973): 6-, 36-37.

Editor of *The Last Things: Essays Presented by His Students to Dr. W.B. West, Jr., Upon the Occasion of His Sixty-fifth Birthday*. Austin, Texas: Sweet, 1972.

"The Revised Standard Version of the Bible after Twenty-Five Years." *Firm Foundation* 89 (Jan. 25, 1972): 7; (Feb. 1, 1972): 7; (Feb. 8, 1972): 7.

"A Sunday Morning in Russia." *Voice of Freedom* 20 (Feb. 1972): 24-25.

"The New English Bible." *20th Century Christian* 34 (March 1972): 36-39.

Review of *The Consequences of the Covenant*, by George Wesley Buchanan. *Journal of Biblical Literature* 91 (March 1972): 108.

"What Is Christian Love?" *The Spiritual Sword* 3 (July 1972): 50, 52.

Review of *The Living Bible Paraphrased*, by Kenneth Taylor. *Christian Bible Teacher* 16 (August 1972): 328, 346-47.

"Some Verses Involving Textual Critical Problems." In *Lubbock Christian College Bible Lectures*, 193-209. Lubbock, Texas: Lubbock Christian College, 1972.

"Inspiration and Authority of the Bible." In *Harding College Bible Lectures*, 90-122. Austin, Texas: Firm Foundation, 1972.

"What the Bible Teaches about God." In *Harding Graduate School of Religion Bible Lectures*, 93-108. Nashville, Tenn.: Gospel Advocate, 1972.

"Following Paul with Hertz." *Restoration Quarterly* 15 (3rd and 4th Quarters, 1972): 129-51.

1973

"Tradition." *Firm Foundation* 90 (Jan. 2, 1973): 3, 12-13.

"A Visit to Philippi." *Voice of Freedom* 21 (Jan. 1973): 4-5.

"Women, Keep Silent in the Church." *Christian Bible Teacher* 17 (April 1973): 138-39, 145.

"A Visit to Ephesus." *Voice of Freedom* 21 (March 1973): 38-40.

Review of *The Quest for Noah's Ark*, by John Warwick Montgomery. *Mission* 6 (April 1973): 314-15; *Christian Bible Teacher* 17 (May 1973): 200.

"What Shall I Major In?" *Firm Foundation* 90 (June 26, 1973): 406; *Harding University Graduate School of Religion Bulletin* 12 (Aug. 1973): 3-4.

"A Visit to Pergamum." *Voice of Freedom* 21 (June 1973): 88-89.

"Shall I Preach a While First?" *Christian Bible Teacher* 17 (July 1973): 266, 273; *Harding Graduate School of Religion Bulletin* 21 (July 1980): 1ff.

Review of *Bible, Archaeology and Faith*, by Harry Thomas Frank. *Christian Bible Teacher* 17 (July 1973): 286, 303.

"As One Having Authority." *Campus Journal* 16 (1973): 14-16.

"Jesus Gave His Blood." In *Bible Foundations*, 9-16, 2:2:273. Nashville, Tenn.: Gospel Advocate, 1973.

"The Preacher Needs to Know the Old Testament." *Harding Graduate School of Religion Bulletin* 12 (Sept. 1973): 3-4.

"What the Old Testament Claims for Itself." *The Spiritual Sword* 5 (Oct. 1973): 24-27.

"The Word of Prophecy Made Sure." In *Pillars of Faith*, 151-74. Edited by Herman O. Wilson and Morris M. Womack. Grand Rapids: Baker, 1973.

"Courage" and "Despair." In *Baker's Dictionary of Christian Ethics*, 146, 176-77. Edited by C.F. Henry. Grand Rapids: Baker, 1973.

"To Study, To Do, and To Teach." *Christian Bible Teacher* 17 (Oct. 1973): 404-7, 409.

1974

"The Louvre and the Bible." *Voice of Freedom* 22 (Jan. 1974): 12-13.

"Berlin and the Bible." *Voice of Freedom* 22 (March 1974): 41-42.

"The Hardest Commandment." *20th Century Christian* 34 (April 1974): 7-9.

"A Look at the New International Version." *The Apostolic Reflector* 1 (April 1974): 56-57.

"That Which Every Joint Supplies." *Firm Foundation* 91 (May 21, 1974): 232; *Christian Bible Teacher* 20 (Oct. 1976): 410.

"The New World Translation of the Holy Scriptures." *The Spiritual Sword* 6 (Oct. 1974): 32-36.

"The Intermediate State of the Dead." In *Harding College Bible Lectures*, 169-90. Austin, Texas: Firm Foundation, 1974. In *Magnolia Bible College Lectures*, 87-96. Kosciusko, Miss.: Magnolia Bible College, 1984.

"The Majority of the Men." In *What Lack We Yet?* 37-42. Edited by J.D. Thomas. Abilene, Texas: Biblical Research, 1974.

1975

"I Must See Africa." *Voice of Freedom* 23 (March 1975): 37-38.

"Genesis 3:15: The Woman's Seed." *Firm Foundation* 92 (April 22, 1975): 248.

"The Biblical Field." *Harding Graduate School of Religion Bulletin* 14 (July 1975): 3, 6.

"Edna," "Ekron, Ekronite," "Elhanan," "Eliab," "Fast, Fasting," "Feasts," "First Fruits," "Food," and "Leaven." In *Zondervan Pictorial Encyclopedia of the Bible*, 201, 259-62, 279, 289, 501-4, 521-26, 541, 581-87, 910-13. Edited by M. Tenney. Grand Rapids: Zondervan, 1975.

"Apocrypha," "Luke," and "Matthew." In *Wycliffe Bible Encyclopedia*, 111-12, 1056-57, 1090-91. Edited by Charles F. Pfeiffer, Howard F. Voss, and John Rea. Chicago: Moody, 1975.

Archaeology and the Bible. Abilene, Texas: Biblical Research, 1975.

"The New Testament in the Twentieth Century." *Restoration Quarterly* 18 (4th Quarter, 1975): 193-215.

1976

"Virgin Daughter." *Firm Foundation* 93 (Jan. 6, 1976): 6.

"Fruit of the Vine." *Firm Foundation* 93 (Feb. 17, 1976): 101.

"Living Soul." *Firm Foundation* 93 (March 16, 1976): 166.

"Only Begotten Son." *Firm Foundation* 93 (June 22, 1976): 388, 395.

The Gospel According to Matthew. 2 vols. The Living Word Commentary. Austin, Texas: Sweet, 1976.

"In Journeyings Often." *Firm Foundation* 93 (Oct. 5, 1976): 629, 634-35.

"Archaeology and the Bible." In *Harding College Bible Lectures*, 140-48. Austin, Texas: Firm Foundation, 1976.

"Topography and Archaeology of the Gospel of John." In *Lubbock Christian College Bible Lectures*, 224-35. Lubbock, Texas: Lubbock Christian College Bookstore, 1976.

"The Zero Milepost." *Firm Foundation* 93 (Dec. 7, 1976): 771, 779.

1977

"Bible Translation and Doctrinal Error." *Firm Foundation* 94 (June 7, 1977): 356, 363.

"Lords Over God's Heritage?" *Firm Foundation* 94 (June 14, 1977): 372, 379.

"When God Says 'You Are Unworthy.'" *20th Century Christian* 39 (Aug. 1977): 25-27.

"The Authority of the Scriptures." In *Harding College Bible Lectures*, 184-203. Austin, Texas: Firm Foundation, 1977.

1978

"A Review of Loraine Boettner's Postmillennialism." *The Spiritual Sword* 9 (Jan. 1978): 8-11.

"Personality of the Month: W.B. West, Jr." *Gospel Advocate* 120 (March 2, 1978): 133, 136.

"From the Beginning It Was Not So." In *Your Marriage Can Be Great*, 410-19. Edited by Thomas B. Warren. Jonesboro, Ark.: National Christian, 1978.

"Love—Its Meaning." In *Your Marriage Can Be Great*, 110-14. Edited by Thomas B. Warren. Jonesboro, Ark.: National Christian, 1978.

"Authority." *Harding Graduate School of Religion Bulletin* 18 (June 1978): 2-3.

"Confused Holy Spirit?" *Firm Foundation* 95 (Aug. 15, 1978): 520; *Voice of Freedom* 27 (March 1979): 36.

"Mark 10:14, Koluein, and Baptizein." *Restoration Quarterly* 21 (3rd Quarter, 1978): 129-34.

1979

"Bible Archaeology and Geography." In *The World and Literature of the Old Testament*, 71-116. Edited by John T. Willis. Austin, Texas: Sweet, 1979.

"When a Man ... : An Exegesis of Deut. 24:1-4." In *Abilene Christian University Annual Bible Lectures*, 144-61. Abilene, Texas: Abilene Christian University Bookstore, 1979.

"The Graduate School as I Remember It." *Harding Graduate School of Religion Bulletin* 19 (Feb. 1979): 1-3.

"First Century Jews and the Messiah." *20th Century Christian* 41 (Feb. 1979): 3-5.

"Inspiration and Authority of the Bible." *Alternative* 5 (Spring 1979): 3-8.

"Greek Words for Elders." *Firm Foundation* 96 (June 26, 1979): 407; (July 3, 1979): 423; (July 10, 1979): 439; (July 17, 1979): 455; (July 24, 1979): 471, 475; (July 31, 1979): 487, 491.

Review of *Where Is Noah's Ark?* by Lloyd R. Bailey. *Biblical Archaeologist* 42 (Summer 1979): 190-91.

Review of *The Noah's Ark Nonsense*, by Howard M. Teeple. *Biblical Archaeologist* 42 (Summer 1979): 190-91.

"The Signs of the Times." *20th Century Christian* 42 (Dec. 1979): 18-21; *Campus Journal* 24 (Spring 1981): 4-6.

"The Bible and Archaeology." In *White's Ferry Road Bible Lectures*, 117-19. West Monroe, La.: School of Biblical Studies, 1979.

"Reflections on Preaching." *Harding Graduate School of Religion Bulletin* 19 (Nov. 1979): 1ff.; *The Harvester* 61 (Feb. 1981): 7-9; *Firm Foundation* 98 (June 2, 1981): 339.

1980

"External Only?" *Firm Foundation* 97 (June 17, 1980): 388.

"Greek Word Studies on the Function and Authority of Preachers." *Firm Foundation* 97 (Sept. 1980): 567, 572, 583, 599, 615, 631, 635.

"Stewards of Our Minds." In *Harding University Bible Lectures*, 140-54. Austin, Texas: Firm Foundation, 1980.

"Archaeological Fictions." *Christian Light* 2 (Nov.-Dec. 1980): 53, 62; 2 (March-April 1981): 86-87, 93.

Review of *Genealogy and History in the Biblical World*, by Robert R. Wilson. *Restoration Quarterly* 23 (4th Quarter, 1980): 249-51.

1981

"Kizzie, Stay Put!" *Firm Foundation* 98 (Jan. 6, 1981): 3.

"Signs of These Times." *Harding Graduate School of Religion Bulletin* 21 (Jan. 1981): 1ff.; *Firm Foundation* 98 (April 28, 1981): 259; *Gospel Light* 51 (Sept. 1981): 135.

'ohel, 'aron, ba'ar, be'er, be'er lahay ro'i, be'er shebac bo'r, bor, bur, gamal gemul, gemula, tagmul, gamal, zaqen, zaqzn, zaqen, zoqen, zigna, zequnim, haqa haqaq, hoq, huqqa, hatam, hotam, tal, yadac, decah, dacat, yiddeconi, modac, modacat, maddac yacad, ceda, moced, massa, qahal, qohelet, qazer, qoser, qasar, qasir. In *Theological Wordbook of the Old Testament*. Edited by R. Laird Harris. Chicago: Moody, 1980.

"The New International Version." *Restoration Quarterly* 24 (1st Quarter, 1981): 1-11.

"Pretexting?" *Firm Foundation* 98 (May 19, 1981): 310.

"Preaching." *Firm Foundation* 98 (June 2, 1981): 339.

The English Bible from KJV to NIV: A History and Evaluation. Grand Rapids: Baker, 1981.

Archaeological Backgrounds to Bible People. Grand Rapids: Baker, 1981. Previously published as *Historical Backgrounds of Bible History*. Grand Rapids: Baker, 1971.

"Translation Questions." *Firm Foundation* 98 (Oct. 6, 1981): 631; (Oct. 13, 1981): 647.

1982

"Difficult Texts from the Psalms and Proverbs." In *Difficult Texts of the Old Testament Explained: the Fifth Annual Fort Worth Lectures*, 311-23. Hurst, Texas: Winkler, 1982.

"W.B. West, Jr." *Harding Graduate School of Religion Bulletin* 22 (Feb. 1982): 1-2.

"What the Restoration Movement Has Accomplished." *Firm Foundation* 99 (March 2, 1982): 135; (March 9, 1982): 151; (March 16, 1982): 167; (March 23, 1982): 183; (March 30, 1982): 199.

"The Old Testament and Homosexual Acts." In *Counseling Homosexuals*, 1-32. Edited by Bill W. Flatt, Jack P. Lewis, and Dowell E. Flatt. Jonesboro, Ark.: National Christian, 1982.

"A Self-Perpetuating Board?" *Firm Foundation* 99 (June 8, 1982): 356, 363.

"Commencements I Remember." *Harding Graduate School of Religion Bulletin* 22 (July 1982): 1, 3.

"Let Me Write Their Songs." *Firm Foundation* 99 (July 13, 1982): 436, 443.

"The Priesthood: 1 Peter 2:5-9." *The Exegete* 1 (May 1982): 1-5.

Review of *Hosea: A New Translation with Introduction and Commentary*, by Francis I. Andersen and David Noel Freedman. *Biblical Archaeologist* 45 (Summer 1982): 190-91.

"Old Testament Ethics." *20th Century Christian* 44 (Sept. 1982): 6-9.

"How Many Times Was Cain Killed?" *Harding Graduate School of Religion Bulletin* 22 (Oct. 1982): 3.

"Why Stop Here? The New King James in Perspective." *Christianity Today* 26 (Oct. 8, 1982): 108, 110.

"Read from the King James or the American Standard." *Bulletin of Harding Graduate School of Religion* 23 (Dec. 1982): 1-2.

1983

"Read from the King James or the American Standard." *The Seed* 1 (Spring 1983): 7; and *Mission Journal* 17 (July 1983): 3-5.

"Mark Them Which Cause Divisions." *Firm Foundation* 100 (Feb. 22, 1983): 118.

"I've Heard That You Do Not Believe that Isaiah 7:14 Predicts the Virgin Birth and Yet Matthew 1 Says That It Does: How Do You Explain This?" *Harding Graduate School of Religion Bulletin* 24 (March 1983): 3.

"Lay up Treasures in Heaven." *Firm Foundation* 100 (March 1, 1983): 135; (March 8, 1983): 151, 156.

"Italics in English Bible Translation." In *The Living and Active Word of God: Studies in Honor of Samuel J. Schultz*, 250-70. Edited by Morris Inch and Ronald Youngblood. Winona Lake, Ind.: Eisenbrauns, 1983.

" 'Spiritual Words' or 'Spiritual Men'? (1 Cor. 2:13)." *Firm Foundation* 100 (April 19, 1983): 262, 267.

"A Cloud of Witnesses: Hebrews 12:1." *Gospel Advocate* 125 (April 21, 1983): 233, 237.

"Baptismal Practices of the Second and Third Century Church." *Restoration Quarterly* 26 (1st Quarter, 1983): 1-17.

Review of *The Prophets.* Vol. 1: *The Assyrian Period*, by Klaus Roch. *Hebrew Studies* 24 (1983): 205-6.

1984

"Ah, Assyria, the Rod of My Anger." *20th Century Christian* 45 (April 1984): 16-19.

"But What Is One among So Many?" *Gospel Advocate* 126 (May 3 1984): 277.

"Great News from Jerusalem." *The World Evangelist* 12 (May 1984): 4.

"The Text of the New Testament." *Restoration Quarterly* 27 (2d Quarter, 1984): 65-74.

"The Intermediate State of the Dead." In *Biblical Doctrine of Last Things*, 87-96. Edited by David Lipe. Kosciusko, Miss.: Magnolia Bible College, 1984.

"1 Corinthians 7 and Remarriage." *Harding Graduate School of Religion Bulletin* 35 (Nov. 1984): 1, 4.

"Noah and the Flood in Jewish, Christian, and Muslim Tradition." *Biblical Archaeologist* 47 (Dec. 1984): 175-76.

Review of *The Plot Against Christianity*, by Elizabeth Dilling. *Voice of Freedom* 32 (Dec. 1984): 175-76.

1985

"Professor Burn-Out." *Harding Graduate School of Religion Bulletin* 36 (Jan. 1985): 1, 4.

"The Office and Function of a Prophet." In *Living Lessons from the Prophets*, 40-55. Edited by John Waddey. Knoxville, Tenn.: East Tennessee School of Preaching and Missions, 1985.

"A Historical Background of the Prophets." In *Living Lessons from the Prophets*, 71-86. Edited by John Waddey. Knoxville, Tenn.: East Tennessee School of Preaching & Missions, 1985.

"Red or Green?" *Image* 1 (June 15, 1985): 28.

Leadership Questions Confronting the Church. Nashville, Tenn.: Christian Communications, 1985.

"Bible Characters Really Lived." *Gospel Advocate* 127 (July 18, 1985): 426, 435.

"Those Who Rule." *Image* 1 (Aug. 15, 1985): 10.

Contributor of Notes to Hosea and Joel. In *The NIV Study Bible*, 1321-44. Edited by Kenneth Barker. Grand Rapids: Zondervan, 1985.

"The Work of the Preacher." In *Jesus Calls Us*, 202-17. Harding University Lectures, 1985. Delight, Ark.: Gospel Light, 1985.

"Bible Study in the Churches of Christ." *Seminary Review* 31 (Dec. 1985): 177-96.

1986

"Pretexting?" *Bulletin of Harding Graduate School of Religion* 27 (Jan. 1986): 1; (Feb. 1986): 3.

"The Ethical Teaching of the Prophets." In *Ethics for Daily Living*, 161-75. Freed Hardeman College Lectures, 1986. Edited by Winford Claiborne. Henderson, Tenn.: Freed-Hardeman College, 1986.

"Faith Only." *Gospel Advocate* 128 (March 6, 1986): 145, 148.

"I Wish She would Stay Here with Me." *Harding Graduate School Bulletin* 27 (March 1986): 1, 3; *Gospel Advocate* 128 (May 15, 1986): 300, 308.

"Only Begotton Son." *Gospel Advocate* 127 (May 1, 1986): 273-74.

"Food," "Fast," "Fasting," "Cup," "Meals," "Banquet," "Bread," "Vinegar," "Drink," "Drunkenness," "Famine," "Leaven," "Table," "Wine," "Winepress." In *Nelson's Illustrated Bible Dictionary*. Edited by Herbert Lockyer, Sr. Nashville, Tenn.: Nelson, 1986.

"The Priority of Bible Study." *Gospel Advocate* 128 (Oct. 12, 1986): 593, 604.

"Putting Away and Divorce." *Gospel Advocate* 128 (Nov. 6, 1986): 665, 668

Review of *Enosh and His Generation: Pre-Israelite Hero and History in Post Biblical Interpretation*, by Steven D. Fraade. *Journal of Biblical Literature* 105 (Dec. 1986): 736-37.

1987

"Cooperative Evangelism." *Bulletin of Harding Graduate School of Religion* 29 (Jan. 1987): 1, 3; *The Christian Chronicle* 44 (Feb. 1987): 23; *Gospel Advocate* 129 (March 18, 1987): 163, 168.

"A Series on the Silence of Scripture." *The World Evangelist* 15 (Jan. 1987): 10, 12; (Feb. 1987): 10, 12.

"The Value and Danger of Bible Cross-References." *Gospel Advocate* 129 (March 5, 1987): 144-46.

"Genesis 3:15: The Woman's Seed." *Gospel Advocate* 129 (April 2, 1987): 209.

"New Testament Authority for Music in Worship." In *The Instrumental Music Issue*, 14-59. Edited by Bill Flatt. Nashville, Tenn.: Gospel Advocate, 1987.

"Building a House for David." In *Adult Bible Quarterly*, 9-13, Spring, 1987. Edited by Rubel Shelly. Nashville, Tenn.: 20th Century Christian, 1987.

"The Division of the Kingdom." In *Adult Bible Quarterly*, 39-43, Spring 1987. Edited by Rubel Shelly. Nashville, Tenn.: 20th Century Christian, 1987.

Understanding Genesis. Nashville, Tenn.: Christian Communications, 1987.

"An Exegesis of Matthew 19:1-12." *Harding Graduate School Bulletin* 28 (Sept. 1987): 1, 2.

"Authority of Elders." *Image* 3 (Nov. 1987): 14-15; (Dec. 1987): 20-21; 4 (Jan. 1988): 22-23, 27; (Feb. 1988): 14-15, 17; (March 1988): 11, 17.

"HGSR at Work." *Harding Graduate School Bulletin* 28 (Nov. 1987): 3.

1988

"We Preach Not Ourselves ... (2 Cor 4:5)." *Harding Graduate School Bulletin* 29 (Feb. 1988): 1-3.

"False Comfort for a Good Man." In *Adult Bible Quarterly, Poetry in Israel,* 11-15. Nashville, Tenn.: 20th Century Christian, Spring, 1988.

"Lemuel's Poem: A Good Wife." In *Adult Bible Quarterly, Poetry in Israel,* 37-41. Nashville, Tenn.: 20th Century Christian, Spring, 1988.

"Quietness or Silence." *Gospel Advocate* 130 (July 1988): 11-12.

"The Ending of Mark." In *The Lifestyle of Jesus According to the Gospel of Mark*, 597-603. Harding University's 1988 Lectures. Searcy, Ark.: Harding University, 1988.

"Love the Lord with All Your Mind." *Gospel Advocate* 130 (Oct. 1988): 17-18.

"Wolf! Wolf!" *Harding Graduate School of Religion Bulletin* 29 (Nov. 1988): 1. Reprinted in *The Christian Catalyst* 3 (March 1989): 1, 6.

Exegesis of Difficult Passages. Searcy, Ark.: Resource Publications, 1988.

"James Turner Barclay, Explorer of Nineteenth-Century Jerusalem." *Biblical Archaeologist* 51 (Sept. 1988): 163-70.

1989

"Questions about Translations." *Harding Graduate School Bulletin* 30 (March 1989): 1, 3.

"Modesty: A Biblical View." *The Christian Catalyst* (March 1989): 1, 6.

"The Semitic Background of the Gospel of John." In *Johannine Studies*, 97-110. Edited by James E. Priest. Malibu, Calif.: Pepperdine University Press, 1989.

"The Centrality of the Resurrection." *20th Century Christian* 51 (March 1989): 5-9.

"Sow the Wind; Reap the Whirlwind." *Harding Graduate School Bulletin* 30 (April 1989): 1, 4; *Image* 5 (May 1989): 26-27, 32; *Gospel Advocate* 131 (July 1989): 8-9.

Editor and Contributor to *Interpretation 2 Corinthians 5:14-21. An Exercise in Hermeneutics*. Vol. 17 of *Studies in the Bible and Early Christianity*. Lewiston, N.Y.: Mellen, 1989.

"An Introduction to Acts." In *Acts: The Flame*, 29-35. Searcy, Ark.: Harding University, 1989.

"The Spirit Comes with Power." In *Acts: The Flame*, 85-92. Searcy, Ark.: Harding University, 1989.

"Archaeology of Acts." In *Acts: The Flame*, 416-29. Searcy, Ark.: Harding University, 1989.

"The Missionary Journey of Paul." In *Acts: The Flame*, 487-93. Searcy, Ark.: Harding University, 1989.

"But What Is One Among So Many?" *Firm Foundation* 105 (June 1989): 46.

"The Value of Timely Translations." *Gospel Advocate* 131 (Oct. 1989): 25-27.

"The Days of Creation: An Historical Survey of Interpretation." *Journal of the Evangelical Theological Society* 32 (Dec. 1989): 433-55.

1990

"Genesis," "Esther," "Exodus," "Isaiah," "Jeremiah," "Job," "John," "Johannine Literature," "Joshua," "Kings," "Minor Prophets," "Noah," "Ruth," and "Samuel." In *Encyclopedia of Early Christianity*. Edited by Everett Ferguson, Michael P. McHugh, and Frederick W. Norris. New York and London: Garland, 1990.

Review of *Noah: The Person and the Story in History and Tradition* by Lloyd Bailey. *Biblical Archaeologist* 55 (June 1990): 120.

"Biblical Archaeology and 1 Corinthians." In *The Church of God in a Pagan World: Studies in First Corinthians*, 233-70. Harding University 67th Annual Lectureship. Searcy, Ark.: Harding University, 1990.

"Marriage and 1 Corinthians." In *The Church of God in a Pagan World: Studies in First Corinthians*, 291-321. Harding University 67th Annual Lectureship. Searcy, Ark.: Harding University, 1990.

"How Hedges Become Traditions, Then Laws." *Gospel Advocate* 132 (Nov. 1990): 18-20.

1991

"The New Revised Standard Version of the Bible." *Gospel Advocate* 133 (Jan. 1991): 42-45.

Review of *God's New Covenant: A New Testament Translation* by Heinz W. Cassirer. *Restoration Quarterly* 23 (1st Quarter, 1991): 53-55.

"Christians Must Know the Old Testament." *Gospel Advocate* 133 (Feb. 1991): 57-58.

"Christ, the Church and the Middle East." *Gospel Advocate* 133 (May 1991): 26-28.

Questions You've Asked about Bible Translations. Searcy, Ark.: Resource Publications, 1991.

The English Bible from KJV to NIV. 2d ed. Grand Rapids: Baker, 1991.

"Archaeology and Biblical Studies" and "Gentiles." In *Holman Bible Dictionary*, 83-93, 542-43. Edited by Trent C. Butler. Nashville, Tenn.: Holman Bible Publishers, 1991.

"Is Forgiveness Conditional?" *Gospel Advocate* 133 (Aug. 1991): 32.

"The Minor Prophets in the NRSV." *Restoration Quarterly* 33 (3d Quarter, 1991): 129-39.

"The Historical and Archaeological Backgrounds to Genesis: Syro-Palestinian Era." In *Where Genesis Meets Life: Promises and Providence*, 133-61. Harding University's 68th Annual Bible Lectureship. Searcy, Ark.: Harding University, 1991.

"God in Genesis." In *Where Genesis Meets Life: Promises and Providence*, 176-92. Harding University's 68th Annual Bible Lectureship. Searcy, Ark.: Harding University, 1991.

"The Woman's Seed (Gen. 3:15)." *Journal of the Evangelical Theological Society* 34 (Sept. 1991): 299-319.

"Joshua Succeeds Moses." Lesson 1 in *Adult Bible Quarterly*, 43-45. Nashville, Tenn.: 20th Century Christian, 1991.

"Orphah, Ruth and Naomi." Lesson 11 in *Adult Bible Quarterly*, 43-45. Nashville, Tenn.: 20th Century Christian, 1991.

"Some Aspects of the Problem of the Inclusion of the Apocrypha." In *The Apocrypha in Ecumenical Perspective*, 161-207. United Bible Society Monograph Series, no. 6. Edited by Siegfried Muerer. New York: United Bible Societies, 1991.

1992

"What is Adultery?" *Gospel Advocate* 134 (Jan. 1992): 19-20.

"¿Que es el adulterio?" *La Voz Eterna* 30 (Noviembre-Diciembre 1992): 23-25.

"Adultery and Repentance." *Gospel Advocate* 134 (Jan. 1992): 21-22.

Review of *The Books of Nahum, Habakkuk, and Zephaniah*, by O. Palmer Robertson. *The New International Commentary on the Old Testament*. Grand Rapids: Eerdmans, 1990. In *Restoration Quarterly* 34 (1st Quarter, 1992): 61-62.

"Her Labor Was Not in Vain." *21st Century Christian* 54 (July 1992): 17-18.

"God and the Prayers of Sinners." *Gospel Advocate* 134 (April 1992): 54-55.

"The Voice on the Phone." *21st Century Christian* 54 (July 1992): 17-18.

"Bible, Bishops'," "Great Bible, The," "Douay Version," "Flood," "Geneva Bible," "Jamnia (Jabneh), Council of," "Versions, English (Pre-1962)," "Wycliffe's Version," "Authorized Versions," and "King James Version." In *The Anchor Bible Dictionary*. Edited by David Noel Freedman. New York: Doubleday, 1992.

"The Bird Cage." *Gospel Advocate* 134 (Sept. 1992): 36-37.

"The Book of Revelation and the Millennium." In *Visions of Victory: The Book of Revelation*, 176-201. Harding University's 69th Annual Bible Lectureship. Searcy, Ark.: Harding University, 1992.

"The Lord's Servant Must Not Strive." *Gospel Advocate* 134 (Oct. 1992): 10-11.

"Anchored in Midstream." *Gospel Advocate* 134 (Oct. 1992): 42-43.

"Archaeology and the Old Testament." *Gospel Advocate* 134 (Dec. 1992): 18-20.

1993

"Bridging the Gap Between the University and the Church." *Restoration Quarterly* 35 (1st Quarter, 1993): 1-8.

"Adulterio y Arrepentimiento." *La Voz Eterna* 32 (Enero-Febrero, 1993): 25-28.

"Repentance: Baby-Boomer Style." *Gospel Advocate* 135 (Feb. 1993): 30-31.

"Quiet Time." *Gospel Advocate* 135 (May 1993): 48-49.

"William Francis Lynch, Explorer of the Dead Sea." *Near East Archaeological Society Bulletin*, n.s. no. 37 (Fall 1992): 2-9.

"Eighth Century Minor Prophets: Historical Background and Archeological Insights." In *Today Hear His Voice: The Minor Prophets Speak*, 117-44. Harding University's 70th Annual Bible Lectureship. Searcy, Ark.: Harding University, 1993.

"Seventh Century Minor Prophets: Historical and Archaeological Background." In *Today Hear His Voice: The Minor Prophets Speak*, 117-43. Harding University's 70th Annual Bible Lectureship. Searcy, Ark.: Harding University, 1993.

"Post-Exilic Minor Prophets: Historical Background and Archaeological Insights." In *Today Hear His Voice: The Minor Prophets Speak*, 145-67. Harding University's 70th Annual Bible Lectureship. Searcy, Ark.: Harding University, 1993.

"Hebrews 1:1-4: Christ the Prophet, Priest and King." In *Great Bible Texts Revisited*, 329-42. Faulkner University Lectures. Edited by M.F. Bailey, Jr. Montgomery, Ala.: Faulkner University, 1993.

1994

"Old Testament Word Studies in Worship." In *Worship in Spirit and Truth*, 230-36. Freed-Hardeman University 1994 Lectures. Edited by D.L. Lipe. Henderson, Tenn.: Freed-Hardeman University, 1994.

"Blessed Are Those Who Read." *Gospel Advocate* 136 (Sept. 1994): 15-17.

"What We Learn about God from Ephesians." In *To God Be the Glory: Ephesians' Call to Unity*, 31-43. Harding University's 79th Annual Bible Lectureship. Edited by Don Shackelford. Searcy, Ark.: Harding University, 1994.

"Ruts." *Gospel Advocate* 136 (Nov. 1994): 24-25.

"Elder's Wives." *Gospel Advocate* 136 (Dec. 1994): 35-36.

"The Offering of Abel (Gen. 4:4): A Historical Interpretation." *Journal of the Evangelical Theological Society* 37 (Dec. 1994): 481-96.

1995

"Discoveries and Bible People." *Gospel Advocate* 137 (Feb. 1995): 34-35.

"He Saw Him A Long Way Off." *Gospel Advocate* 137 (April 1995): 31-32.

"If You Mess Up with Your Children." *Gospel Advocate* 137 (June 1995): 50-51.

"Worth a Thought?" *Server* 42 (July 26, 1995): 1, 3.

"The Things That Have Been Fulfilled among Us." In *Touched By the Master: Luke Presents Jesus*, 91-103. Harding University's 72nd Annual Bible Lectureship. Edited by Allan Isom. Searcy, Ark: Harding University, 1995.

"The Capable Wife (Prov. 31:10-31." In *Essays on Women in Earliest Christianity*, 2:155-80. Edited by C.D. Osburn. Joplin, Mo.: College Press, 1995.

"The Gates of Hell Shall Not Prevail Against It (Matt. 16:18): A Study of the History of Interpretation." *Journal of the Evangelical Theological Society* 38/3 (Sept. 1995): 349-67.

"Claude R. Conder, Surveyor of Palestine." *Near East Archaeological Society Bulletin*, n.s. 39-40 (1995): 41-47.

1996

"Challenges to Messianic Prophecies." In *Settled in Heaven: Applying the Bible to Life*, 304-8. 1996 Annual Freed-Hardeman University Lectureship. Edited by David L. Lipe. Henderson, Tenn.: Freed-Hardeman University, 1996.

"Exegesis of Relevant Texts 1 Cor. 2:7-13." In *Settled in Heaven: Applying the Bible to Life*, 309-12. 1996 Annual Freed-Hardeman University Lectureship. Edited by David L. Lipe. Henderson, Tenn.: Freed-Hardeman University, 1996.

"An Analysis of 1 Timothy 2:8-15." *Spiritual Sword* 27 (Jan. 1996): 34-38.

"The Silence of Scripture in Reformation Thought." *Gospel Advocate* 138 (Jan. 1996): 18-19.

"Worship: Biblical or Cultural?" *Gospel Advocate* 138 (Aug. 1996): 26-27.

"The Importance of Biblical Languages." In *Men of God*, 161-71. Edited by Shawn D. Mathis. Nashville, Tenn.: Gospel Advocate, 1996.

"Metaphors in Hosea." In *Festschrift in Honor of Charles Speel*, 71-87. Edited by T.J. Sienkeqicz and J.E. Betts. Monmouth, Ill.: Monmouth College, 1996.

"Sir Charles Wilson Discoverer of Wilson's Arch." *Near East Archaeological Society Bulletin*, n.s. 41 (1996): 38-49.

"Clermont-Ganneau and 19th Century Discovery." *Near East Archaeological Society Bulletin*, n.s. 41 (1996): 51-60.

"Around the Curve in the Road." *Server* 43 (July 24, 1996): 1, 3.

"Substitutes." *Server* 48 (Dec. 4, 1996): 1-2.

1997

"Esther," "Exodus," "Genesis," "Isaiah," "Jeremiah," "Job," "Joshua," "Kings," "Minor Prophets," "Noah," "Ruth," and "Samuel." In *Encyclopedia of Early Christianity*. 2d ed. Edited by Everett Ferguson. New York and London: Garland, 1997.

"Sela Merrill: 19th Century American Explorer-Diplomat." *Near East Archaeological Society Bulletin* 42 (1997): 15-22.

"Cycles of Apostacy & Restoration." *Gospel Advocate* 139 (May 1997): 15-16.

"The Less-Traveled Road." *Gospel Advocate* 139 (July 1997): 36-38.

"The Tithe." *Gospel Advocate* 139 (Dec. 1997): 15-18.

1998

"A Cappella Worship in the Assembly." *Harding University Graduate School of Religion Bulletin* 39 (Jan. 1998): 1, 4.

"Revelation 20: The Millennium." In *At His Coming*, 235-42. 1998 Freed-Hardeman University Lectureship. Edited by David L. Lipe. Henderson, Tenn.: Freed-Hardeman University, 1998

"Metaphorical Standing." *Gospel Advocate* 140 (Feb. 1998): 35-36.

"The Kingdom of God … Is Righteousness, Peace, and Joy in the Holy Spirit (Rom. 14:17): A Survey of Interpretation." *Restoration Quarterly* 40 (4th Quarter, 1998): 53-68.

"A Time for Worship." *Gospel Advocate* 140 (April 1998): 35-35.

"El Silencio de las Escriptura: El Pensamiento de la Reforma." *La Voz Eterna* 36 (March-April 1998): 10(46)-15(51).

"Introduction." In *Directions for the Road Ahead*, xii-xvi. Edited by Jim Sheerer and Charles Williams. Chickasha, Okla.: Yoeman, 1998.

"See What You Made Me Do!" *Server* 46 (April 22, 1998): 1-2.

"The Duties of Grandparenting." *21st Century Christian* 61 (May/June, 1998): 24-27.

"A Light to the Nations." In *Celebrating 75 Years: Focusing on Things That Count*, 165-81. Edited by Don Shackelford. Searcy, Ark.: Harding University Institute for Church and Family Resources, 1998.

Historical Backgrounds to Bible People. Henderson, Tenn.: Hester Publications, 1998. Originally published as *Historical Backgrounds of Bible History*. Grand Rapids: Baker, 1971. Second publication as *Archaeological Backgrounds to Bible People*. Grand Rapids: Baker, 1981.

1999

"Proverbs as General Rules." In *Hearing Wisdom's Voice: Proverbs at the Millennium*, 233-38. Edited by David L. Lipe. Henderson, Tenn.: Freed-Hardeman University, 1999.

"Proverbs and Woman." In *Hearing Wisdom's Voice: Proverbs at the Millennium*, 239-43. Edited by David L. Lipe. Henderson, Tenn.: Freed-Hardeman University, 1999.

"Follow Me." *Server* 46 (March 3, 1999): 1-2.

"Losing Life." *Server* 46 (July 21, 1999): 1-2.

"May Thy Will and Mine Be One." *Gospel Advocate* 141 (April 1999): 39-40.

"Preaching from the Acts of the Apostles." In *Understanding the Times*, 85-108. Edited by Howard W. Norton. Searcy, Ark.: Institute for Church and Family, 1999.

2000

"That Is How I Learned." *Server* 47 (Jan. 12, 2000): 1-2.

"The Teaching." *Firm Foundation* 115 (Feb. 2000): 23-24.

"Desire of the Nations (Hag. 2:7): A Messianic Title?" In *A Heart to Study and Teach the Law of the Lord, Essays Honoring Clyde M. Woods*, 52-68. Edited by Dale W. Manor. Henderson, Tenn.: Freed-Hardeman University, 2000.

"Predestination: Who Answers to God?—Romans 9:20." In *Receiving God's Righteousness, Grace and Glory in Romans*, 151-55. Edited by D.L. Lipe. Henderson, Tenn.: Freed-Hardeman University, 2000.

"The Priest in the Biblical World." *Firm Foundation* 115 (March 2000): 15-16.

"A Holy Priesthood." *Firm Foundation* 115 (April 2000): 6-11.

"Thank You." *Server* 47 (May 31, 2000): 1-2.

"The Priesthood of Believers." *Firm Foundation* 115 (June 2000): 7-9.

"The Stork and the Fox." *Gospel Advocate* 142 (June 2000): 36-38.

"Misconceptions of the Priesthood of Believers." *Firm Foundation* 115 (Aug. 2000): 20-22.

"Spiritual Service." *Firm Foundation* 115 (Sept. 2000): 23-24.

"Bridging the Translation Gap." *The Bridge* 41/5 (Sept. 2000): 1, 4.

"Jamnia after Forty Years." *Hebrew Union College Annual* 70-71 (1999-2000): 233-59.

2001

"Interpreting Genesis." In *New Beginnings: God, Man and Redemption in Genesis*, 307-15. 65th Annual Freed-Hardeman University Lectureship. Edited by David L. Lipe. Henderson, Tenn.: Freed-Hardeman University, 2001.

"Saturday Night Communion?" *Firm Foundation* 116 (March 2001): 17-21.

Ethics of the Prophets. Henderson, Tenn.: Hester Publications, 2001.

"John Lewis (Johann Ludwig) Burckhardt: Explorer in Disguise." *Near East Archaeological Society Bulletin* 45 (2000): 13-21.

"A Challenge to New Elders." *Gospel Advocate* 143 (May 2001): 34-35.

"Back to Basics: Faith." *Firm Foundation* 116 (June 2001): 18-21.

"Back to Basics: The Human Situation." *Firm Foundaton* 116 (July 2001): 12-14.

"Women in the New Testament." *Gospel Advocate* 143 (Sept. 2001): 18-19.

"No Small Service." *Gospel Advocate* 143 (Sept. 2001): 20-22.

"Only a Tomato!" *Server* 48 (Oct. 3, 2001): 1.

"Minister." *Server* 48 (Sept. 26, 2001): 1, 4.

2002

"Back to Basics: Born Again." *Firm Foundation* 117 (Jan. 2002): 12-15.

"In Christ: How Chosen and Predestined? Ephesians 1:3-14." In *Exalting Christ in the Church*, 257-61. Edited by David L. Lipe. Henderson, Tenn.: Freed-Hardeman University, 2002.

"In Christ: How Are Barriers Removed? Ephesians 2:14-19." In *Exalting Christ in the Church*, 262-66. Edited by David L. Lipe. Henderson, Tenn.: Freed-Hardeman University, 2002.

"Back to Basics—Confession." *Firm Foundation* 117 (April 2002): 10-13.

"The Good of One's Neighbor." *Server* 49 (May 1, 2002): 1.

"Today's New International Version." *Gospel Advocate* 144 (June 2002): 29-33.

"The Center of the Message." *Gospel Advocate* 144 (Nov. 2002): 26-27.

"In a Foxhole." *Server* 49 (Nov. 6, 2002): 1.

"Jamnia Revisited." In *The Canon Debate*, 146-62. Edited by L.M. McDonald and J.A. Sanders. Peabody, Mass.: Hendrickson, 2002.

2003

"The Nature of Hebrew Poetry." In *When We Hurt: Tragedy and Triumph in Job*, 185-93. Edited by David L. Lipe. Henderson, Tenn.: Freed-Hardeman University, 2003.

"Back to Basics: A Capella Singing." *Firm Foundation* 118 (March 2003): 1, 4-6.

"More Than You Think You Will Need." *Server* 50 (April 23, 2003): 1.

"A Fasting Meditation." *Firm Foundation* 118 (June 2003): 6-9.

"Archibald Henry Sayce: Decipherer of Inscriptions." *Near East Archaeological Society Bulletin* 48 (2003): 33-41.

2004

"God Is Free," *Firm Foundation* 119 (Jan. 2004): 14-15.

"Paul's Vow." In *Opening Our Eyes to Jesus from Darkness to Light in Acts*, 264-67. Edited by David L. Lipe. Henderson, Tenn.: Freed Hardeman University, 2004.

"Rebaptism." In *Opening Our Eyes to Jesus from Darkness to Light in Acts*, 268-70. Edited by David L. Lipe. Henderson, Tenn.: Freed-Hardeman University, 2004.

"Fulfillment of Joel's Prophecy." In *Opening Our Eyes to Jesus from Darkness to Light in Acts*, 271-74. Edited by David L. Lipe. Henderson, Tenn.: Freed-Hardeman University, 2004.

"Eating Meat." *Firm Foundation* 119 (March 2004): 1, 5-9.

"Your Credit." *Server* 51 (March 24, 2004): 1.

"Studies in the Pre-Literary Prophets: Abraham the Intercessor." *Firm Foundation* 119 (April 2004): 11-14.

"Studies in the Pre-writing Prophets—2: Moses as a Prophet." *Firm Foundation* 119 (May 2004): 1-8.

"Congregational Membership." *Gospel Advocate* 146 (June 2004): 36-40.

"Studies in the Pre-literary Prophets—3: Women Who Were Prophetesses." *Firm Foundation* 119 (June 2004): 16-19.

"Studies in the Pre-literary Prophets: The Prophet Samuel." *Firm Foundation* 119 (July 2004): 1, 5–8.

"Historical Accuracy of the Bible." In *A Humble Defense: A Special Tribute Honoring Dr. Lynn Gardner*, 75-88. Edited by Mark Scott and Mark More. Joplin, Mo.: College Press, 2004.

"God Works for Good." *Server* 51 (Aug. 11, 2004): 1.

"Studies of the Pre-literary Prophets: The Prophets and the Kings." *Firm Foundation* 119 (Sept. 2004): 9-12.

"Studies in Pre-literary Prophecy." *Firm Foundation* 119 (Oct. 2004): 12-15.

"Studies in the Pre-Literary Prophets: Young and Old Prophets—Jehu—Azariah—Hannani." *Firm Foundation* 119 (Nov. 2004): 1, 5-7.

"Persis." *Server* 52 (Dec. 8, 2004): 1.

"Studies in the Pre-literary Prophets: Elijah." *Firm Foundation* 119 (Dec. 2004): 8-11.

Hebrew Wisdom and Poetry. Henderson, Tenn.: Hester Publications, 2004.

"Bible, Versions and Translation of the." In the *Encyclopedia of the Stone-Campbell Movement*, 87-89. Edited by D.A. Foster, P.M. Blowers, A.L. Dunnavant, and D.M. Williams. Grand Rapids: Eerdmans, 2004.

2005

"Eternal Punishment: The Book of Revelation." *The Spiritual Sword* 36 (Jan. 2005): 13-15.

"The Pre-literary Prophets: Second Lesson on Elijah." *Firm Foundation* 120 (Jan. 2005): 12-14.

"The Gift of Forgiveness." *Server* 52 (Feb. 9, 2005): 1.

"The Peaceable Kingdom." In *A Light to the Nations*, 221-30. Edited by D.L. Lipe. Henderson, Tenn.: Freed-Hardeman University, 2005.

"The Virgin Birth." In *A Light to the Nations*, 231-39. Edited by D.L. Lipe. Henderson, Tenn.: Freed-Hardeman University, 2005.

"A Highway in the Wilderness." In *A Light to the Nations*, 240-49. Edited by D.L. Lipe. Henderson, Tenn.: Freed-Hardeman University, 2005.

"Studies in Pre-literary Prophets: An Anonymous Prophet." *Firm Foundation* 120 (Feb. 2005): 16-19.

"The Pre-Writing Prophets—Elisha." *Firm Foundation* 120 (April 2005): 22-25.

"The Pre-Writing Prophets—Elisha 2." *Firm Foundation* 120 (May 2005): 22-24.

"A Low Maintenance Wife." *Server* 52 (June 1, 2005): 1.

"Studies in the Pre-Literary Prophets: Miscellaneous Prophets." *Firm Foundation* 120 (June 2005): 12-16.

"A Day of Small Things (cf. Zech. 4:10)." *Firm Foundation* 120 (Aug. 2005): 10.

"New Testament Authority for Music in Worship." *Firm Foundation* 120 (Sept. 2005): 1, 5-20.

"Yahweh: The God of Israel." In *Restoring the First-Century Church in the Twenty-First Century: Essays in the Stone Campbell Restoration Movement in Honor of Don Haymes*, 29-41. Edited by Warren Lewis and Hans Rollmann. Eugene, Ore.: Wipf and Stock, 2005.

2006

"How Does the Gospel Fulfill Jeremiah's Promise?" In *A Call to Faithfulness*, 286-96. Edited by David L. Lipe. Henderson, Tenn.: Freed-Hardeman University, 2006.

"Where Was the Altar of Incense?" In *A Call to Faithfulness*, 307-14. Edited by David L. Lipe. Henderson, Tenn. Freed-Hardeman Universtiy, 2006.

"What Are the Patterns of Things in the Heavens?" In *A Call to Faithfulness*, 307-14. Edited by David L. Lipe. Henderson, Tenn.: Freed-Hardeman University, 2006.

Studies in the Non-Writing Prophets of the Bible. Henderson Tenn.: Hester Publications, 2006.

"Silence of Scripture in Reformation Thought." *Restoration Quarterly* 48 (2006): 73-90.

"My Pilgrimage." *Gospel Advocate* 148 (Oct. 2006): 21-23.

"The Slippery Slope." *Firm Foundation* 121 (Nov. 2006): 15-17.

"Unbaptized Children and the Lord's Supper." *Firm Foundation* 121 (Nov. 2006): 17-20.

2007

"Deuteronomy: Ancient Near Eastern Backgrounds: Social Customs." In *Hear O Israel*, 86-96. Edited by David L. Lipe. Henderson, Tenn.: Freed-Hardeman University, 2007.

"Deuteronomy: Ancient Near Eastern Backgrounds: Covenants." In *Hear O Israel*, 97-105. Edited by David L. Lipe. Henderson, Tenn.: Freed-Hardeman University, 2007.

"Deuteronomy: Ancient Near Eastern Backgrounds: Law Codes." In *Hear O Israel*, 106-13. Edited by David L. Lipe. Henderson, Tenn.: Freed-Hardeman University, 2007.

"Deuteronomy: Ancient Near Eastern Backgrounds: Religions." In *Hear O Israel*, 114-23. Edited by David L. Lipe. Henderson, Tenn.: Freed-Hardeman University, 2007.

" 'A Prophet's Son' (Amos 7:14) Reconsidered." *Restoration Quarterly* 49 (2007): 229.

"Pilgrimage of Mind and Heart." In *Feasting on Assurance*, 94-95. Edited by Lynette C. Gray. Rockford, Tenn.: Gospel Focus, 2007.

2008

"Did John Write 'John 7:53-8:11'?" In *Behold the Lamb: John's Gospel of Belief*, 132-38. Edited by David L. Lipe. Henderson, Tenn.: Freed-Hardeman University, 2008.

"Does the 'Wind Blow' or the 'Spirit Breathe'?" In *Behold the Lamb: John's Gospel of Belief*, 180-87. Edited by David L. Lipe. Henderson, Tenn.: Freed-Hardeman University, 2008.

"The Bishops' Bible." *Bible Editions and Versions: Journal of the International Society of Bible Collectors* 9 (April-June 2008): 4-12.

The Question of Instrumental Music in Worship. Searcy, Ark.: Truth for Today World Mission School, 2008.

"Did Moses Write the Pentateuch?" *Gospel Advocate* 150 (July 2008): 15-18.

"A Note on Bible Translation." *Restoration Quarterly* 50 (2008): 169-79.

"Conrad Schick: Architect-Archaeologist." *Near East Archaeological Society Bulletin* 53 (2008): 15-23.

2009

"Punishment of the Innocent." In *Crying Out to God: Prayer and Praise to God*, 64-71. Edited by David L. Lipe. Henderson, Tenn.: Freed-Hardeman University, 2009.

"Conceived in Sin." In *Crying Out to God: Prayer and Praise to God*, 71-79. Edited by David L. Lipe. Henderson, Tenn.: Freed-Hardeman University, 2009.

"The King James Bible Editions: Their Character and Revision History." In *Translation That Openeth the Window: Reflections on the History and Legacy of the King James Bible*, 97-117. Edited by David G. Burke. Atlanta: Society of Biblical Literature, 2009.

"A Challenge to New Elders." Reprinted from May 2001. *Gospel Advocate* 151 (Oct. 2009): 19.

2010

"The Lord Has Created a New Thing on the Earth." *Restoration Quarterly* 52 (2010): 19-28.

"Deliver Unto Satan." *In Perfecting God's People*, 260-69. Edited by David L. Lipe. Henderson, Tenn.: Freed-Hardeman University, 2010.

2011

The Encouragement of the Scriptures. Henderson, Tenn.: Hester Publications, 2011.

"Authorized Version Has Stood Test of Time." *Memphis Commerical Appeal* (Nov. 5, 2011): M3-4.

"Whom Do You Call When You Are Sick? (James 5:14)." In *The Behavior of Belief: Faith and Life in James to Jude*. Edited by David L. Lipe. Henderson, Tenn.: Freed-Hardeman University, 2011.

2012

"Prophecy in Recent New Testament Scholarship." Accepted for publication in *Sufficient Evidence: A Journal of Christian Apologetics* 2 (Fall 2012).

Archaeology for the Bible Student. Searcy, Ark.: Resource Publications. Proposed for publication in 2012.

These Things Are Written: Fifty-Eight Years at the Harding Bible Lectureship. Searcy, Ark.: Resource Publications. Proposed for publication in 2012.

Early Explorers of Bible Lands. Abilene, Texas: ACU Press. Accepted for publication in 2012.

As I Remember It: An Autobiography. Nashville, Tenn.: Gospel Advocate, 2012.

And So We Speak: Sermons from Five Decades. Nashville, Tenn.: Gospel Advocate. Proposed for publication in 2012.

Vita

Jack P. Lewis was born in Midlothian, Texas, March 13, 1919. He attended Abilene Christian College, Sam Houston State Teachers' College, Harvard University, and Hebrew Union College. He received a Ph.D degree each from Harvard and from Hebrew Union. He has received numerous fellowship grants. The most recent was from the American Schools of Oriental Research for a year (1967-1968) at its Jerusalem School. He was Senior Fellow at the W.F. Albright Institute of Archaeological Research, Jerusalem, Israel, 1982-1983.

Lewis has done local work in churches in Throckmorton and Huntsville, Texas, in Providence, R.I., and in Covington, Ky. He has preached in congregations in Arkansas, Mississippi, Tennessee and Texas and has appeared on numerous lecture programs at the Christian colleges. He is on the editorial board of *Restoration Quarterly*. He is honorary dean of the Japan School of Evangelism. He was a member of the board of directors of University Christian Center, Oxford, Miss., and is an elder of the White Station congregation, Memphis, Tenn. He was the chairman (1969-1970) of the Southern Section of the Evangelical Theological Society and was a member of the American Academy of Religion. He is a member of the Society of Biblical Literature and the Evangelical Theological Society.

Lewis is the author of *The Minor Prophets, A Study of the Interpretation of Noah and the Flood in Jewish and Christian Literature, The Gospel of Matthew* (2 vols.), *Archaeology of the Bible, Understanding Genesis, Exegesis of Difficult Passages, Archaeological Backgrounds of Bible History, The English Bible from KJV to NIV, Questions You've Asked about Bible Translations, Leadership Questions Confronting the Church, The Major Prophets, Ethics of the Prophets*, and *Archaeological Insights into the Interpretation of the Minor Prophets*.

Lewis has made about 33 trips to the Holy Land. He made a trip around the world in 1974, to Mexico in 1975, to Scandinavia in 1975, to the British Isles in 1977 and 1983, to Eastern Europe in 1978, to Spain in 1979, to mainland China in 1982, to Australia in 1983, and to Alaska in 1985. He has visited Kenya, Ghana, and Nigeria.

Lewis has taught Bible at Harding since 1954. He was four years in Searcy, Ark., but has been at the Memphis Graduate School since 1958. After his retirement, he taught one class a semester for several years.

Lewis and his deceased wife (Lynell Carpenter) have two sons: John Robert and Jerry Wayne. He has two grandchildren: Karen Lewis and Jeffery Lewis. He was married to the late Annie May Alston.

Lewis received the Twentieth Century Christian Education award in 1968. Lewis was honored by his former students and his friends with a Festschrift, March 1986, titled *Biblical Interpretation*. He has received citations from Pepperdine, Western Christian, Freed-Hardeman University, and Harding University.

Jack Pearl Lewis
FAMILY TREE

Married December 21, 1876
William Donnel Lewis (1859-1907)
Amanda Jane Hackworth (1859-1950)

Fred Cleveland Lewis (1884-1968)
Walter Scott Lewis, Sr. (1886-1967)
Pearl Gonce Lewis (1888-1952)
William Jasper Lewis (1889-1976)
Bettie Amber Lewis (1891-1983)
Donald A. Lewis (1896-1976)
Robert E. Lewis (1901-1940)

Married September 30, 1883
Henry Thomas Holland (1846-1912)
Margaret Elizabeth Jones (1852-1924)

Clara Claudia Holland (1878-1959)
Henry Walter Holland (1880-1948)
James Edwin Holland (1884-1965)
Anna Elizabeth Holland (1888-1962)
Gillie Louisa Holland (1891-1895)

Married September 10, 1912
Pearl Gonce Lewis (1888-1952)
Anna Elizabeth Holland (1888-1962)

LeMoine Gaunce Lewis (1916-1987)
Amber Loreta Lewis (1918-Living)
Jack Pearl Lewis (1919-Living)
Homer Clyde Lewis (1922-2009)
Roy Lewis (1925-2007)
James Wendel Lewis (1929-1929)

Jack Pearl Lewis (1919-Living)

Married August, 1943
Lynell Carpenter (1921-1975)

Married November 23, 1978
Annie May Alston (1917-2006)

Married December 29, 1973
John Robert Lewis (1947-Living)
Kathleen Sue Wright (1950-Living)

Karen Frances Lewis (1979-Living)

Married January 1, 2005
Jeffrey David Lewis (1982-Living)
Rachel Ann Rozmarynowycz (1982-Living)

Married October 23, 1999
Jerry Wayne Lewis (1953-Living)
Pamela Jean Perella (1953-Living)

CPSIA information can be obtained at www.ICGtesting.com
Printed in the USA
LVOW072021270912

300658LV00002B/2/P